Harivaṁśa Purāṇa

ISBN 81-8403-034-7
Published by: Rasbihari Lal & Sons.
Loi Bazar, Vrindaban-281121
(U.P.) India.
Phone: 91-565-2442570
Fax: 91-565-2443970
E-mail: brijwasi2001@hotmail.com
Our Other Division Brijwasi Exports

Our Other Publications

The Glories of Advaita Acarya
Mystical Stories from the Bhagavatam
Vedic Stories from Ancient India
Aisvarya Kadambini
Simple for Simple
Srimad Bhagavat Tatparya
Dasa Mula Tattva
Gita Mala Song Book
Gitavali Song Book
Kalyan Kalpataru Song Book
Sarnagati Song Book
Sri Bhagavatarka Marici Mala
Sri Harinama Cintamani
Sacred Cow
The twelve Mahajanas
Vrndavana Dhama Ki Jaya
Rasaraja Sri Gauranga
Sanskrit Bhagavad-Gita Grammar:
Vol.-1 "Introduction"
Vol-2 "Exercise"
Vol-3 "The Gita"
Advaita Prakash
Prema Vivarta
Gita Govinda (By Gadadhara Prana)
A Garland of Verses
Caitanya Upanishad
Genesis Renovated
Katha & Kena Upanishads
Sri Gaura Ganoddesa Dipika
Devadasa
Govinda Lilamrata
Sri Gaudiya Kanthahara
Dhamali (By Gadadhar Prana)
Sri Gopal Sahasra Nama
Sri Krsna Astottara Satnama
Sri Radha Sahasra-Nama- Stotra
The Life of Ramanujacarya
Namamrta Samudra
Narottama Vilasa
Sri Prem Bhakti Chandrika
Lessons From The Ayurveda
Sanskrit Gramar
Caitanya Candramrtam
Garuda Purana
Life of Madhavacharya
Padama Purana
Skand Purana
Sri Narad Puran

Braja-Vilasa Stavah
Mukta Caritra (The Perl Story)
Sri Manah Siksa
Sri Sri Dana Keli Cintamanih
A Handbook of Vaisnava Songs & Practices
A Vaisnava Harmonium and Singing Method (With 2 tape)
Practical Mrdanga Lessons (With One Tape)
Food for Peace (Cook Book)
Astakala Lila Padavali
Lalit Madhava
Mathura Mahatmaya
Sri Krsna Caitanya Divya Sahasra-Nama
Sri Radha Krsna Ganoddesa Dipika
Vidagdha Madhava
Hari Bhaktivilas Vol. l-5
Sri Krsna Lila Stava
Sri Sikastaka
The Mahabharata
The Songs of Lochan Dasa Thakura
Harivamsa Purana: Vol. 1-3
Sri Narad Pancaratra: Vol. 1-2
Srimad Bhagavadgita
The Glories of Ekadasi
From Nothingness to Personhood
Narasimha Avatar
The Four Principal of Freedam
The Heart of Devotion
The Life and Times of Lord Caitanya
The Lives of Vaishnava Saints
The Six Goswamies of Vrindavan
Vedic Archeology & Assorted Essays
Sri Gopala Tapani Upanisad
Sri Krsna Bhavanamrta Mahakavya
Sri Prem Samput
The Bhakti Trilogy
Sri Caitanya Bhagavata - Complete Edition
Sri Vrndavana Mahimamrta - only 17th Chapter.
Sri Vrndavana Mahimamrta - Complete Edition
Garga Samhita
Bhakti Ratnakara
Sri Krsna Karnamrta
Jagannatha Vallabha Nataka
Camatkara Candrika
Sri Vrajariti Cintamani
Sri Caitanya Carita Mahakavya Vaisnava Saints
Bhagavad Gita by Bhaktivinoda Thakura
Sri Uddhava-Sandesa & Sri Hamsaduta
Sri Krisna's Names In Bhagavad Gita
Ujjvala-Nilamani
Jaiva Dharma
Bhavishya Purana, vol. 1, 2
Sri Krishna-sandarbha vol. 1-3
Sri Paramatma-sandarbha vol. 1, 2
Sri Nrisimha sahasrara-Nama
Sri Sri Stava Mala

Harivaṁśa Purāṇa

Śrīla Kṛṣṇa Dvaipayāna Vyāsadeva

Volume Four

Śrī Viśṇu-parva

Chapters 37-61

Translated by Bhumipati Dāsa

Edited by Purṇaprajña Dāsa

RAS BIHARI LAL & SONS
RBL&S
VRINDABAN

Dedicated to

His Divine Grace
A. C. Bhaktivedanta Swami Prabhupāda
founder-ācārya
International Society for Krishna Consciousness

Harivaṁśa Purāṇa

Śrī Kṛṣṇa Dvaipāyana Vedavyāsa

Harivaṁśa and Mahābhārata are complementary to each other. Harivaṁśa especially describes the pastimes of the Supreme Lord that took place after the battle at Kuruksetra, including His pastimes of disappearance. Harivaṁśa is considered to be a supplement of Mahābhārata. It is divided into three parts–Harivaṁśa-parva, Viṣṇu-parva and Bhaviśya-parva. Harivaṁśa-parva has fifty-five chapters, Viṣṇu-parva has one hundred twenty-eight chapters and Bhavisya-parva has one hundred thirty-five chapters. Harivaṁśa consists of about sixteen thousand verses.

Harivaṁśa was first recited by the great sage, Vaiśampāyana, to King Janmejaya. In that assembly, Ugraśravā or Sauti was also present. Later on, by the request of the sages at Naimiṣāraṇya, headed by Śaunaka, Sauti again recited it. Many Gauḍiya-vaiṣṇava ācāryas have quoted evidence from Harivaṁśa in their writings. There is no doubt that the readers of this book will find it both interesting and beneficial for their cultivation of Kṛṣṇa consciousness.

Contents

Śrī Viśṇu-parva
Chapters 37-61

CHAPTER 37

King Haryaśva banished and his son, Yadu, awarded benedictions by the serpent king, Dhumravarna

Text 1

vaiśampāyana uvāca
sa kṛṣṇa tatra valavān
rauhiṇeyena saṅgataḥ
mathurāṁ yavad ākīrṇām
purīṁ tāṁ sukham āvasat

Vaiśampāyayana said: My dear Janamejaya, the supremely powerful Lord Kṛṣṇa, along with Balarāṁa, the son of Rohiṇī, very happily continued to reside at Mathurā, the city of the Yādavas.

Text 2

prāpto yauvana dehastu
yukto rājaśriyā vibhuḥ
cacāra mathurāṁ prītaḥ
savanākara bhūṣaṇām

To those who observed Them, it appeared as if They had entered the prime of Their youth. The two Lords dressed like kings as They happily wandered about Mathurā, which was decorated with very beautiful gardens.

Text 3

kasyacit tvatha kālasya
rājā raja gṛheśvaraḥ

sasmāra nihataṁ kaṁsaṁ
jarāsandhaḥ pratāpavān

At that time, the greatly powerful King Jarāsandha, while residing in his palace, continually remembered how King Kaṁsa had been killed.

Text 4

yuddhāya yojito bhūyo
duhitṛbhyāṁ mahipatiḥ
dalca sapta ca saṅgrāmān
jarāsandhasya yādavāḥ
dudurna cainaṁ samarae
hantuṁ śekur mahārathāḥ

His two daughters continuously induced Jarāsandha to get revenge. Thus, he attacked the Yādavas seventeen times but was unable to attain victory.

Text 5

tato māgadharāt śrīmāṁs
caturaṅga valānvitaḥ
bhūyo'pi aṣṭādaścam kartuṁ
saṅgrāmaṁ sa samārabhāt

Thereafter, Jarāsandha, the king of Magadha, decided to attack the Yadu dynasty for the eighteenth time, accompanied by his army, which consisted of four divisions.

Text 6

vailaksyāt punarevāsau
rājā raja gṛheśvaraḥ

jarāsandho bale śrīmān
pāka śāsana vikramaḥ

King Jarāsandha was as powerful as Indra. Being very embarrassed because of his previous defeats, he diligently prepared for war.

Text 7

sa sādhanena mahatā
bṛhadratha wuto bale
kṛṣṇasya vadhamanvicchan
bhūyo vai saṅyavartata

Finally, the powerful son of Bṛhadratha departed for Mathurā, harboring a desire to kill Kṛṣṇa, and for this purpose, he was armed with all kinds of terrestrial and celestial weapons.

Text 8

taṁ śrutvā sahitaḥ sarve
nivṛttaṁ magadheśvaraṁ
yādavā mantra yāmāsur
jarāsandha bhayārditāḥ

When they received the news of the Magadha king's attack upon Mathurā, the members of the Yadu dynasty, being fearful, consulted one another as to how to content with him.

Text 9

tataḥ prāha mahāteja
vikadrur naya kovidaḥ
kṛṣṇaṁ kamala patrākṣam
ugrasenasya śṛṇvataḥ

In that assembly, the greatly powerful Vikadru, who was an expert strategist, spoke to the lotus-eyed Lord Kṛṣṇa, in the presence of King Ugrasena.

Text 10

śrūyatāṁ tāta govinda
kulasyāsya samudbhavaḥ
śrūyatāṁ abhidhyāsyāmi
prapta kālaṁ ahaṁ tataḥ
yuktaṁ cenmayase sādho
karisyasi vaco mama

My dear Govinda, I wish to describe to You the history of this glorious dynasty. Now is the proper time for me to disclose some confidential information so that You can act accordingly.

Text 11

yādavasyāsya vaṁśasya
samudbhavaṁ aśeṣataḥ
yathā me kathitaḥ purvam
vyāsena viditātmanā

I will repeat to You what I had previously heard regarding the Yadu dynasty from the great literary incarnation of Godhead, Śrīla Vyāsadeva.

Text 12

āsīd rājā manas vaṁśe
śrīmān īkṣvāku sambhavaḥ
harayaśva iti vikhyāto
mahendra sma vikramaḥ.

There was a celebrated king named Harayaśva, the son of Ikṣvāku, who had appeared in the dynasty of Vaivasvata Manu. He was considered to be as powerful as Indra, the king of heaven.

Text 13

tastyāsīd dayitā bhāryā
madhyo daitasya vai sūtā
devī madhumati nāma
yathendrasya śacī tathā

His wife was Madhumatī, the daughter of the demon Madhu. As Śacī was very dear to Indra, this Madhumatī was very dear to Haryaśva.

Text 14

sā yauvaṇa guṇopeto
rūpena apratimā bhuvi
manoratha kari rājñaḥ
praṇebhyo'pi garīyasī

She was in the prime of her youth and very talented. Indeed, she was considered to be the most beautiful woman in the world. Because she fully dedicated herself to the service of her husband, Haryaśva, she was dearer to him than his very life.

Text 15

danvendra kule jātā
suśroṇi kāma rūpinī
eka patni vrata dharā
khecarā rohiṇi yathā

Madhumatī, the daughter of the demon Madhu, had a very thin waist. She was the only wife of her husband, and she could traverse the airways like Rohiṇī-devī.

Texts 16-17

sā tam ikṣvāku śārdūlaṁ
kāmayā māsa kāminī
sa kadacit naro śreṣtho
bhrātā jyeṣthena mādhava

rājyān nirasto viśvastaḥ
so'yodhyāṁ samparityajat
sa tadālpa parivāro
priyayā sahito vane.

Being very lusty by nature, Madhumatī was enchanted with Haryaśva, a great hero in the dynasty of Ikṣvāku. However, it came to be that Haryaśva's brother banished him from the kingdom. Thus, Haryaśva was forced to leave Ayodhyā, along with his wife and children, and reside in the forest.

Text 18

reme sametya kālajñaḥ
priyayā kamalekṣaṇaḥ
bhrātrā viniskṛtaṁ rājyāt
provāca kamalekṣaṇāḥ

Lotus-eyed Haryaśva accepted the fact that he had been banished by his brother as the will of destiny and so he happily passed his days in the forest. One day, his wife approached him and spoke as follows.

Text 19

ehyāgaccha nara śreṣtha
tyaja rājya kṛtāṁ spṛhāṁ
gacchāvaḥ sahitau vīra
madhor mama pitur gṛham

O King ! O great hero, give up all hope of returning to Ayodhyā. Let us go to the house of my father, Madhu.

Text 20

ramyaṁ madhu vanaṁ nāma
kāma puṣpa phala drumam
sahitau tatra raṁsyābo
yathā divi gatau tathā

My father resides in a very pleasant forest known as Madhuvana. The trees and plants of that forest produce flowers and fruit at will. We can live there and enjoy life like the inhabitants of the heavenly planets.

Text 21

piturme dayitastvaṁ hy
māthur mama ca pārthiva
mat priyārthaṁ priyataro
bhrātuśca lavaṇasya vai

O lord of the earth, You are highly respected by my mother and father and my brother, Lavaṇāsura, always desires to please me and so he will also treat you very nicely.

Text 22

raṁsāvas tatra sahitau
rājasthāviva kāma gau
tatra gatvā nara śreṣtha
hyamarā viva nandane
yathā deva pure tathā

O foremost of human beings, at that place we can reside among other loving couples, enjoying the fruits of nature just like the demigods and their consorts in the Nandana garden.

Text 23

taṁ tyajāva mahārāja
bhrātaraṁ te' bhimāninam
āvayor dveṣiṇaṁ nityaṁ
mattaṁ raja madena vai

O King, your brother is very proud, thinking himself to be the lord of all he surveys. I know that he is envious of us and so we should completely sever all ties with him.

Text 24

dhigimaṁ garhitaṁ vāsaṁ
bhṛtyavat ca parāśrayam
gacchāvaḥ sahitau vīra
piturme bhavanāntikam

It is a terrible life when one is treated like a slave by his relatives. To hell with such a life! O heroic king, let us go to the house of my father without delay.

Text 25

tasya samyak pravṛttasya
pūrvajaṁ bhrātaraṁ prati
kāmārtasya narendrasya
patnyāstad ruruce vacaḥ

My dear Lord Kṛṣṇa, even though Haryaśva still had respect for his elder brother, being impelled by lusty desires, as a henpecked husband he readily agreed to his wife's proposal.

Text 26

tato madhuraṁ rājā
hayarśvaḥ sa jagāma ca
bhāryayā saha kāmīnyā
kāmī puruṣa puṅgavaḥ

Thereafter, the lusty King Haryaśva traveled to Madhupurī with his equally lusty wife.

Text 27

madhunā dānavendreṇa
sa sāmnā samudāhṛtaḥ
svāgataṁ vatsa haryaśva
prīto'smi tava darśanāt

When the king of the demons, Madhu, saw him approach, he affectionately said, "My dear son, Haryaśva, you are welcome. I am very glad to see you."

Text 28

yadetan mama rājyaṁ vai
sarvaṁ madhuvanaṁ vinā
dadāmi tava rājendra
vāsaśca pratigṛhyatām

O emperor, except for this forest of Madhuvana, I now hand over my entire kingdom to you. Simply reside here peacefully.

Text 29

vane'smillavaṇaś cāyaṁ
sahāyaste bhaviṣyati
amitra nigrahe caiva
karṇa dhāratvam eṣyati

My son, Lavaṇa, will assist you in every way. He will especially be able to protect you from your enemies.

Text 30

pālayainaṁ śubhaṁ rāṣtraṁ
samudrān ūpabhūṣitam
gosamṛddhaṁ śriyā juṣṭam
ābhīra pṛāya mānuṣam

You should rule this beautiful kingdom, which is surrounded by sea. Here you will find innumerable cows and all kinds of opulence. In fact, the inhabitants of this kingdom are mostly cowherds.

Texts 31-33

atra te vasatas tāta
durgaṁ giri puraṁ mahat
bhavitā pārthivāvāsaḥ
surāṣtra viṣayo mahān

anūpa viṣayas caiva
samudrānte nirāmayaḥ
ānartaṁ nāma te rāṣtraṁ
bhaviṣyat yāyataṁ mahat

tad bhaviṣyam ahaṁ manye
kāla yogena pārthiva
adhyāsyatāṁ yathā kālaṁ
pārthivaṁ vṛttam uttamam

Dear one, your capital will be the flourishing city of Surāṣṭra, which is near the towering Girnar Mountain, situated by the sea. In this kingdom, which will be known as Ānarta, no one will suffer from disease. O ruler of men, in due course of time, your fame will be established if you maintain the citizens righteously.

Text 34

yāyātama_pi vaṁśaste
sameṣyati ca yādavam
anu vaṁśaṁ ca vaṁśaste
somasya bhavitā kila

Your family will come to be considered part of the dynasties of Yadu and Yayāti. You will be known as a king of the Candra dynasty and not of the Sūrya dynasty, as previously.

Text 35

eṣa me vibhavas tāta
tavemaṁ viṣayottamam
datvā yāsyāmi tapase
sāgaraṁ lavaṇālayam

My dear son, my kingdom is filled with opulence. After handing over the kingdom to you, I will go the Lavaṇa Ocean (the ocean of salt) to perform penance.

Text 36

lavaṇena samāyuktas
tvamimaṁ viṣayottamam
pālayasva khilaṁ tāta
svasya vaṁśasya vṛddhaye

O gentle one, please stay here with Lavaṇa and nicely maintain this kingdom, and thus increase the reputation of your family.

Text 37

vādaṁ ityeva haryaśvaḥ
pratigrāha tat puram
sa ca daityastapovāsaṁ
jagāma varuṇālayam

King Haryaśva gave his consent, saying, "so be it," and in this way, formally accepted the kingdom from his father-in-law. Thereafter, the demon Madhu left his palace so that he could perform austerities in the ocean.

Text 38

haryaśvaśca mahātejā
divye girivara uttame
niveśayā māsa puraṁ
vāṣarthaṁ amaropamaḥ

Thereafter, King Haryaśva, whose prowess was on the level of the demigods, established his most enchanting capital near the shore of the ocean.

Text 39

ānartaṁ nāma tad rāṣtraṁ
surāṣṭraṁ godhanāyutam
acireṇaiva kālena
samṛddhaṁ pratyāpadyata

Later on, that city became known as the capital of Surāṣtra. The countryside will filled with innumerable cows, thus exhibiting its great prosperity.

Texts 40-41

anūpaviṣaye caiva
velāvana vibhuṣitam
vicitraṁ kṣetra śasyāḍhyaṁ
prākāra grāma saṇkulam

śaśāsa nṛpatiḥ spahitaṁ
tad rāṣṭraṁ rāṣṭra varadhanaḥ
raja dharmena yaśasā
prajānāṁ nandi vardhanaḥ

This kingdom was decorated with seas, forests, fertile agricultural fields, ample production of grains, villages, towns, and ever-increasing wealth. King Haryaśva ruled the citizens righteously, giving them great delight.

Text 42

tasya samyak pracāreṇa
haryaśvasya mahātmanaḥ
vyavardhata tad kṣobhyaṁ
rāṣṭraṁ rāṣṭra gunair yutam

As a consequence of the good conduct of the exalted king Haryaśva, the undisturbed kingdom soon prospered and the citizens also exhibited godly qualities.

Text 43

sa hi rājā sthito rājye
rāja vṛttena śobhitaḥ
prāptaḥ kuloccitāṁ lakṣmīṁ
vṛttena ca nayena ca

King Haryaśva, who exhibited the behavior of a saintly king, became the possessor of great wealth and prestige, as would be expected.

Text 44

tasyaiva ca suvṛttasya
putra kāmasya dhīmataḥ
madhumatyāṁ suto yajñe
yadur nāma mahāyaśṣḥ

In due course of time, the pious and intelligent King Haryaśva begot a son in the womb of his wife, Madhumatī. This boy was given the name Yadu.

Text 45

so'vardhata mahātejā
yadur dundubhi niṣvanaḥ
rāja lakṣana saṁpannaḥ
sapatnair duratikraṁaḥ

When he grew up, Yadu's voice became very grave, like the sounding of a drum. Like his father, he became decorated with all good qualities, and he proved to be a noble ruler of men. His prowess was unmatched and thus none of his enemies could even hope to conquer him.

Text 46

yadur nāma abhavat putro
rāja lakṣana pūjitaḥ
yathāsya pūrvajo rājā
puruḥ sa sumahāyaśāḥ

This son of Haryaśva became famous throughout the world and because he was a reservoir of godly qualities, he was often compared to his ancestor, King Puru.

Text 47

sa eka eva tasyāsit
putraḥ parama śobhanaḥ
urgitaḥ pṛthivībhartāṁ
haryaśvasya mahātmanaḥ

Yadu was the only son of the noble-minded King Haryaśva. He was a very powerful and righteous ruler of men and was thus respected by one and all.

Text 48

dāśa varṣa sahasrāṇi
sa kṛtvā rājyaṁ avyayam
jagāma tridivaṁ rājā
dharmeṇa apratimo bhuvi

After piously ruling his kingdom for ten thousand years, King Haryaśva ascended to the heavenly planets. Indeed, he had exhibited the behavior of an ideal saintly king.

Text 49

tato yadura dīnātmā
prajābhīs tvabhaṣicyata
pitur uparate śrīmān
krameṇārka ivoditaḥ

After the death of Yadu's father, the elderly residents of Surāstra installed him upon the royal throne. Thereafter, he ruled the kingdom in an exemplary manner so that it appeared as if another sun had risen after the sun of Haryaśva had set.

Text 50

śaśāsa cemāṁ vasudhāṁ
praśānta bhaya pratikāśo
nṛpo yennasma yādavāḥ

Yadu's prowess was equal to that of Indra, the king of

heaven. It is because of Yadu that his descendents are known as Yādavas. During his rule, fear, thieves, and plunderers were never to be seen.

Text 51

sa kadācin nṛpaścake
jala krīḍāṁ mahodadhau
dāraiḥ saha guṇodāraiḥ
satāra iva candramāḥ

One day, King Yadu was enjoying in the ocean, along with his wives, so that he appeared like the moon surrounded by many stars.

Texts 52-54

sa tatra sahasā kṣiptas
titīrṣuḥ sāgarāmbhasi
dhumra varṇena nṛpatiḥ
sarparājena vīryavān

so'pākṛṣyata vegena
jala sarpapuraṁ mahāt
maṇistambha gṛha dvāraṁ
muktā dāma vibhūṣitam

kīrṇaṁ saṅkha kūlaiḥ śubhrai
ratna rāśi vibhūṣitam
pravāla aṅkura patrāḍhai
pādapai rūpa śobhitam

Although he was very powerful, King Yadu was suddenly taken deep within the ocean, as if by force. The serpent king,

Dhumravarna, had exercised his superior strength within the water to take him to his city of Nāgas. There, it was seen that the city gates, the doors of the houses, and the pillars were bedecked with jewels, and the residents were adorned with pearl necklaces. Conch shells were seen here and there, the city gates were lavishly decorated, and innumerable trees bearing fruit and flowers lined the streets.

Text 55

kīrṇaṁ pannaga nāyordhaiḥ
samudra udara vāṣibhiḥ
svaraṇa varṇena bhāsvantaṁ
svastikena indu varcasā

In this city deep within the ocean, there were seen many beautiful daughters of the serpents. Auspicious drawings of *svastikas* and other such symbols decorated the streets and houses.

Text 56

sa taṁ dadarśa rājendro
vimale sāgarāmbhasi
pannagendra puraṁ toye
jagatyāmiva nirmitam

O best of kings, King Yadu was astonished to see how, although within the ocean, the city of the serpents exactly resembled the cities of the earth.

Text 57

svacchaṁ caiva puraṁ tatra
praviveśa nṛpo yaduḥ

agādhaṁ toyadākāraṁ
pūrṇaṁ sarpa vadhugaṇaiḥ

While gazing at the buildings, which appeared somewhat transparent, like the water, King Yadu leisurely entered the city.

Text 58

tasya dattaṁ maṇimayaṁ
jalajaṁ paraāsanam
svāstīrṇaṁ padma patraiśca
padma sutrottara cchadam

After entering the city, King Yadu was offered a seat made of lotus flowers and leaves, and covered by cloth made of lotus threads.

Text 59

tamāsinaṁ nṛpaṁ tatra
parame pannagāsane
dhijihva patiravyagro
dhumra varṇe'bhya bhāṣata

After King Yadu was comfortably seated on this *āśana* offered by the serpents, the king, Dhumravarṇa, began to speak in a gentle voice.

Text 60

pita te svargatiṁ prāptaḥ
kṛtvā vaṁśaṁ imaṁ mahāt
bhavantaṁ tejasā yuktam
utpādya vasudhā dhipam

O King, your father had taken birth in a glorious dynasty in which many powerful and influential kings had appeared, and then departed for his heavenly abode.

Text 61

yādavānā mayaṁ vaṁśas
tvannāmnā yadu puṅgava
pitrā te maṅgalārthāya
sthāpitaḥ pārthivākaraḥ

O Yadu, this dynasty will come to be called by your name and it will be famous throughout the world. Indeed, your father had enhanced the glory of this dynasty simply for your benefit.

Text 62

vaṁśe cāsmistava vibho
devānām tanayāvyayāḥ
ṛṣināṁ uragānāṁ ca
utpātsyante nṛyonijāḥ

O powerful one, in the future, many demigods, sages, and serpents will appear in your dynasty in human forms.

Text 63

tan mamemāḥ sutāḥ pañca
kumāryo vṛtta sammatāḥ
utpannā yauvanśvasya
bhaginyāṁ nṛpasttama

O foremost ruler of men, I have five very beautiful daughters, born from the womb of Yauvanāśva's sister, who are talented and well-behaved.

Text 64

praticchemāḥ svadharmeṇa
prājāpatyena karmaṇā
varaṁ ca te pradāsyami;
varārhastvaṁ mato mama

I would like you to marry them according to religious principles, because I consider you to be the most suitable husband for them. Besides this, I would like to award you the benediction of your choice.

Text 65

bhaimaśca kukurāś caiva
bhojāśca andhaka yadavāḥ
dāśārhā vṛṣṇayasceti
khyātiṁ yāsyanti sapta te

Because of you, seven branches of your dynasty will become very famous. They will be known as Bhima, Kukura, Bhoja, Andhaka, Yādava, Dāśārha, and Vṛṣṇi.

Text 66

sa tasmai dhūmra varṇe vai
kanyāḥ kanyavṛte sthitāḥ
jala purṇena yogena
dadāvindra samāya vai

After saying this, King Dhumravarṇa placed some water in his palm and then formally handed over his five daughters in marriage to King Yadu, who was as powerful as Indra, the king of heaven.

Text 67

varaṁ cāsmaidadau prītaḥ
sa vai pannaga puṅgavaḥ
śrāvayan kanyakāḥ sarvā
yathā kramam adīnavat

Thereafter, the magnanimous Dhumravarṇa, who was the crest jewel of all serpents, happily awarded benedictions to King Yadu in the presence of his wives.

Text 68

etāsu te sutāḥ pañca
sutāsu mama manada
utpatsyante pitus tejo
mātuś caiva samāśrītāḥ

He said: O gentle king, you will receive five sons from my five daughters. These sons will be endowed with all the virtues of their parents.

Text 69

asmāt samaya vaddhāśca
salila abhyantare carāḥ
tava vase bhavisyati
pārthivāḥ kāma rūpiṇaḥ

Because of my benediction, all the future kings in your dynasty will be able to reside within water and assume any form they desire.

Text 70

sa varaṁ kanyakāś caiva
labdhā yaduvaras tadā
udatiṣthata vegena
salilāt candramā iva

Thereafter, King Yadu and his five wives emerged from the ocean, like the rising of the moon on the horizon.

Text 71

sa pañca kanyā madhyastho
dadṛśe tava pārthivaḥ
pañca tārena saṁyukto
nakṣatreṇeva candramāḥ

Surrounded by his five beautiful wives, King Yadu appeared like the moon encircled by five auspicious planets.

Text 72

sa tad antapuraṁ sarvaṁ
dadarśa nṛpasattamaḥ
vaivāhikena veṣeṇa
divya srag anulepanaḥ

When that foremost of kings, who was beautifully decorated with his wedding garments, flower garlands, and sandalwood paste, emerged from the water, he saw that his flourishing kingdom awaited his guidance.

Text 73

samāśvāsya ca tāḥ sarvāḥ
sa patniḥ pavakopamāḥ
jagāma sa puraṁ rājā
prītyā paramayā yutaḥ

Taking his wives, who appeared as bright as fire, King Yadu cheerfully entered his capital.

Thus ends the translation of the thirty-seventh chapter of the Viṣṇu Parva of Śrī Harivaṁsa.

Chapter 38

Vikadru's description of the Yadu dynasty and advice about handling the attack of Jarāsandha

Text 1

vaiśampāyana uvāca
sa tāsunāga kanyāsu
kālena mahatā nṛpaḥ
janayāmāsa vikrāntān
pañca pūtran kulodvahān

Vaiśampāyana said: O Janamejaya, in due course of time, King Yadu begot five powerful sons, who were capable of carrying the burden of their family, in the womb of his five wives.

Text 2

mucukundaṁ mahāvāhuṁ
padama varaṇaṁ tathaiva ca
mādhavaṁ sārasaṁ caiva
haritaṁ caiva pārthivam

The names of these sons were the mighty-armed Mucukunda, Padmavarṇa, Mādava, Sārasa, and Harita.

Text 3

etān pañca sutān rājā
pañca bhūtopamān bhuvi
ikṣamāṇo nṛpaḥ prīthīṁ
jagāma atula vikramaḥ

They were considered to be like the five gross material elements found on this earth. The unlimitedly powerful King Yadu was very pleased to receive such exceptional sons.

Text 4

te prapta vayasaḥ sarve
sthitā pañca yathadrayaḥ
tejitā bala darpābhyām
ūcuḥ pitaraṁ agrataḥ

When these five boys grew up, they appeared like five great hills. One day, being very confident of their prowess, the boys approached their father and spoke as follows.

Text 5

tāta yuktāṇ sma vāyasā
bale mahati saṁsthitāḥ
kṣipram ājñaptum icchāmaḥ
kiṁ kurmas tava śāsanāt

Our dear father, now that we are grown up and very powerful, we await your order. Kindly tell us what we can do to serve you.

Text 6

sa tān nṛpati śārdūlaḥ
śārdūlaniva vegitāṇ
prītyā paramayā prāhā
sutān vīrya kutūhalāt

In order to ascertain their actual strength, King Yadu, who was as powerful as a lion, spoke as follows.

Text 7

vindhyarkṣavan tāvabhito
dve puryau parvatāśraye
niveśayatu yatnena
mucukundaḥ suto mama

Let my son, Mucukunda, take shelter of the Vindhya and Ṛkṣavān mountains and there establish two cities in the valley between them.

Text 8

sahyasya copariṣṭattu
dakṣiṇāṁ diśam āśritaḥ
padma varṇo'pi me putro
niveśayatu mā ciram

Let my son, Padmavarṇa, establish a city on the peak of Sahya mountain in the southern direction.

Text 9

tatraiva parataḥ kānte
deśe campaka bhūṣite
sāraso me puraṁ rāmyaṁ
niveśayatu putrakaḥ

Let my son, Sārasa, establish a beautiful city in the western direction where jasmine flowers are found in abundance.

Text 10

harito'yaṁ mahāvāhuḥ
sāgare haritodake
dīpaṁ pannaga rājasya
suto me pālayiṣyati

Let my son, the mighty-armed Harita, become the ruler of the island of serpents that is situated within the ocean.

Text 11

madhavo me mahāvahur
jaiṣṭha putraśca dharmavit
yauvarājyeva saṅyuktaḥ
sa puraṁ pālayiṣyati

My fifth son, the mighty-armed Mādhava, who is the eldest, is a very pious soul. As the true heir to my throne, he should carefully rule the kingdom.

Texts 12-13

sarve nṛpaśriyaṁ prāptā
abhiṣiktaḥ sa cāmarāḥ
pitrānu śiṣṭās catvāro
loka pālopamā nṛpāḥ

svaṁ svaṁ nivesanaṁ sarve
bhejire nṛpasattamāḥ
purasthānāni ramyāṇi
mṛgayanto yathākramam

In this way, all five sons received great opulence and the

rule of a kingdom. Each was installed upon a royal throne, being covered by an umbrella and fanned by *cāmaras*. On the order of their father, each established his capital in a suitable place.

Text 14

mucukundaśca rājarṣir
vindhyamadhyama rocayat
svasthānaṁ narmadā tīre
dāruṇo pala saṅkaṭe

For his capital, the saintly king Mucukunda chose a beautiful place within the Vindhya mountain range, by the side of the River Narmadā. It was very rocky terrain and thus practically inaccessible.

Text 15

sa ca taṁ śodhayāmāsa
viviktaṁ ca cakāra ha
setuṁ caiva samaṁ cakre
parikhās ca amitodakāḥ

He first made that solitary land flat and then dug a deep moat all around his fort, filled it with water, and constructed bridges in several places.

Text 16

sthāpayāmāsa bhāgeṣu
devatāyatana anyapi
rathyā vīthīr nana mārgāś
catvarāni vanāni ca

King Mucukunda then built many temples of the Supreme

Lord in various places throughout the city. That city was nicely planned with broad highways, beautiful gardens, and ample residential areas.

Text 17

sa tāṁ puriṁ dhanvatīṁ
purūhūta puri prabhām
nāti dīrghena kālena
cakāra nṛpa sattamaḥ

That foremost king had the entire city constructed within a very short time and it exhibited all kinds of opulence. Indeed, someone might mistake his kingdom for the abode of Indra in the heavenly planets.

Text 18

nāma cāsyāḥ śubhaṁ cakre
nirmitaṁ svena tejasā
tasyāḥ purya nṛpa śreṣṭho
deva śreṣṭha parakrama

The exalted King Mucukunda, who in terms of prowess was on the level of the demigods, named the beautiful city he had created after himself.

Text 19

mahāśma saṅghāta vatī
yatheyaṁ vindhya sanugā
māhiṣmati nāma pure
prakāśam upayāsati

This prosperous city was located on the peak of the

Vindhya Mountain, and it was encircled by rocky terrain. In the future, it came to be known as Māhiṣmatīpurī.

Text 20

ubhayor vindhyoḥ pāde
nagayostāṁ mahā purīm
madhye niveśaya māsa
śrīyā paramayā vṛtām

King Mucukunda's opulent realm was thus established between two of the Vindhya mountains.

Text 21

purīkāṁ nāma dharmātmā
purīṁ deva purī prabhām
udyāna śata sambadhāṁ
samṛddhāpaṇa catvarām

Thereafter, the pious king founded another city named Purīkā, which was as enchanting as an abode of the demigods. That city contained thousands of gardens, market places, and wide boulevards.

Text 22

ṛkṣavantaṁ samabhitas
tīre tatra nirāmaye
nirmitā sā pure rājñā
purīkā nāma nāmata

The city of Purīkā, whose inhabitants were free from disease and lamentation, was constructed on the bank of the river Narmadā, near the Ṛkṣavān Mountain.

Text 23

sa te dve vipule puryau
deva bhogyopame śubhe
pālayāmāsa dharmātmā
rājā dharma vyavasthitaḥ

The pious King Mucukunda, who faithfully followed religious principles, thus founded two very beautiful cities that rivaled the abodes of the demigods, from which he ruled his extensive kingdom.

Text 24

padma varṇo'pi rājarṣiḥ
sahya pṛṣṭhe purottamam
cakāra nadyā veṇāyās
tīre taruu latā kūle

The saintly king Padmavaraṇa also established an excellent city on the bank of Vena River, near the Sahya Mountain, in a region rich in vegetation.

Text 25

viṣayasya alpatāṁ jñatvā
sampurnaṁ rāṣtrameva ca
niveśayāmāsa nṛpaḥ sa
vapra prāyam uttamam

Knowing that the extent of his kingdom was much smaller than those of his brothers, Padmavaraṇa concentrated on making his capital a city of beauty beyond imagination, the buildings a veritable showcase of architecture.

Text 26

padmāvataṁ javapadaṁ
karavīraṁ ca tat puram
nirmitaṁ padma varṇena
prājāpatyena karmaṇā

His kingdom became known as Padamāvata, and the capital was called Karavīrapura. King Padmavaraṇa constructed the city strictly according to the rules prescribed in the scriptures governing architecture.

Text 27

sārasenāpi vihitaṁ ramyaṁ
krauñca puraṁ mahat
campaka aśoka vahulaṁ
vipulaṁ tāmra mṛtikam

Similarly, King Sāras founded a vast and beautiful city known as Krauñchapura as his capital. This delightful city was noted for being filled with *champaka* and *aśhoka* trees. The inhabitants of the extensive kingdom were mainly engaged mining copper and producing copper utensils.

Text 28

vanavāsiti vikhyātaḥ
sphīto janapada mahān
purasya tasya tu śrīmān
drumaiḥ sārvartukai vṛtaḥ

The king also established another beautiful city known as Vanavāsī, which was decorated with innumerable plants and trees that supplied fruit and flowers in all seasons.

Text 29

harito'pi samudrasya
dvīpaṁ samabhi pālayat
ratna sañcaya sampurṇaṁ
nārī jana manoharam

King Harita established a beautiful city bedecked with innumerable gems on an island within the ocean. Because of its opulence, the city was greatly appreciated by ladies.

Text 30

tasya dāśā jale magnā
madgurā nāma viśrutāḥ
ye haranti sadā śaṅkhān
samudra udara cāriṇaḥ

King Harita employed many experienced fishermen known as *madguras* to dive into the depths of the ocean and collect beautiful conch shells.

Text 31

tasyāpare dāśa janāḥ
pravālāñjala sambhavān
saṅ cinvanti sadā yuktā
jāta rūpaṁ ca mauktikam

He also employed many expert divers to collect brilliant pearls and coral from the depths of the ocean to use as offerings to visiting kings.

Text 32

jalajāni ca ratnāni
niṣadās tasya mānavāḥ
pracinvanto'ṛṇave yuktā
naubhi saṅyāna gāminaḥ

King Harita had an expert assistant by the name of Iṣadā who had a fleet of small boats that would scout the depths of the ocean for precious jewels.

Text 33

matsya māṁsena te sarve
vartante sma sadā narāḥ
gṛhynantaḥ sarva ratnāni
ratna dīpa ṇivāsinaḥ

Being inhabitants of this bejeweled island city were mostly sailors and fishermen who earned their living by fishing and collecting jewels.

Text 34

taiḥ saṅyāna gatair dravyair
vaṇijo dūra gāminiḥ
haritaṁ tarpayantekaṁ
yathaiva dhanadaṁ tathā

The *vaiṣya* community would purchase these jewels and pearls and then sell them in far-off countries. Whatever wealth these merchants managed to collect would be deposited with King Harita, just as the Yakṣas place all of their wealth in the care of their master, Kuvera.

Text 35

evam ikṣvāku vaṁśāt tu
yadu vaṁśa vinisṛtaḥ
caturdhā yadu putraistu
caturbhir bhidyate punaḥ

Thus it is seen that the Yadu dynasty branched off from the Ikṣvāku dynasty. Later on, the kingdom of Mahārāja Yadu was divided into parts by his four sons.

Text 36

sa yadur mādhave rājyaṁ
visṛjya yadu puṅgave
triviṣṭapaṁ gato rājā
dehaṁ tyakvā mahītale

After King Yadu had thus divided his kingdom amongst his sons, beginning with his eldest son, Mādhava, who was considered to be the light of the Yadu dynasty, he relinquished his material body and attained his heavenly destination.

Text 37

vabhuva mādhava sutaḥ
satvato nāma vīryavān
sattva vṛtir guṇopetaṁ
rājā rāja guṇe sthitah

King Mādhava had a powerful son named Satvata. He was a pious ruler of men who displayed all godly qualities, being firmly situated in the mode of goodness.

Text 38

sattva tasya suto rājā
bhīma nāma mahāna bhut
yena bhaimāḥ susaṁvṛttāḥ
sattvatāt sātvatāḥ smṛtāḥ

Satvata's son was the magnanimous King Bhīma, whose descendents therefore became known as Bhīmas. They were also known as the Sātvata dynasty because they had descended from Satvata.

Text 39

rājye sthite nape tasmin
rāme rājyaṁ praśāsti
śatrughṇo lavaṇaṁ hatvā
ciccheda sa madhor vanam

When King Bhīma was ruling the kingdom of Ānarta, Lord Rāmacandra was the king at Ayodhyā. During His rule, His son, Śātrughna, killed Madhu's son, Lavaṇa, and destroyed his city.

Text 40

tasmin madhu vane sthāne
puriṁ ca mathurā mimām
niveśayāmāsa vibhuḥ
sumitrā nanda vardhanaḥ

Thereafter, near the forest of Madhuvana, Sumitrā's son, Śatrughna, established the city of Mathurā.

Texts 41-42

paryaye caiva rājasya
bharatasya talhiva ca
sumitrā sutayoś caiva
sthānaṁ prāptam ca vaiṣṇavam

bhīmeneyaṁ pure tena
rājya samvandha kāraṇāt
svavaśe sthāpitā pūrvaṁ
svayam addhāsitā tathā

After Lord Rāmacandra had completed His mission and departed for His own abode, along with Lakṣmaṇa, Bharata, and Śatrughna, King Bhīma ascended the throne at Mathurā, the transcendental abode of Lord Viṣṇu. After the killing of Lavaṇāsura, King Bhīma was the rightful heir of Mathurā and so he took up residence there.

Text 43

tataḥ kuśe sthite rājye
lave tu yuva rajani
andhako nāmo bhīmasya
suto rājyam kārayāt

Thereafter, as Kuśa ruled his kingdom from Ayodhyā, with Lava the heir apparent, Bhīma's son, Andhaka, was installed upon the throne at Mathurā.

Texts 44-45

andhakasya suto yajñe
revato nāma pārthivaḥ

ṛkṣo'pi revatā yajñe
ramie parvata murdhani

tato raivata utpannaḥ
parvataḥ sāgarāntike
nāmnā raivatako nāma
bhūmau bhūmīdharaḥ smṛtaḥ

The son of Andhaka was Revata, who begot Raivata on the beautiful peak of Ṛkṣavān Mountain. Later on, that mountain, which was situated by the seashore, became known as Raivataka Mountain.

Text 46

raivatasya ātmaja rājā
viśvagarbho mahā yaśāḥ
vabhuva pṛthivī pālaḥ
pṛthivyāṁ prathitaḥ prabhuḥ

The son of Raivataka was the well-known King Viśvagarbha, who was a very powerful ruler of men.

Text 47

tasya tisṛṣu bhāryāsu
divya rūpāsu keśava
catvāro yajñire putrā
coka pālopamāḥ śubhāḥ

O Keśava, King Viśvagarbha had three wives who were very pleasing and qualified, and within their wombs, he begot four sons who became powerful rulers of men.

Text 48

vasur vabhruḥ suṣeṇaśca
sabhākṣaś caiva vīryavān
yadu pravīrāḥ prakhyātā
loka pālā ivāpare

These sons were named Vasu, Vabhru, Suṣeṇa, and Sabhākṣa, and these great heroes of the Yadu dynasty were on the level of demigods in terms of prowess.

Texts 49-51

tairayaṁ yadavao vaṁśaḥ
pārthivair vahuli kṛtaḥ
yai sākaṁ kṛṣṇa loke'smin
prajāvantaḥ prajeśvarāḥ

vasostu kunti viṣaye
vasudeva suto vibhuḥ
tataḥ sa janayāmāsa
suprabhe dve ca dārike

kuntiṁ ca pāṇḍor mahiṣīṁ
devatāmīva bhūcarīṁ
bhāryā ca dama ghoṣasya
cedirājasya suprabhām

O Kṛṣṇa, in this way, the Yadu dynasty flourished as each king had many sons and grandsons. From Vasu, who was also called Suraseṇa, Vasudeva was born. He was a very influential personality. After the birth of Vasudeva, Surasena begot two daughters named Pṛthā, who also became known as Kuntī, and Śrutasravā. Kuntī, who was like a goddess of the heavenly planets, was married to King Paṇḍu, and the charming Śrūtasravā was married to Damaghoṣa, the king of Cedi.

Text 52

eṣa te svasya vaṁśasya
prabhavaḥ saṁ prakīrtitaḥ
śruto mayā purā kṛṣṇa
kṛṣṇa dvaipāyanāntikāt

My dear Lord Kṛṣṇa, I have thus described to You the descendents of King Yadu, in whose dynasty I have also appeared, just as I had heard from Kṛṣṇa Dvaipāyana Vyāsa.

Text 53

tvaṁ tvidānīṁ praṇaṣṭe'smin
vaṁśe vaṁśabhṛtāṁ vara
svayambhūriva saṁprāto
bhavāyāsmat jayāya ca

O Kṛṣṇa, this most exalted dynasty is greatly harassed at present but You have appeared within this world like the self-manifested Brahmā to insure that the Yadu dynasty comes out victorious in all respects.

Text 54

na tu tvāṁ paura mātreṇa
śaktā gūhayituṁ vayam
deva gṛheṣvapi bhagnān
sarvajñaḥ sarva bhāvanaḥ

It is not possible for us to convince others that You are an ordinary human being. It is obvious to everyone that You have appeared to accomplish the mission of the demigods, being the omniscient Supreme Personality of Godhead.

Text 55

śaktaścāpi jarā saṅdhaṁ
nṛpaṁ yodhayituṁ vibho
tvad buddhi vaśagāḥ sarve
vayaṁ yodhavrate sthitāḥ

My dear Lord, You are certainly able to contend with Jarāsaṅdha single-handedly. We simply wish to fight his army under Your guidance.

Text 56

jarāsaṅdhas tu valavāṇ
nṛpāṇāṁ murdhni tisthati
aprameya valaścaiva
vayaṁ ca kṛśa sādhanāḥ

We know that King Jajarāsaṅdha is extremely powerful and is surrounded by a vast army that appears to be superior to us.

Text 57

na ceyam ekāham api
pure rodhaṁ sahiṣyati
kṛśa bhakten dhana kṣāmā
durgair pariveṣtitāḥ

The city of Mathurā is not very strongly fortified and due

to a shortage of stocks of food, fuel, and potable water, it cannot survive more than a single day's siege.

Text 58

asaṅskṛtāmbu parikhā
dvārayanta vivarjitā
vapra prākāra nicayā
kartavyā vahu viṣtarā

The moat surrounding the city is now dry and the gates of the city are not very well stocked with weapons. We recommend that for the protection of the city, high walls with platforms should be constructed.

Text 59

saṅskartavya āyudha āgāra
yoktavyā cestikā cayaiḥ
kaṁsasya bala bhogyatvān
nāti guptā purā janaiḥ

The stores of arms should be replenished and fortifications should be made throughout the city. These arrangements were not previously made because it was feared that this would strengthen Kaṁsa's position.

Text 60

sadyo nipatite kaṁse
rājye's smākaṁ navodaye
puri pratyagra rodheva
na rodhaṁ visahiṣyati

Kaṁsa was slain only recently, and so our rule of the kingdom has freshly begun. Just as a king's army surrounds a village to collect taxes, we appear to be surrounded by the formidable enemy.

Text 61

balaṁ samarda bhagnaṁ ca
kṛśyamānaṁ pareṇa ha
asaṁsayam idaṁ rāṣṭraṁ
janaiḥ saha vinaṅkṣati

Our army has been beleaguered by numerous battles and so the enthusiasm of the soldiers is not high. Due to repeated attacks, our morale has slackened. Thus, we must fear for both the city and its inhabitants.

Text 62

yādavānāṁ virodhena
ye jitā rajya kamukaiḥ
te sarve dvaidham icchanti
yat kṣamaṁ tat vidhīyatām

While securing the rule of this kingdom, we have created many enemies, even amongst the Yādavas. Now they will certainly take advantage of our precarious condition and so please carefully consider what should be done.

Text 63

vañcanīyā bhaviṣyāmo
nṛpaṇāṁ nṛpa kāraṇāt
jarāsandha bhayārtānāṁ
dravatāṁ rājya sambhrame

Out of fear of Jarāsaṅdha, many other kings will neglect us and align themselves with him, just to protect their kingdoms.

Text 64

ārtā vakṣanti naḥ sarve
ruddhamānāḥ pure janāḥ
yādavānāṁ virodhena
vinaṣṭā smeti keśave

O Keśava, if the people of this city suffer great losses on account of this attack of Your enemy, they will place all the blame on the Yādavas.

Text 65

etan mama mataṁ Kṛṣṇa
viśrambhāt samudāhṛtam
tvaṁ tu vijñāpitaḥ pūrvaṁ
na punaḥ sampravodhitaḥ

My dear Lord Kṛṣṇa, this is my opinion. I have revealed my feeling to You because I have complete faith in Your judgment. I have informed you of the situation and am not trying to convince You of anything, one way or another.

Text 66

yadatra vaḥ kṣamaṁ kṛṣṇa
tacca vai saṁ vidhīyatām
tvamasya netā sainyasy
vayaṁ tvacchāsne sthitāḥ
tvam mūlaśca virodha'yaṁ
rakṣās mānātmanā saha

O Kṛṣṇa, do whatever You feel is best because You are the leader of the Yādavas, and so we are all Your obedient servants. It is You who have created this enmity and so You must ascertain what is best both for Yourself and for the rest of us.

Thus ends the translation of the thirty-eighth chapter of the Viṣṇu Parva of Śrī Harivaṁsa.

Chapter 39

Kṛṣṇa and Balarāma flee Mathurā, going south. They meet Paraśurāma at Karavīrapura, and are advised by him

Text 1

vaisampayana uvāca
vikarastu vacaḥ śrutvā
vasudeva mahāyaśāḥ
parituṣṭena manasā
vacanaṁ cetam avravit

Vaiśampāyana said: O Janmejaya, after hearing Vikadru's speech, Vasudeva, who was famous for his truthfulness, spoke as follows with great conviction.

Text 2

rājā ṣāḍgunyavaktā vai
rājā mantrārtha tattvavit
satattvaṁ ca hitaṁ caiva
kṛṣṇoktaṁ kila dhīmatā

O Kṛṣṇa, a king is a man who knows the six qualities of political science, and how to apply them, and he must also know the efficacy of chanting *mantras*. The wise Vikadru has spoken the truth for our benefit.

Text 3

bhāṣitā rāja dharmāśca
satyāśca jagato hitāḥ

vikraduṇā yadu śrestha
yaddhitaṁ tad vidhīyatām

O foremost descendent of Yadu, Vikadru has indicated the actual duty of a king and how he must act for the welfare of the world. Now, do whatever You feel to be proper.

Text 4

eṭacchrutvā pitur vākyaṁ
vikradrośca mahātmanaḥ
vākyam uttamam ekagr
vabhāṣe puruṣottamaḥ

After hearing these words of His father, Vasudeva, as well as the speech of Vikadru, the Supreme Personality of Godhead, Lord Kṛṣna, spoke as follows.

Text 5

vruvatāṁ vaḥ śrutaṁ vākyaṁ
hetutaḥ kramatas tathā
nyāyataḥ śāstrataś caiva
daivaṁ civānu pasyatām

I have carefully noted all that you both have said about the cause of the present enmity, the prowess of our enemies, the duties of a righteous king, the orders of the scriptures, and what should be expected in the future by the arrangement of providence.

Texts 6-7

śruyatām uttaraṁ vākyaṁ
śrutvā ca parigrhyatām

nayena vyavahartavyaṁ
pārthivena yathā kramam

sandhiṁ ca vigrahaṁ caiva
yānam āsanam eva ca
dvaidhi bhavaṁ saṁ śrayaṁ ca
ṣāḍaguṇyaṁ cintayet sadā

Now hear what I have to say and if you think that it is acceptable, tell Me. There is no doubt that a king should act according to the science of diplomacy and that he should possess the six qualities of a ruler of men. He should perfectly understand the strengths and weaknesses of his enemies and if he is confident of victory, he should not hesitate to attack them. Everything depends upon finding the right opportunity, and there is no harm in acting with duplicity to attain victory. However, if one's enemy is clearly more powerful, a wise king will surrender without a fight.

Text 8

balina saṅnikrṣṭe tu
na stheyaṁ paṇḍitena vai
apakramedbhi kālajñaḥ
samartho yuddham udvahet

An intelligent king should never challenge an enemy who is more powerful than him. One should be confident that an opportune time will come, and thus he should acquiesce to a strong enemy for the time being. One should engage in battle only if he is confident of attaining victory.

Text 9

ahaṁ tāvat sahāryeṇa
mūhurte'smin prakaśite
jīvitārthaṁ gamisyāmi
śaktimān api śaktavat

In spite of being supremely powerful, I will pretend to be weak by running away, along with Balarāma, and wait for the opportune time.

Text 10

tataḥ sahyācala yutaṁ
sahāryeṇa aham kṣayam
ātma dvitīyaḥ śrīmantaṁ
pravekṣe dakṣiṇā patham

After fleeing the city, Balarāma and I will proceed toward the southern province which is very beautifully situated adjacent to the Sahya Mountain.

Text 11

karavīra puraṁ caiva
ramyam krauñca puraṁ tathā
drakṣyāvas tatra sahitau
gomantaṁ ca nagottamam

We will first visit Karavīrapura, then the beautiful city of Krauñcapura, and finally arrive at the best of mountains, Gomantaka.

Text 12

āvayor gamanaṁ śrutvā
jita kāśi sa pārthivaḥ
apraviṣya purṁ darpād
anusāraṁ karisyati

When Jarāsandha comes to know that We have fled to the South, he will surely exhibit great pride, thinking himself to be very powerful, so that rather than attacking Mathurā, he will follow Us.

Text 13

tataḥ sahya vaneṣveva
rājā yāti sa sānugāḥ
āvayor grahaṇe caiva
nṛpatiḥ prayatisyati

Accompanied by his army, the king will enter the forest surrounding the Sahya mountain, hoping to capture Us.

Text 14

eṣā naḥ śreyasī yātrā
bhavisyati kūlasya vai
paurāṇām atha puryāśca
deśasya ca sukhāvahā

I think that this plan will be in the best interests of the Yādavas, the people of Mathurā, and everyone in the country ruled by King Śuraseṇa.

Text 15

na ca śatroḥ paribhraṣṭā
rājāno vijigiṣavaḥ
para rāṣṭrreṣu mṛṣyanti
mṛdhe śatroḥ kṣayaṁ vinā

When an enemy flees from a king who is very eager for victory, he will never rest peacefully until he has sought him out and killed him.

Text 16

evaṁ uktvā tu tau vīrau
kṛṣṇa saṅkarṣaṇā vubhau
prapeda tura sambhrāntau
dakṣiṇau dakṣiṇāpatham

After saying this, the two most expert strategists, Kṛṣṇa and Balarāma, departed the city, going toward the South, although They were not at all afraid.

Text 17

tau tu rāṣṭrāni śataśas
carantau kāma rūpinau
dakṣiṇāṁ diśamāsthāya
ceratur mārgagau sukham

These two most exalted personalities, who could assume any form at will, traversed a great distance by the highway and finally arrived at the Southern province.

Text 18

sahya pṛstheṣu ramyeṣu
moda mānā vubhau tathā
dakṣiṇā pathagau vīrāvat
dhānaṁ saṁprapedatuḥ

After traversing the Sahya mountain range, which was pleasing to see, They continued walking along the highway further south.

Text 19

tau ca svalpena kālena
sahyācala vibhūṣitam
karavīra puraṁ praptau
sva vaṁśena vibhūṣitam

After some time, the two brothers arrived at the city of Karavīrapura, which appeared to be decorated with a garland of mountains of the Sahya mountain range. Their were many members of Their dynasty residing there.

Text 20

tau tatra gatvā veṇāyā
nadyās tīrāṇtam āśritam
āsedatuḥ prarahāḍhyaṁ
nyagrodhaṁ taru puṅgavam

Before entering the city, the two brothers sat beneath a *varagada* tree with many roots extending downward that grew on the banks of Veṇā River.

Texts 21-25

ahas tāt tasya vṛkṣasya
muniṁ dīpta tapodhanaṁ
aṁsāvasakta paraśuṁ
jaṭā valkala dhāriṇam

gauram agni śikhākāram
tejasā bhāskaro pamam
kṣatrānta kara okṣabhyaṁ
vapuṣmantam ivārṇavam

nyasta saṅkucitādhānaṁ
kale hūta hūtāśanam
klinnaṁ triṣa varṇābhyo
virādhyaṁ deva guruṁ yathā

savastsāṁ dhenukāṁ śvetāṁ
homa dhuk kāma dohanām
kṣirāraṇiṁ karṣamāṇam
mahendra giri gocaram

dadrśatustau sahitāva
pariśrāntam avyayam
bhārgavaṁ rāmam āsīnam
mandarasthaṁ yathā ravim

While seated beneath that huge tree, the two brothers saw the greatly effulgent ascetic, Paraśurāma of the Bhṛgu dynasty, sitting nearby. He had matted hair and was dressed in tree bark, and he held an axe in his left hand. His complexion was fair and he was illuminating, like fire. Paraśurāma, the annihilator of the *kṣatriyas*, appeared to be as grave and unfathomable as the ocean. Although he had completed his daily performance of fire sacrifice, he was seen offering oblations into the sacrificial fire from time to time. Because he bathed three times daily, his clothing remained wet. He resembled Brhaspati, the spiritual master of the demigods. He had a white cow whose milk was only used for his sacrificial performances, and so she was called Homadhenu. She was also known as Kāmadhenu because she would supply anything the sage desired. Paraśurāma, who never feels fatigue, was preparing to take his glorious cow somewhere. Kṛṣṇa and Balarāma thus saw Paraśurāma, who normally remains on the peak of Mount Mahendra, just like a bright sun risen above the mountains.

Text 26

nyāyatastau tu taṁ dṛṣtvā
pādamūle kṛtāñjali
vasudeva sutau vīrau
sadhiṣṇāviva pavakau

When the two sons of Vasudeva saw Paraśurāma, They devotedly offered obeisances with folded hands. At that time, the sage appeared like the blazing fire within the sacrificial pit.

Text 27

krsnastam ṛṣi śārdulam
uvāca vadatāṁ varaḥ
ślakṣaṇaṁ madhurayā vācā
rāmaṁ munināṁ ṛṣabhaṁ
kṣatriyānāṁ kūlāntakam

Thereafter, Lord Kṛṣṇa, the most eloquent of speakers, who is most expert in all departments of knowledge, spoke with great affection to that topmost sage, Paraśurāma, the annihilator of the *kṣatriyas*.

Text 28

bhagavan jāmadagnaṁ tvām
avagacchāmi bhārgavam
rāmaṁ munināṁ ṛṣabhaṁ
kṣātrīyānāṁ kūlāntakam

O Lord, I can understand that you are the son of Jamadagni, the foremost of sages, Paraśurāma, the ornament in the Bhṛgu dynasty, who annihilated all the *kṣatriyas* of the world.

Text 29

tvayā sayaka vegena
kṣipto bhārgava sāgaraḥ
iṣupātena nagaraṁ
kṛtaṁ surpārakaṁ tvayā

O descendent of Bhṛgu, you pushed back the waves of the ocean by the force of your arrows and then established the city of Surpāraka on that reclaimed land.

Text 30

dhanuḥ pañcaśatāyām
amiṣupañca śatocchṛayam
sahyasya ca nikuñjeṣu
sphito janapada mahān

This city was five hundred bow-lengths in length and half that in breadth and was located within the groves beneath the Sahya mountain.

Texts 31-33

atikramya dadher belām
aparānte niveśitaḥ
tvayā tat kārtavīryasya
sahasra bhuja kānanam

chinnaṁ paraśu naikena
smaratā nidhanaṁ pituḥ
iyaṁ adyāpi rūdhiraiḥ
kṣatriyānāṁ etad viṣām

snighais tatoparaśut sṛṣtai
rakta paṅkā vasundarā
rainukeyaṁ vijāne tvāṁ
kṣitau kṣiti paroṣaṇam

You had forcefully taken this land that belonged to the ocean to establish this prosperous city. To avenge the killing of your father, you had cut off Kārtavīryārjuna's one thousand arms. Thereafter, the soil became soaked with the blood of the dead bodies of the *kṣatriyas* who were slain by your powerful axe. I am confident that you are the same Paraśurāma, the son of Reṇukā.

Texts 34-36

paraśu pragrahe yuktaṁ
yathaiveha raṇe tathā
tad icchāvas tvayā vipra
kaṭcid arthaṁ upaśrūtam

uttaṁ ca śrutārthena
pratyuktam aviśaṅkayā
āvayor mathurā rāma
yamunā tīra śadhinī

yādavau svo muni śreṣtha
yadi te śrutim āgatau
vasudeva yadu śreṣṭhaḥ
pita nau hi dhṛtavrataḥ

O exalted *brāhmaṇa*, because you still hold your axe, as if you are prepared to enter the battlefield, We wish to ask you something and are eager to hear your reply. O foremost of sages, Paraśurāma, We are members of the Yadu dynasty and residents of Mathurā which is situated by the side of the Yamunā River. You may be familiar with Our names. We are sons of Vasudeva, the great descendent of Yadu and performer of religious vows.

Text 37

janma prabhṛti caivāvāṁ
vrageṣveva niyojitau
tau svaḥ kaṁsa bhayāt
tatra saṅkitau parivarddhitau

We two brothers had grown up in Vraja incognito, due to fear of Kaṁsa, who had terrorized the members of Our dynasty.

Texts 38-39

vayaśca prathamaṁ prāptau
mathurāyāṁ praveśitau
tāvāvāṁ vyuthitaṁ hatvā
samāje kaṁsa mojasā

pitaraṁ tasya tatraiva
sthāpayitvā janeśvaram
svameva karma cārabdhau
gavāṁ vyāpāra kārakau

When We grew up, we went to Mathurā and killed sinful Kaṁsa, who had deviated from the principles of religion. We then installed his father, Ugrasena, on the royal throne at Mathurā. Thereafter, although We had intended to return to Vraja to take care of Our cows, We were delayed due to the threat of Our enemies.

Texts 40-41

athāvayoḥ puraṁ rodhyuṁ
jarāsandho vyavasthitaḥ
saṅgrāmān su vahun kṛtvā
labdha lakṣāvapi svayaṁ

tataḥ svapupra rakṣārthaṁ
prajānāṁ ca dhṛtavrata
akrtārthāva anudyogau
kartavya bala sādhanau

After some time, King Jarāsandha decided to attack Our city of Mathurā. Although We both fought valiantly and defeated him again and again, He returned with renewed enthusiasm, so that the residents of Mathurā are once again threatened. O sage, as a tactic, We fled the city to avoid another confrontation and in that way We have arrived here.

Text 42

arathau pattinau yuddhe
nistanutrau nirāyudhau
jarāsandhodyam bhayāt
purād dvāveva niḥsṛtau

We fled from the attack of Jarāsandha on foot and so We are without a chariot or any weapons or armor.

Text 43

evamāvā manu prāptau
muni śreṣṭha tvavāntikam
āvayor mantra mātreṇa
kartum arhasi sat kriyāt

O foremost of sages, in this condition We have approached you, hoping that you will guide Us for our benefit.

Text 44

śrutvaitad bhārgavau rāmas
tayor vākyam aninditam
raiṇukeyaḥ prativaco
dharma saṁhitaṁ avravit

After hearing this sincere appeal, Paruśurāma, the son of Reṇukā and descendent of Bhṛgu, replied according to religious principles.

Text 45

aparāntā dahaṁ kṛṣna
sampratīhā gataḥ prabho
eka eva vinā śiṣyair
yuvayair mantra kāraṇāt

O all-powerful Lord Kṛṣṇa, simply to assist You in this pastime by giving You sage advice, I have come to this secluded place without any of my disciples or associates.

Text 46

vidito me vraje vāsas
tava padma nibhekṣaṇa
dānavānāṁ vadhaścāpi
kaṁsasyāpi durāṭmanaḥ

O lotus-eyed Lord, I am well aware of Your appearance and Your pastimes in Vraja, and I know that the sinful Kaṁsa and many other demons have been killed by You.

Text 47

vigrahaṁ ca jarāsandhe
viditvā puruṣatoma
tava sa bhāṭṛkasyeha
saṁprāpto'smi varānana

O Supreme Lord having an enchanting face, after learning of Jarāsandha's assault on Your city, I came here to meet You and Your brother.

Text 48

jāne tvāṁ Kṛṣṇa goptāraṁ
jagataḥ prabhum avyayam
deva kāryārtha siddharthaṁ
bālaṁ balata gatam

O Kṛṣṇa, I know that You are the eternal master of the universe. To accomplish Your mission on behalf of the demigods, You have assumed a human-like form, although you are never conditioned by material nature.

Text 49

na tvayā viditaṁ kincit
triṣu lokeṣu vidyate
tathāpi bhakti mātrena
śṛṇu vakṣami te vacaḥ

There is nothing within the three worlds that is unknown to You. Still, being inspired by my devotion for You, I will advise You as You have requested. Please hear me with attention.

Text 50

pūrvajasi tava govinda
pūrvaṁ puramidaṁ kṛtam
karavīra puraṁ nāma
rāṣṭraṁ caiva niveśitam

O Govinda, long ago Your ancestor had established this city of Karavīrapura, from where he ruled his kingdom.

Text 51

pure'smin nṛpatiḥ kṛṣṇa
vāsudeva mahāyaśāḥ
śṛgāla iti vikhyāto
nityaṁ parama kopanoḥ

My dear Lord Kṛṣṇa, at present the king of Karavīrapura is named Śṛgāla, and he also goes by the name of Vāsudeva. He is a very arrogant person, easily prone to fits of anger.

Text 52

nṛpeṇa tena govinda
tava vaṁśa bhavā nṛpāḥ
dāyadā nihatāḥ sarve
vīra dveṣānu śāyinā

O Govinda, this king, Śṛgāla Vāsudeva is very envious of others. Indeed, he has killed many kings of Your exalted dynasty.

Text 53

ahaṅkāra paro nityam
ajitātma ati matsarī
rājyaiśvarya madāviṣṭaḥ
putreṣuvapi ca dāruṇaḥ

Being arrogant and puffed-up, he constantly inspires fear in others. Being overly proud of his kingdom and wealth, he even treats his own sons without mercy.

Text 54

tanneha bhavataḥ sthānaṁ
rocate me narottama
karavīra pure ghore
mityaṁ pārthiva dūṣite

O foremost of great personalities, for this reason I think that it is not wise for You to remain here at Karavīrapura. Only further enmity awaits You in the form of King Śṛgāla.

Text 55

śrūyatāṁ kathayisyāmi
yatrobhau śatru badhanau
jarāsandhaṁ balodagraṁ
bhavantauyodhayiṣyataḥ

I will suggest to You a place where You brothers can remain to confront Jarāsandha so that his attack on Mathurā can be thwarted.

Text 56

tīrtvā veṇāmīmāṁ puṇyāṁ
nadī madhyaiva bāhubhiḥ
viṣayānte nivāsāya
giriṁ gacchāma durgamam

Let us depart at once, crossing the River Veṇā without difficulty, and go to an impassible mountain that is situated near Karavīrapura. It is there that I suggest we reside.

Text 57

ramyaṁ yajñagiriṁ nāma
sahyasya praruhaṁ girim
nivāsaṁ māṁsa bhakṣānāṁ
caurānāṁ ghora karmanām

This mountain is called Yajñagirī, and it is part of the Sahya mountain range. It is a very pleasant place, but it is mostly inhabited by meat-eating plunderers who engage in all kinds of sinful activities.

Texts 58-59

nānā druma latā yuktaṁ
citraṁ puṣpita padapam
proṣye tatra niśāmekāṁ
khaṭvāṅgāṁ nāma nimnagām

bhadraṁ te saṅtariṣyāṁo
nikaṣo pala bhūṣanām
gaṅgā pratāpa pratimāṁ
bhraṣṭā ca mahato gireḥ

This mountain is always decorated with flowering trees so that it appears very beautiful. We should remain there for one night and then cross the Khaṭvāṅgā River, which is filled with impressive rocks. O Lord, may You attain auspiciousness! This beautiful river resembles the Ganges in all respects.

Texts 60-61

tasyāḥ prapātaṁ drakṣāmas
tāpa sāraṇya bhūṣaṇam
upabhujyatvi mān kāmān
gatvā tān dharaṇī dharān

drakṣāmas tatra viprān
sāmyato vai tapo dhanān
ramyaṁ krauñch puraṁ nāma
gamiṣyāmaḥ purottamam

There is a beautiful waterfall on the Khaṭvāṅgā River that is decorated with beautiful forests on both sides. We will go there, have our meal, and spend some time wandering through the lovely forests. We can meet the *brāhmaṇas* who live in those forests, undergoing severe austerities. Thereafter, we will go to the city of Krauñcapura.

Text 62

vaṁśajas tatra te rājā
kṛṣṇa dharma rataḥ sadā
mahā kapiriti khyato
vanavāsī janādhīpaḥ

O Kṛṣṇa, Krauñcapura is ruled by a very pious king named Mahākapi who belongs to Your dynasty. He also rules the city of Vanavāsī and the surrounding district.

Text 63

tama dṛṣṭaiva rājānaṁ
nivāsāya gate'hani
tīrtha māna ḍuhaṁ nāma
tatrasthā śyāma saṅgatā

There is no need for us to meet this king. We can bypass the city and proceed on so that by evening we can reach the holy place called Āṇḍuha, where the three of us can stay for some time.

Text 64

tataścyutā gamiṣyāmaḥ
sahyasya vivare girim
gomantam iti vikhyātaṁ
naika śṛṅga vibhūṣitam

Thereafter, we can travel further into the forest where there are caves in the Sahya mountains and thus finally arrive at the well-known Gomanta Hill, which has beautiful peaks.

Text 65

svarga taika mahā śṛṅgaṁ
durā rohaṁ khagairapi
viśrāma bhūta devānāṁ
jyotir bhirabhi saṁ vṛtam

One of the hill's peaks is so high that it seems to reach the heavenly planets. Even powerful birds cannot cross over it. That mountain peak is effulgent and a resting place of the demigods.

Text 66

sopāna bhūtaṁ svargasya
gaganādriivocchitam
taṁ vimāna avataranaṁ
giriṁ veruṁ ivāparam

Indeed, this mountain peak is considered to be a stairway to heaven. The demigods come there in their celestial chariots. It appears like a mountain floating in the sky and not a mere hill of this earth. Thus it resembles Mount Sumeru.

Texts 67-68

tasyotame mahāśṛṅge
bhāsvantau deva rūpinau
udayās tamaye sūryam
somaṁ ca jyotiṣāṁ patim

ūrmimantaṁ samudraṁ ca
apāra dvīpa bhūṣanam
prekṣa mānau sukhaṁ tatra
nagāgre vicariṣyataḥ

You two brothers have wonderfully beautiful forms, just befitting the residents of heaven. You can happily reside on the peak of Gomanta Hill for some time. From there, You will have a good view of the sea, with its islands and sparkling waves, and You can enjoy watching the sunrise and sunset, as well as the moonlit nights.

Text 69

śṛṅgasthau tasya śaulasya
gomantasya vane carau
dūrga yuddhena dhavantau
jarāsandhaṁ vijeṣvathaḥ

You can set up camp on the peak of Gomanta Hill and enjoy wandering throughout the surrounding forests. From the peak of Gomanta Hill, You two great heroes can contend with Jarāsandha and thus defeat him.

Text 70

tatra śaulagatau dṛṣṭvā
bhavantau yuddha dūrmadau
āsakrtaḥ śaula yuddhe vai
jarāsandho bhavisyati

When Jarāsandha arrives and sees how You are eager to fight from the top of the hill, he will certainly accept the challenge, being intoxicated by false pride.

Text 71

bhavantorapi yuddhe tu
pravṛtte tatra dāruṇe

āyudhaiḥ saha saṅyogaṁ
pasyāmi nacirādiva

When a fierce battle commences, I will have the opportunity to witness Your use of celestial weapons against the mighty Jarāsandha.

Text 72

saṅgrāmaśca mahān kṛṣṇa
nirdiṣṭas tatra daivataiḥ
yadunāṁ pārthivānām ca
māṁsa śoṇita kardamaḥ

O Lord Kṛṣṇa, the demigods had predicted that there would be a terrible battle between the Yādavas and their enemies, so that a river of blood from the slain soldiers would be created.

Texts 73-74

tatra cakraṁ halaṁ caiva
gadāṁ kaumadakīṁ tathā
saunandaṁ muṣalaṁ caiva
vaiṣṇavāṇ āyudhāni ca

darśayiṣyanti saṅgrāme
pāsyanti ca mahīkṣitām
rudhīraṁ kāla yuktanāṁ
vapurbhiḥ kāla sannibhau

I am confident that You two will employ Your Sudarśana *cakra*, Samvartaka plough, Kaumadakī club, and Saunanda *muṣala*, as well other imperishable weapons of Lord Viṣṇu. These transcendental weapons will certainly drink the blood of all who oppose You, thus ending their sinful lives.

Text 75

sa cakra muṣalo nāma
saṅgrāma kṛṣṇa viśrutaḥ
daivatairiha nirdiṣṭaḥ
kālasya ādeśa saṁjñitaḥ

O Kṛṣṇa! The demigods indicated that the conflict that will take place here, conducted within the jurisdiction of Yamarāja, will later on be known as the *cakra muṣala* battle.

Text 76

tatra te kṛṣṇa saṅgrāme
suvyaktaṁ vaiṣṇavaṁ vapuḥ
drakṣyanti ripavaḥ sarve
surāśca sura bhāvana

My dear Kṛṣṇa, You are the shelter of the demigods and indeed the entire material creation. While witnessing this terrible battle, the demigods will have the opportunity to gaze upon Your transcendental form.

Text 77

tāṁ bhajasva gadāṁ kṛṣṇa
cakraṁ ca cira vismṛtam
bhajasva svena rūpena
surānāṁ vijayāya vai

O Kṛṣṇa, whose transcendental form never deteriorates, although You have come here without weapons, to insure Your victory on behalf of the demigods, You should invoke Your invincible *cakra* and club.

Text 78

balaścāyaṁ halaṁ ghoraṁ
muṣalaṁ cāri bhedanam
vadhāya sura śatrunāṁ
bhajatāl loka bhāvanaḥ

Balarāma, who always acts for the welfare of the world, should also invoke his divine weapons, the plough and *muṣala*, which easily tear apart the lives of the enemies.

Text 79

eṣa te prathamaḥ kṛṣṇa
saṅgrāma bhuvi pārthivaiḥ
pṛthivyarthe samākhyato
bhārāvatarane suraiḥ

O Kṛṣṇa, this will be Your first major battle against the demoniac kings who are enemies of the demigods, and thus it will help diminish the burden of the earth.

Text 80

āyudhā vyaptir atraiva
vapuṣo vaiṣṇavasya ca
lakṣamāśca tejaśas caiva
vyuhānāṁ ca vidāranam

Now is the time for You to employ Your personal weapons, exhibit Your transcendental form, and reveal Your unlimited opulence while contending with Your enemies.

Text 81

ataḥ prabhṛti saṅgrāme
dharaṇyāṁ śastra murcchitaḥ
bhavisyati mahān kṛṣṇa
bhārataṁ nāma vaiśasam

My dear Lord Kṛṣṇa, ultimately there will come to be a great war between all the kings of the world that will be the subject of a great literary classic known as *Mahābhārata*.

Text 82

tad gaccha kṛṣṇa śaulendraṁ
gomantaṁ ca nagottamam
jarāsandha mṛdhe cāpi
vijayastvām upasthitaḥ

O Kṛṣṇa, You should therefore proceed to Gomanta Hill without delay. Victory over Jarāsandha in a fierce battle is awaiting You there.

Text 83

idaṁ caivāmṛtaṁ prakhyaṁ
homa dhenoḥ payo'mṛtaṁ
pītvā gacchata bhadraṁ vo
mayā'diṣṭena vartamanā

May You achieve auspiciousness. Please accept some milk from my celebrated Homadhenu cow. It is my wish that You execute all the instructions that I have given You.

Thus ends the translation of the thirty-ninth chapter of the Viṣṇu Parva of Śrī Harivaṁsa.

Chapter 40

Kṛṣṇa, Balarāma, and Paraśurāma travel to Gomanta Hill

Text 1

vaiśampāyana uvāca
tattu dhenvāḥ payaḥ pītvā
bala darpa samanvitau
tatastau rāma sahitau
prasthitau yadu puṅgavau

Vaiśampāyana said: O Janamejaya, after drinking the milk of the Homadhenu cow, Kṛṣṇa and Balarāma, the scions of the Yadu dynasty, feeling invigorated with prowess and enthusiasm, departed, along with Paraśurāma.

Text 2

gomantaṁ parvataṁ draṣṭuṁ
matta nāgendra gāmīnau
jāmadagnya pradiṣṭena
mārgena vadatām varau

Eager to see the beauty of Gomanta Hill, which had been portrayed by Paraśurāma, Kṛṣṇa and Balarāma, the foremost of eloquent speakers, set out, walking like two maddened elephants.

Text 3

jāmadagnya tṛtiyāste
trayastraya ivāgnayaḥ

śobhayanti sma panthānaṁ
tridivaṁ tridaśā iva

Paraśurāma accompanied the two brothers. They appeared very brilliant and enchanting, so that they enhanced the beauty of the surroundings, just as the demigods enhance the beauty of the heavenly planets.

Text 4

te ccādhya vidhinā sarve
tato vai divasa kramāt
gomantaṁ acalaṁ prāptā
mandaraṁ tridaśā iva

In due course of time, they arrived in the vicinity of Gomanta Hill, appearing like the demigods of heaven approaching the peak of Mandara Mountain.

Text 5

lata cāru vicitraṁ ca
nānā druma vibhūṣitam
nānā guru pinadāṅgaṁ
citraṁ citrair manoharaiḥ

The mountain was pleasing to behold because of its numerous flowering trees and plants. Everywhere the scent of *aguru* was perceived, as well as that of other fragrant substances. Peacocks strutting here and there added to the beauty of the surroundings.

Text 6

dvirepha gaṇa saṅkīrṇaṁ
śilā saṅkaṭa pādapam
matta varhiṇa nirghoṣair
nāditaṁ meghanādibhiḥ

Everywhere was seen humming bumblebees, rocks of various colors, and varieties of trees, and masses of dark clouds hung over the mountain, increasing its beauty. The crowing of the peacocks echoed in the mountain caves.

Text 7

gaganālagni śikharaṁ
jalada āsakta pādapam
matta dvīpa viṣāṇāgraiḥ
paridhṛsto palāṅkitam

The mountain peak seemed to touch the sky and clouds appeared to be embracing the trees. Some of the gigantic protruding boulders appeared like tusks of elephants. In this way, the mountain provided a feast for the eyes.

Text 8

kūjadbhiś cāṇdaja gaṇaiḥ
samantāt pratināditam
dūri prapāta amburabaiś
cchannaṁ śārdula tallajaiḥ

Varieties of birds sang in their distinctive styles, filling the atmosphere with pleasant sounds. Waterfalls issued forth from the caves of the mountain and in some places, the falling water produced a loud sound like the roaring of a tiger.

Text 9

nīlāsma caya saṅghātair
vahu varṇaṁ yathā dhanam
dhātu visrāva digdhāṅgaṁ
sānu prasrava bhūsitam

There were masses of bluish rocks here and there that made the mountain appear as if it were decorated with colorful clouds. The water of the streams was saffron colored, making the mountain appear as if it had been smeared with sandalwood paste. Numerous waterfalls added to the beauty of that mountain.

Text 10

kīrṇaṁ suraganaiḥ kāntair
mainākaṁ iva kāṁagam
ucchṛtaṁ suviśālāgraṁ
samūlāmbu parisravam

That mountain was a place of pleasure pastimes for the demigods, who were thus seen to be like so many luminous moons, delighting in the numerous streams that fell from the peak.

Texts 11-13

sa kānana dari prasthaṁ
svetābhra gaṇa bhūṣitam
panasā mrātakāmrai ghair
vatrasyandana candanaiḥ

tamālai lavana yutaṁ
marīca kṣupa saṅkulam
pippali valli kalilaṁ
citrāmaṅgudi pādapaiḥ

drumaiḥ sarjarasānāṁ ca
sarvataḥ pari śobhitam
prāṁśu śāla vanair yuktaṁ
vahu citra vanair yutam

That king of mountains, which was decorated with nice caves, forests, and peaks, was also adorned with white clouds. There were seen everywhere numerous jackfruit, mango, hog-plum, *tamāla*, and sandalwood trees, and also many bushes full of cardamom, chilies, and black peppers. There were also fig trees, banyan trees with roots extending downwards, thorny plants, and varieties of spices. The mountain was surrounded by tall *sarjaras* and *śāla* trees, giving it a very lush appearance.

Text 14

sarja nimbārjuna vanaṁ
pātali kula saṅkulan
hintālaiśca tamālaiśca
punnāgaiśca upaśobhitam

There were also *neem*, *arjuna* and numerous other trees in those forests. *Patāla* trees especially made the forests appear enchanting, as did trees such as the *oripment*, *tamāla* and nutmeg, which thrived near the peak.

Text 15

jaleṣu jalajaiśchannaṁ
sthaleṣu sthalajair api
paṅkajair druma khaṇḍaiśca
sarvataḥ prati bhūsitam

In the numerous ponds surrounding the mountain there

were lotus flowers and water lilies, and in the fields there were land lotuses and many other flowering plants that seemed to be the mountain's decorations.

Text 16

jambu jambula vṛkṣadhyām
kadru kandala bhūsitam
campaka aśoka bakulaṁ
bilva tinduka śobhitam

The mountain was also adorned with blackberry, betel nut, wood apple, banana, jasmine, *aśoka*, *vakula*, *bilva* and *tinduka* trees and plants.

Text 17

kuñjaiśca nāga puṣpaiśca
samantād upaśobhitam
nāga yuthā samākīrṇaṁ
mṛga saṅghāta śobhitam

Secluded groves with *nāgakeśara* plants surrounding the mountain enhanced its beauty. Many elephants and deer were seen wandering in the forests.

Text 18

siddha cāraṇa rakṣobhiḥ
sevita prastara antaraṁ
gandharvaiśca samāyuktaṁ
guhyakaiḥ pakṣibhiś tathā

Amid the rocks, many perfected beings, Cāraṇas and

Rākṣasas were seated. Gandharvas, Guhyakas, and birds came to enjoy the pleasant atmosphere of the mountain.

Text 19

vidyādhara ganair nityam
anukīrṇa śilātalam
siṁha śārdula saṅnadaiḥ
satataṁ pratināditam
sevitaṁ vāri dhārābhiś
candra pādaiśca sobhitam

The Vidyādharas also took great pleasure in roaming about that rugged terain. The roaring of lions and tigers reverberated throughout the region. The flowing water of the numerous streams and the lovely rays of the moon reflected upon it increased the beauty of that scenic mountain.

Text 20

stutaṁ tridaśa gandharavair
apsarobhir alaṅkrtam
vanaspatināṁ divyānāṁ
puṣpair uccāvaccaiḥ śritam

The demigods and Gandharvas take pleasure in praising that wonderful hill, and Apsarās were seen roaming at will. Fragrant flowering plants and creepers, as well as medicinal herbs grew everywhere in abundance.

Text 21

śakra vajra prahārāṇam
anabhijñaṁ divyānāṁ

dāvāgni bhaya nirmuktaṁ
mahā vāta bhayojjhitam

This mountain has never experienced the attack of Indra's thunderbolt and the subsequent pain. This mountain has no fear of a fire or devastating storm.

Text 22

pratāpa prabhavabhiśca
saridbhir upaśobhitam
kānanair ānanākārair
viśeṣadbhir iva śrītam

Many rivers are formed by the ample water that pours from the mountain streams that are decorated with nice waterfalls. The forests on the slopes of the mountain appear to be its mouths.

Text 23

jala śaibala śṛṅgāgair
unmiṣantam iva śrīyā
sthalibhir mṛga juṣṭabhiḥ
kāntābhir upaśobhitam

The lofty mountain peak, which is covered with dew-laden moss, appears to be attempting to see Lakṣmī-devī face to face. The numerous forests and gardens teeming with animals and birds provide great delight to those that behold them.

Texts 24-26

pārśvair upala kalmāṣair
meghair iva vibhūṣitam

pādapacchanna bhūmibhiḥ
sa puṣpāhi samantatah

maṇḍitaṁ vanarājibhiḥ
pramadabhi patir yathā
sundaribhir darībhiśca
kaṇḍarābhis tathaiva ca

teṣu teṣu avakāseṣu
sa dāraṁ iva śobhitam
auṣadhī dīpta śikharaṁ
vānaprastha niṣevitam
jāta rūpair vana deśaiḥ
kṛtṛmairiva bhūṣitam

The stones of many colors dotting the mountain make it appear as if it is covered by clouds of varying hues. In the gardens surrounding the mountain, the vegetation is so thick that the sunlight does not reach the ground in most places. These gardens appear like many chaste wives surrounding their husband. There are nice caves in the mountain and the adjoining valleys provide suitable places of residence for many saintly persons in the *vānaprastha* order of life. Various medicinal herbs grow profusely on the top of the mountain, which is nicely decorated with lush forests.

Text 27

mūlena suviśālena
śira sāpyucchṛtena ca
pṛthiviṁ antarikṣaṁ ca
grāhayantam iva sthitam

The mountain, whose peak seemed to touch the sky, its

base firmly planted in the earth, appeared as if it were measuring the distance from the earth to the highest reaches of outer space.

Text 28

te samāsādya gomantaṁ
ramyaṁ bhūmi dharottamam
rūciraṁ rūrūcuḥ sarve
vāsāyā mara sannibhāḥ

After witnessing the enchanting beauty of Gomanta Hill, which is considered the best of all mountains, the three exalted personalities decided to reside there for some time.

Text 29

rūrūhaste girivaraṁ
khamurdham iva pakṣiṇaḥ
asajjamānā vegena
vainateya parākramāḥ

The three best of all great personalities, who were as powerful as Garuḍa, climbed the excellent mountain without impediment, just as a bird flies into the sky, without stopping or looking back.

Text 30

te tu tasyottaraṁ śṛṇgaṁ
ārudhā stridaśā iva
agāraṁ sahasā cakrur
manasā nirmitopamam

They soon reached the summit, appearing like three demigods descended upon the earth, and They constructed Their residence with the speed of mind.

Text 31

niviṣṭau yādavau dṛṣṭvā
jāmadagnyo mahāmatiḥ
rāmo'bhi matam akliṣṭam
āpraṣṭum upacakrame

After seeing how the two descendents of Yadu were nicely situated, the greatly intelligent Paraśurāma made up his mind to return home. With that in mind, he began speaking as follows.

Text 32

kṛṣṇa yāsyāmyahaṁ tāta
puraṁ surpārakaṁ vibhau
yuvayor nāsti vaimukhyaṁ
saṅgrāme daivatair api

My dear Kṛṣṇa! O supremely powerful Lord, I will now return to the city of Śurpāraka. What to speak mere human beings, even the demigods cannot defeat You two brothers in battle.

Text 33

praptavānasmi yāṁ prītiṁ
mārgānu gamanād api
sā me krsnānu gṛhnāti
sariraṁ idaṁ avyayam

O Kṛṣṇa, I have experienced great happiness while following the path traversed by You two. Your association is a great favor upon me, whose body is indestructible.

Text 34

idaṁ tat sthānam uddiṣṭaṁ
yatrāyudha samāgamaḥ
yuvayor vihito devaiḥ
samaya sāmparāyikaḥ

This is the place that I had told You about and it is here that You should invoke Your personal weapons. Indeed, the demigods are very eager to bestow these weapons upon You, for the welfare of the world.

Text 35

devānāṁ mukhya vaikuṇṭha
viṣṇo devair abhiṣṭutaḥ
kṛṣṇa sarvasya lokasya
śṛṇu me naiṣṭhikaṁ vacaḥ

O foremost of universal controllers! O Lord of Vaikuṇṭha, I know that You are the all-pervading Lord Viṣṇu, who is perpetually worshiped by the demigods. O Kṛṣṇa, please hear these confidential words that are meant for everyone's benefit.

Texts 36-38

yadidaṁ prastutaṁ karma
tvayā govinda laukikam
mānuṣāṇāṁ hitārthāya
loke mānuṣa dehinā

tasyāyaṁ prathamaḥ kalpaḥ
kālena tu niyojitaḥ
jarāsandhena vai sārddhaṁ
sangrāme samupasthite

tatrāyudha balaṁ caiva
rūpaṁ ca raṇa karkaśam
svayam evātmanā kṛṣṇa
tvamātmānam vidhatsva ha

O Govinda, this is the first time in this millennium that You have descended in a human-like form, for the benefit of human society. Certainly, by the will of providence, Your mission will be accomplished. O Kṛṣṇa, in preparation for Your battle with Jarāsandha, You should summon Your personal weapons, thereby rendering Yourself invincible.

Text 39

cakrodhata karaṁ dṛṣtvā
tvāṁ gadā pāṇim āhave
catur dviguṇa pināṁsaṁ
vibhyed api śatakratuḥ

When You invoke Your *cakra* and club, holding them in Your strongly-built arms, as Indra, the king of heaven, gazes upon You, he will surely feel great fear enter his heart, and so what to speak of others.

Text 40

adya prabhṛti te yātrā
svargoktā samupasthitā
pṛthivyāṁ pārthivendrānāṁ
kṛtāsre tvayi mānada

As soon as You pick up Your weapons in preparation for battle, the path to the heavenly planets for all the kings of the earth will become cleared of all obstacles.

Text 41

vainateyasya cāhvānaṁ
vāhanaṁ dhvaja karamani
kuru śighraṁ mahābāho
govinda vadatāṁ vara

O might-armed Govinda! O foremost of eloquent speakers, as the first step on the path of hoisting Your victory flag, You should summon Your carrier, Garuḍa, the son of Vinatā.

Text 42

yuddha kāmā nṛpatayas
tridivābhi mukhodyatāḥ
dhārtarāṣṭrasya vasagās
tisthanti raṇa vṛttayaḥ

All the kings who oppose You have taken shelter of Duryodhana, the son of Dhṛtarāṣṭra. They are hoping to ascend to the heavenly planets by sacrificing their lives on the battlefield.

Text 43

rājñāṁ nidhana dṛṣṭarthā
vaidhavenādhi bāsitā
eka veṇī dharā ceyaṁ
vasudhā tvāṁ pratikṣate

Very soon, all the kings of the world will be destroyed.

Realizing this, mother earth has dressed herself as a widow and has not tied her hair, anxiously waiting for You to enact this pastime.

Text 44

saṁgrahaṁ kṛṣṇa nakṣatraṁ
saṅkṣipyāri vimardana
tvayi mānuṣya māpanne
yuddhe ca samupasthite

O slayer of Your enemies! O Kṛṣṇa, You have appeared in this world in a human-like form, to relieve the earth of her burden. Now, the time for battle has arrived. All the *kṣatriyas* of the earth are prepared to give up their lives, being without fear of death. Indeed, they are impatient for battle because they know that their deaths are inevitable.

Text 45

tvarasva kṛṣṇa yuddhāya
dānavānāṁ vadhāya ca
svargāya ca narendrāṇāṁ
devatānāṁ sukhāya ca

My dear Lord Kṛṣṇa, please prepare Yourself for battle. By killing the demoniac kings and thus sending them to the heavenly planets, the demigods will certainly be most appreciative.

Text 46

satkṛto'haṁ tvayā kṛṣṇa
lokaiśca sa carācaraiḥ
tvayā sat kṛta rūpena
yena satkrtavān aham

My dear Kṛṣṇa, You are the eternal Lord, full of knowledge and bliss. You are the supreme object of everyone's service. I am very pleased how You have treated me with great kindness. Indeed, it is only by Your mercy that I have become famous within the world and worshiped by those who are actually pious.

Text 47

sādhayāmi mahāvāho
bhavataḥ kārya siddhaye
smartavyas cāsmi yuddheṣu
kāntāreṣu mahīkṣitām

O mighty-armed one, I will personally assist You, just to insure that Your mission turns out successful. Whenever a saintly king is opposed by a very strong enemy, he should remember me and thus attain auspiciousness.

Text 48

ituktvā jāmadagnyastu
kṛṣṇam akliṣṭa kāriṇam
jayāśisā varddhayitvā
jagāma bhipsitāṁ diśam

After saying this, Paraśurāma heartily blessed Lord Kṛṣṇa, the performer of very wonderful activities, and then departed for his own abode.

Thus ends the translation of the fortieth chapter of the Viṣṇu Parva of Śrī Harivaṁsa.

Chapter 41

Vāruṇī, Kānti, and Śrīdevī arrive to serve Lord Balarāma atop Gomanta Hill

Text 1

vaiśampayana uvāca
jāmadagnye gate rāme
tau yādava kūlodvahau
gomanta śikhare ramye
ceratuḥ kāma rūpinau

Vaiśampāyana said: O Janamejaya, after the departure of Paraśurāma, Kṛṣṇa and Balarāma who had appeared to relieve the Yadu dynasty of their oppression, assumed the forms that They desired and then began wandering about the peak of Gomanta Hill.

Text 2

vanamālā kuloraskau
nīla pitāmbarā vubhau
nīla sveta vapuṣmantau
gaganastha vivāmbudau

Kṛṣṇa was dressed in yellow garments, Balarāma was dressed in blue, and both were decorated with nice garlands of flowers. Having fair and dark complexions, They appeared like two clouds suspended in the sky.

Text 3

tau śaila dhātu digdhāṅgau
yuvanau śikhare sthitau
ceratus tatra kānteṣu
vaneṣu rati lālasau

They decorated their bodies with the colored minerals found at that mountain. While standing on the peak, They appeared like two young heroes about to engage in sporting pastimes.

Text 4

udayantaṁ nirikṣantau
śasinaṁ jyotiṣāṁ varam
udayāsta mane caiva
grahanāṁ dharaṇidhare

That night, Kṛṣṇa and Balarāma sat quietly and watched the rising of the moon, which is the best among the luminaries in the sky. They also enjoyed gazing at the planets and prominent stars.

Text 5

atha saṅkarṣaṇaḥ śrīmān
vinā kṛṣṇena vīryavān
cacāra tasya śikhare
nagasya naga sannibha

One day, the unlimitedly powerful Lord Balarāma walked to the top of the mountain without Kṛṣṇa. While standing atop the mountain, Lord Balarāma appeared like a second formidable hill.

Text 6

prafullasya kadambasya
succhāye niṣasāda ha
vāyunā manda gandhena
vījyamānaḥ sukhena vai

As he wandered about on top of the hill, Lord Balarāma came upon a beautiful *kadamba* tree in full bloom. He sat in the shade of this tree and became refreshed by the cool, fragrant breezes.

Text 7

tasya tenānilaughena
sevyamānasya tatra vai
madya saṅsparśajo gandhaḥ
saṅspṛṣān ghrānam āgataḥ

As Lord Balarāma relished the cool breeze beneath the *kadamba* tree, He perceived the sweet scent of honey.

Text 8

tṛṣṇā cainaṁ viveṣāśu
vāruṇī prabhavā tadā
śuśoṣa ca mukhaṁ tasya
matta sevā pare'hani

Lord Balarāma remembered His *vāruṇī* beverage and became mad after it so that He appeared as if intoxicated and His mouth became dry.

Text 9

smāritaḥ sa purāvṛttam
amṛta prāśanaṁ vibhuḥ
tṛṣito madirānveṣī
tatastaṁ taru maikṣataḥ

While absorbed in remembering His previous pastimes of drinking honey, Lord Balarāma got up and began searching for it, here and there. Finally, His gaze scanned the *kadamba* tree.

Text 10

tasya prāvṛṣi phullasya
yadambho jalajojhitam
tat koṭarasthaṁ madirā
saṁjāyata manoharā

It was the rainy season and so the *kadamba* flowers were covered with raindrops. Mixing with the honey of those flowers, the drops fell to the ground.

Text 11

tāṁ tu tṛṣṇābhi bhūtātmā
pivannārtaṁ ivāsakṛt
mohacca litākārāḥ
samajayata sa prabhuḥ

Being exceedingly thirsty, Lord Balarāma drank the water as it fell from the flowers. Finally, after drinking a lot of honey, He felt overcome by sleep, as if overwhelmed by the illusory energy of the Supreme Personality of Godhead.

Text 12

tasya mattasya vadanaṁ
kiñcic calita locanam
ghurṇitā kāram abhavat
śāratkālendu saprabhum

Being intoxicated by the honey, Lord Balarāma's eyes began to roll and yet the beauty of His face defeated the full moon of autumn.

Text 13

kadamba koṭare jātā
nāmnā kādambariti sā
rūpiṇī vāruṇī tatra
devanāṁ amṛtaraṇī

This nectarean honey oozed from the holes of the *kadamba* tree, and it was therefore known as *kādambarī*. As Lord Balarāma was in this apparently intoxicated condition, Vāruṇī in her personified form appeared there, along with her associates. Vāruṇī is the goddess who supplies nectar to the demigods.

Text 14

kādambarī madakalaṁ
viditvā kṛṣṇa pūrvajam
tisra tridaśa nāryas tam
upatasthuḥ priyaṁvadāḥ

Seeing how Lord Kṛṣṇa's elder brother, Balarāma, was unable to speak due to being intoxicated by drinking *kādambarī*, three celestial damsels began serving Him with great care and attention.

Texts 15-16

madirā rūpinī bhūtvā
kantiśca śaśinaḥh priyā
śrīśca devī variṣṭhā strī
svayam evāmbuja dhvajā

sāñjali pragrahā devī
rauhiṇeyam upasthitā
vāruṇyā sahitaṁ vākyaṁ
uvāca mada viklavam

These three celestial women were Vāruṇī the predominating deity of nectar, Kānti the predominating deity of moonlight, and Śrīdevī the predominating deity of beauty and opulence, who is considered one of the foremost of women, and whose flag bears the symbol of a lotus flower. The three stood with folded hands, ready to serve Rohiṇī's son, Balarāma, who appeared to be intoxicated and in a mood of transcendental enjoyment.

Text 17

balaṁ jayasva daitanāṁ
baladeva divīśvara
ahaṁ te dayitā kāntā
vāruṇī samupasthitā

Vāruṇī was the first to speak, saying: O master of the demigods! O Baladeva, may you attain victory over the army of demons. I am your beloved Vāruṇī, having come here to render service.

Text 18

tvāmeva antarhitaṁ śrutvā
śāśvataṁ vaḍavā mukhe
kṣīṇa puṇyeva vasudhāṁ
paryemi vimalānana

O Lord with a most enchantingly beautiful face, I had thought that You eternally reside below Pātāla-loka in the form of Ananta-śeṣa. However, since You have incarnated in this world, You are no longer seen there. Feeling myself to be most unfortunate, I have searched for You throughout the three worlds.

Text 19

puṣpa cakrānu lipteṣu
kesare suṣitaṁ mayā
ati mukteṣu cākṣobhya
puṣpa stavaka vatsu ca

My dear invincible hero, I reside within the pollen of these *kadamba* flowers, as well as within the *vasantī* creepers that produce bunches of fragrant flowers.

Text 20

ahaṁ kadamba mālinā
megha kāle mukha priyā
tṛṣitam margamāṇā tvāṁ
svena rūpeṇa chhāditā

While searching for You everywhere, I sometimes, during the rainy season, rest within the holes of these *kadamba* trees.

My residence of preference, however, is within Your lotus-like mouth.

Texts 21-22

sāsmi pūrṇena yogena
yathaivamṛta manthane
samīpaṁ preṣitā pitrā
varuṇena tavānagha

sā yathaivarṇa vagatā
tathiva vaḍavāmukhe
tvayopa bhaktuṁ icchāmi
sammatastvaṁ hi me guru

O sinless Balarāma, long ago, during the churning of the ocean of milk for the purpose of producing nectar, my father, Varuna, sent me to You. Thereafter, I resided with You in the ocean below Pātāla-loka, and now, once again, I have presented myself before You, to engage in Your service. I am You most obedient maidservant because within my heart, I accept You as my husband.

Texts 23-24

na tvānantaṁ parityakṣe
bhartsi tāpi tvāyanagha
nahaṁ tvayā vinā lokām
utsahe deva sevitum

adipadmaṁ ca padmāṅkaṁ
divyaṁ śravaṇa bhūṣaṇam
kauśeyāni ca nīlāni
samudrārhaṇi vibhrati

O sinless one, if You so desire, You may chastise me, but I will never leave Your service. My dear Lord, I have dressed in this fine blue silk *saree* and have adorned my ears with celestial lotus-shaped earrings, desiring to engage in Your devotional service. I have no desire to serve anyone else within the three worlds.

Texts 25-26

madirānantaraṁ kāntiḥ
saṅkarṣaṇam upasthitā
madenāgalita śroṇī
kiñcidā ghurṇi tekṣaṇā

provaca praṇayāt kāntir
vaddhāñjali puṭā sati
jaya pūrvena yogena
sasmitaṁ vākyam arthavat

After Vāruṇī had finished speaking, Kāntī-devī was the next to speak. As she came before Balarāma, she also appeared somewhat intoxicated with her eyes rolling, although she folded her palms in supplication. She said: All glories to Lord Balarāma. She smiled most beautifully and then continued to speak as follows.

Text 27

ahaṁ candrādapi guruṁ
sahasra śirasaṁ prabhum
svair guṇair anuraktā tvāṁ
yatheva madirā tathā

My dear Lord having thousands of heads, You are the Lord of the universe. Your transcendental form illuminates all directions in a manner that is more pleasing than the moon. Like Vāruṇī, I am attracted by Your transcendental qualities and personality. I have come to engage in Your service and so please accept me.

Texts 28-29

śrīśca padmālayā devī
nidheyā vaiṣṇavair asi
rauhiṇeyor asi śubhā
male cāmalatāṁ gatā

sā mālāmamalāṁ gṛhya
balasyor asi daṁśitā
padmāsyā padma hastā vai
saṅkarṣaṇaṁ athāvravit

Thereafter, Śrīdevī, who eternally resides on the chest of Lord Viṣṇu, next approached Rohiṇī's son, Balarāma, with folded hands, in that forest adorned with lotus flowers. Her face was as beautiful as a lotus flower, and she held a garland of lotus flowers in her hand. She was gorgeously dressed and wore a wonderful garland of lotus flowers. As she stood before Lord Balarāma with a garland of lotus flowers in her hand, she spoke as follows.

Text 30

rāma rāmābhi rāmastvaṁ
vāruṇyā samalaṅkṛtāḥ
kāntyā mayā ca deveśa
saṅgataś candramā yathā

O Lord Balarāma, master of the demigods, You the foremost of attractive males. In the company of Vāruṇī, Kānti, and myself, You appear even more enchanting, like the full moon surrounded by twinkling stars.

Text 31

iyaṁ ca sā mayā mauliḥ
proddhatā varuṇālayāt
murdhni śirsa sahasrasya
yā te bhānur ivāvabhau

The thousand-headed Lord Ananta is adorned with a crown that is as brilliant as the sun. I have brought that crown with me as my humble presentation to You.

Text 32

jāta rūpa mayaṁ caikaṁ
kuṇḍalaṁ vajra bhūṣitam
ādi padmaṁ ca padmākṣaṁ
divya śravaṇa bhūṣaṇam

I have also brought a golden earring inlaid with diamonds, which is known as Ādipadma or Padmākṣa. It is my wish that You decorate Yourself with this earring.

Text 33

kauśeyāni ca nīlāni
samudrārhāṇiḥ bhāvataḥ
hāraṁ ca pīna taralaṁ
samudraa bhyantaroṣitam

These ornaments were produced by the ocean. I have also brought fine blue silk cloth, and a beautiful necklace that was also produced from the ocean. Kindly accept them.

Text 34

devemāṁ pratigṛhnāṣva
pauraṇīṁ bhūṣaṇa kriyām
samayasye mahābāho
bhūṣanānāṁ alaṅkriyām

My dear Lord, these are Your eternal ornaments. O mighty-armed one, please accept them. This is a most suitable time for You to decorate Yourself, although You have no need for them. After all, it is the ornaments that become more beautiful by Your presence, and not that Your beauty increases because of them.

Text 35

saṁgṛhya tamalaṅkāraṁ
tāśca tisraḥ surastriyaḥ
śuśubhe baladevo hi
śāradendu sama prabhaḥ

Lord Balarāma not only graciously accepted these transcendental ornaments, but the three celestial women as well. At this time, He appeared more beautiful than the full moon of autumn.

Text 36

sa samāgamya kṛṣṇena
jalajāmbo davarcasā
mudaṁ paramikāṁ lebhe
graham yuktaḥ śaśī yathā

Thereafter, Lord Balarāma rejoined Lord Kṛṣṇa, whose

complexion resembled the color of a dark rain cloud or a blue lotus flower. They appeared highly delighted and were like two full moons that had risen over Gomanta Hill.

Text 37

tābhyāṁ ubhābhyāṁ saṅlāpe
vartamāne gṛhe yathā
vainateyas tato'dhyānam
ati cakrāma vegataḥ

Kṛṣṇa and Balarāma sat together and conversed with one another, just as if They were seated at home. At that time, Vinata's son Garuḍa appeared in the sky overhead.

Text 38

saṁgrāma muktas tejasvī
daitya praharaṇāṅkitaḥ
devatānāṁ jayaślāghī
divya sraganu lepanaḥ

The extraordinarily powerful Garuḍa had come from a fierce battle on behalf of the demigods and the wounds of the demons' weapons were clearly visible on his body. He was decorated with a nice flower garland and smeared with sandalwood paste.

Text 39

suptasya sayane divye
kṣirode varuṇālaye
viṣṇoḥ kīriṭaṁ daityena
hṛtaṁ vairacanena vai

Once, as Lord Viṣṇu was lying on a divine bed within the ocean of milk, wherein Varuṇa resides, a demon who was the son of Virocana came and stole His crown.

Text 40

tadarthastena saṁgrāmaḥ
kṛto gurvartham ojasā
kirīṭārthe samudrasya
madhye daityagaṇaiḥ saha

To retrieve the crown of his worshipable Lord and spiritual master, Garuḍa fought with the demons within the ocean.

Text 41

mokṣayitvā kirīṭaṁ tu
vaiṣṇavaṁ patatāṁ varaḥ
vyatya kramata vegena
gaganaṁ devatālayam

After a fierce battle, Garuḍa, the king of birds, snatched the Lord's crown from the demons and swiftly rose up to the abodes of the demigods.

Text 42

sa dadarśa guruṁ śaile
viṣṇuṁ kāryāntarā gatam
tena krīḍāvalambena
kirīṭena virājatā

While flying through the sky, Garuḍa happened to see his master, Lord Viṣṇu, sitting on the peak of this mountain. At that time, Garuḍa held the Lord's beautiful crown in his beak.

Texts 43-44

sa dṛṣṭvā mānuṣaṁ viṣṇuṁ
śaila rāja śirogatam
prakāśa ceṣṭā nirmuktaṁ
vimaulimiva mānuṣam

abhijñastasya bhāvānāṁ
garutmān patatāṁ varaḥ
cikṣepa khaṁ gato mauliṁ
viṣṇoḥ śirasi dṛḍhavrata

Thus it came to be that Garuḍa saw his worshipable Lord, present in the human-like form of Lord Kṛṣṇa, on the peak of Gomanta Hill, the king of all mountains, without His crown. Having arrived in the presence of Kṛṣṇa and Balarama, Garuḍa carefully went and placed the Lord's crown upon His head.

Text 45

upendra mūrghni sā maulir
apindddhā ivāpatat
śirasaḥ sthāna niryuktā
kṛṣṇaṁ caivān vaśobhayat
yathaiva meruśikhare
bhānur madhyadine yathā

The crown fell from the beak of Garuḍa and gently landed on Lord Kṛṣṇa's head, in a way that appeared most wonderful. Being adorned with this crown, Lord Kṛṣṇa appeared magnificent. The crown sparkled gloriously, like the rays of the sun reflected on the peak of Mount Sumeru.

Text 46

vainateya prayogeṇa
viditvā maulimāgatām
kṛṣṇaḥ prahṛṣṭa vadano
rāmaṁ vacanam avravīt

Lord Kṛṣṇa was very pleased to see how Garuḍa had returned His crown. He turned to Balarāma and spoke as follows.

Text 47

tvarete khalu kāryārthe
devatānāṁ na saṁśayaḥ
yatheyam āvayoḥ śaile
saṁgrāma racanā kṛtā

My dear brother, We have been supplied nice garments and other paraphernalia, indicating that the time is soon approaching for Us to accomplish Our mission on behalf of the demigods, to relieve the burden of the earth.

Texts 48-49

vairocanena suptasya
mama maulir mahodadhau
śakrasya sadṛśaṁ rūpaṁ
divyaṁ āsthāya sāgarāt

grāha rūpeṇa yo nīta
ānīto'sau garutmatā
mamāhi śayatān maulir
hṛtvā kṣipto garutmatā

I was sleeping on the ocean of milk when Virocana's son assumed the form of Indra and took My crown. Just see how Garuḍa has recovered My crown and returned it to Me.

Text 50

syuvyaktaṁ saṁnikṛṣṭaḥ
sa jarāsandho narādhipaḥ
lakṣyante hi dhvajāgrāṇi
rathānāṁ vātaraṁ hasām

I think that Jarāsandha must be approaching, because I can see the top of the flag that adorns his chariot, which moves faster than the speed of wind.

Text 51

etāni vijigī ṣūṇāṁ
śaśikalpāni bhūbhṛtām
chatrāṇyārya virājante
daṁśitāni mitāni ca

O sinless one, I can see the white umbrellas covering the *kṣatriyas* who desire victory over Us. However, it appears as if their numbers are limited.

Text 52

aho nṛparatho dagrā
vimalāśchatra paṅktayaḥ
abhi vartanti na śubhrā
yathā khe haṁsapaṅktayaḥ

Indeed, the rows of white umbrellas shielding the chariots

of the *kṣatriyas* from the rays of the sun look like swans flying in formation in the sky.

Text 53

aho dyaur vimalābhānāṁ
śastrāṇāṁ vimalānanā
prabhā bhāskara bhāmiśrā
carantīva diśo daśa

Because of the countless brightly-shining weapons in the hands of the enemy, the whole sky has become illuminated. Combining with the effulgence of the sun, the ten directions have been very brightly lit.

Text 54

etāni nūnaṁ samare
pārthivairāyudhāni ca
kṣiptāni vinaśiṣyanti
mayi sarvāṇi saṁyuge

Still, I am confident that when these kings attack Me, it will simply be their weapons that will meet with destruction.

Text 55

kāle khalu nṛpaḥ prāpto
jarāsandho mahīpatiḥ
āvayor yuddha nikaṣaḥ
prathamaḥ samarātithiḥ

King Jarāsandha has come at a time that will act in Our favor. Now is the proper time to begin removing the burden of the earth, and he should be the first casualty.

Text 56

ārya tiṣṭhāva sahitau na
khalvānāgate nṛpa
yuddhārambhaḥ prayoktavyo
balaṁ tāvad vimṛśyatām

O sinless one, We should always fight side-by-side. Let Us not be impatient. We should wait for Jarāsandha to come before s. Meanwhile, let Us ascertain the strengths and weaknesses of his army.

Text 57

evamuktvā tataḥ kṛṣṇaḥ
svasthaḥ saṁgrāma lālasaḥ
jarāsandha vadhaṁ prepsuś
cakāra baladarśanam

After saying this, Lord Kṛṣṇa carefully controlled His anger, waiting for the proper time to combat Jarāsandha, while observing the strength of his army.

Texts 58-59

vīkṣamāṇaśca tān sarvān
nṛpān yaduvaro'vyayaḥ
ātmānam ātmanovāca
yatpūrvaṁ divi mantritam

ime te pṛthivīpālāḥ
pārthive vartmani sthitāḥ
ye vināśaṁ gamiṣyanti
śāstradṛṣṭena karmaṇā

As He observed the army of his enemy, Lord Kṛṣṇa, the crest jewel of the Yadu dynasty, thought to Himself: Our mission on behalf of the demigods is about to be accomplished. As a result, all of these sinful kings will meet with destruction. This has also been predicted in the scriptures and thus the outcome cannot be otherwise.

Text 60

prokṣitān khalvimān manye
mṛtyunā nṛpasattamān
svargagāmīni cāpyeṣāṁ
varuṁṣi pracakāśire

I think that Death personified has already accepted these kings as oblations in the sacrificial fire of battle. Indeed, I can see that their celestial bodies are already being formed.

Text 61

sthāne bhāra pariśrāntā
vasudheyaṁ divaṁ gatā
eṣāṁ nṛpati siṁhānāṁ
balau ghairam ipīḍitā

Mother earth has been heavily burdened by these demoniac kings and in response to her prayers, I have appeared to give her relief.

Text 62

alpena khalu kālena
viviktaṁ pṛthivītalam
bhaviṣyati narendrau ghair

akīrṇaṁ ca nabhastalam

Very soon, the earth will be relieved of these sinful kings and thus the condition of human society will be transformed. Even the atmosphere will become cleansed and everything will assume its natural aspect.

Thus ends the translation of the forty-first chapter of the Viṣṇu Parva of Śrī Harivaṁsa.

Chapter 42

After surrounding Gomanta Hill, Jarāsandha and his allies set it on fire. Kṛṣṇa and Balarāma jump from the peak of the mountain

Text 1

vaiśampāyana uvāca
jarāsandhas tataḥ prāpto
nṛpaḥ sarva mahīkṣitām
narādhibair balayutair
anuyāto mahādyutiḥ

Vaiśampāyana said: O Janamejaya, shortly thereafter, that foremost of powerful kings, Jarāsandha, arrived at the base of Gomanta Hill, accompanied by many subordinate kings and their armies.

Text 2

vyāyato dagra turagair
vispaṣṭārtha samāhitaiḥ
rathaiḥ saṅgraḥmikair yuktair
asaṅgatibhiḥ kacit

These kings were all masters of the arts of battle, and they rode upon mighty chariots filled with all kinds of weapons and driven by swift horses.

Text 3

hemakakṣair mahāghaṇṭair
vāraṇair vāridomamaiḥ

mahāmātrottam ārūḍhaiḥ
kalpitai raṇagarvitaiḥ

Some proud warriors rode upon mighty elephants decorated with gold and bells hanging from their ears. They appeared like dark clouds ranging across the sky.

Text 4

svārūḍhaiḥ sādibhir yuktaiḥ
preṅkhamāṇaiḥ pravalgitaiḥ
vājibhir vāyusaṁkāśaiḥ
plavadbhiriva patribhiḥ

There were countless warriors mounted upon horses that were faster than the speed of wind. Sometimes they ascended into the sky, so that they appeared like giant birds in flight.

Text 5

kahṅgacarma balodgraiḥ
pattibhir balināṁ varaiḥ
sahasra saṁkhyair nimuktair
utpatadbhiri voragaiḥ

In that vast army there were innumerable infantry soldiers equipped with swords and shields. They appeared very ferocious as they marched forward impetuously, sometimes jumping with excessive energy, as if they were snakes shedding their sloughs.

Text 6

evaṁ caturvidyaiḥ sainyaiḥ
pracaladbhiri vāmbudaiḥ

nṛpo'bhiyāto balavāñ
jarāsandho dhṛtavrataḥ

Thus there were four divisions of soldiers in the army of King Jarāsandha, and they had taken a vow to fight until death. Like a rumbling cloud, they marched toward the enemy, eager to attack.

Texts 7-8

sa rathair nimighoṣaiśca
gajaiśca madasaṁyutaiḥ
heṣadbhiścāpi turagaiḥ
kṣveḍitograiśca pattibhiḥ

saṁnādayan diśaḥ sarvāḥ
sarvāṁścāpi guhāśayān
sa rājā sāgarākāraḥ
sasainyaḥ pratyadṛśyata

There was a great rattling sound created by the wheels of the chariots, combined with the screaming of countless intoxicated elephants, the neighing of the horses, and the loud roaring of the lion-like soldiers of King Jarāsandha's army, which appeared like an impassable ocean. This sound filled the ten directions and echoed in the caves of the mountain.

Text 9

tadvalaṁ pṛthivīśānāṁ
hṛṣṭayodha janākulam
kṣveditas phoṭitaravaṁ
megha sainyam ivābabhau

All of the warriors were very powerfully built and made thundering sounds like a mass of clouds in the rainy season.

Texts 10-11

rathaiḥ pavana saṁpātair
gajaiśca jaladopamaiḥ
turagaiśca sitābhrābhaiḥ
pattibhiścāpi daṁśitaiḥ

vyāmiśraṁ tadvalaṁ bhāti
mattad vipa samākulam
dharmānte sāgaragataṁ
yathābhra paṭalaṁ tathā

The chariots could move with the speed of wind, the elephants appeared like dark clouds, the horses looked like white clouds, and the armor of the infantry increased the beauty of the army. The approach of this formidable army was like the onslaught of a terrible storm, creating fear within the minds of all who witnessed it.

Text 12

sabalāste mahīpālā
jarāsandha purogamāḥ
parivārya giriṁ sarve
niveśāyopa cakramuḥ

Under the leadership of Jarāsandha, the army surrounded the entire mountain and then began setting up their camps.

Text 13

babhau tasya niviṣṭasya
balaśrīḥ śivirasya vai
śukle parvaṇi pūrṇasya
yathā rūpaṁ mahodadheḥ

That army was like a great ocean and when the full moon rose high in the sky, it appeared as if it had come to see the beauty of the tossing of numerous waves in the form of the warriors' camps.

Text 14

vītarātre tataḥ kāle
nṛpāste kṛtakautukāḥ
ārohaṇārthaṁ śailasya
sametā yuddhalālasāḥ

Early the next morning, the soldiers woke up and performed their religious duties. When these were concluded, they began preparations for the impending conflict.

Text 15

samavāyī kṛtāḥ sarvaṁ
giriprastheṣu te nṛpāḥ
niviṣṭā mantrayāmā sur
yuddhakāla kutūhalāḥ

The commanders then met to discuss their strategy, should the opportunity for combat present itself, while the soldiers awaited their command.

Text 16

eṣāṁ tu tumulaḥ śabdaḥ
śuśruve pṛthivīkṣitām
yugānte bhidyamānānāṁ
sāgarāṇāṁ yathā svanaḥ

The army covered the land as far as the eye could see and the warriors created a roaring sound that rivaled the tumult at the time of the annihilation of the universe, or the ocean during a terrible storm.

Text 17

teṣāṁ sakañcu koṣṇīṣāḥ
sthavirā vetrapāṇayaḥ
cerurmā śabda ityevaṁ
bruvanto rājaśāsanāt

The spies and other servants of the kings were nicely decorated with fine clothing and turbans, and they carried heavy staffs. It was their duty to keep order within the camps.

Text 18

tasya rūpaṁ balasyāsīn
niḥśabdas timitasya vai
līnamīna bhujaṅgasya
niḥśabdasya payodadheḥ

The order was given that the army should remain silent and at that time, it appeared as grave as the ocean. Although appearing calm at times, huge aquatics remain active deep within the sea. Similarly, the army, although silent, remained poised for action.

Text 19

tasmin stimita niśabde
yogādiva mahārṇave
jarāsandho vṛhadvākyaṁ
bṛhaspatir ivādade

When all of the warriors had settled down, Jarāsandha, who was a master strategist, like Bṛhaspati, began to speak as follows.

Text 20

śīghraṁ samabhi vartantāṁ
balānīha mahīkṣitām
sarvataḥ parvataś cāyaṁ
balaudhaiḥ parivāryatām

We should quickly surround the mountain and prepare to attack the enemy as soon as the order is given.

Text 21

aśmayantrāṇi yujyantāṁ
kṣepaṇīyāśca mudgarāḥ
ūrdhvaṁcāpi pravāhyantāṁ
prāsā vai tomarāṇi ca

Let us take up our weapons and remain alert, in case the enemy mounts a surprise attack. Get ready to engage in battle and remain fixed in your determination to gain victory.

Text 22

ūrdhvaṁ prakṣepaṇārthāya
ḍṛḍhāni ca laghūni ca
śastrapāta vidhātāni
kriyantā māśu śilpibhiḥ

Our engineers can clear the field so that there are no obstacles as we march to battle. Be ready to counter any attack our enemy might spring upon us.

Text 23

śūrāṇāṁ yuddha mānānāṁ
prramattānāṁ parasparam
yathā narapatiḥ prāha
tathā śīghraṁ vidhīyatām

All of you are certainly the foremost of warriors. When the fight commences, you should never show leniency, but instead fight as if enraged, for this is my solemn order.

Text 24

dāryatāmeṣa ṭaṅkaudhaiḥ
khanitraiśca narottamaḥ
nṛpāśca yuddha mārgajñā
vinyasyan tāmadūrataḥ

When we launch our attack, everyone should be informed of our strategy, and all should be prepared to invoke their most powerful weapons, even if that involves smashing the mountain to atoms.

Text 25

adyaprabhṛti sainyairme
girirodhaḥ pravartyatām
yāvadetau pātayāmo
vasudeva sutāvubhau

When all preparations are completed, we will surround the mountain so that there will be no chance for the two sons of Vasudeva to escape.

Text 26

acalo'yaṁ śilāyoniḥ
kriyatāṁ niścalāṇḍajaḥ
ākāśam api bāṇoghair
niḥsampātaṁ vidhīyatām

The rocky terrain of this mountain certainly makes it very difficult to attack, but if we cover the sky with our arrows so that even a bird will be unable to escape, then surely we will attain our objective.

Text 27

mayānu śiṣṭās tiṣṭhanu
giribhūmiṣu bhūmipā
teṣu teṣvava kāśeṣu
śīghram āruhyatāṁ giriḥ

My order is that we should first surround the mountain, and then begin our ascent to the top, leaving no room for our enemies to penetrate our ranks.

Texts 28-29

madraḥ kaliṅgādhipatiś
cekitānaśca bāhlikaḥ
kāśmīra rājo gonardaḥ
karūṣādhi patistathā

drumaḥ kiṁpuruṣaścaiva
parvatīyāśca mānavāḥ
parvatasyā paraṁ pārśvaṁ
kṣipram ārohayantvamī

Śalya the king of Madra, Śrutāyu the king of Kaliṅga, Cekitāna, Bāhlika, Gonarda the king of Kaśmīra, Dantavakra the king of Karuśa, and Druma the king of the Kinnaras, as well as all the other kings present here, who are all very expert warriors who are experienced in mountain combat, should climb Gomanta Hill from the west.

Texts 30-33

pauravo veṇudāriśca
vaidarbhaḥ somakastathā
rukmī ca bhojādhipatiḥ
sūryākṣaścaiva mālavaḥ

pāñcālādhi patiścaiva
drupadaśca narādhipaḥ
vindānu vindā vāvantyau
dantavaktraśca vīryavān

chāgaliḥ puramitraśca
virāṭaśca mahīpatiḥ
kauśāmbyo mālavaścaiva
śatadhanvā vidūrathaḥ

bhūriśravāstri gartaśca
bāṇaḥ pañcana dastathā
uttaraṁ parvatoddeśa
mete drugasahā nṛpāḥ
ārohantu vimardanto
vajrapratima gauravāḥ

Veṇudārī of the Puru dynasty, Somaka from Vidarbha, Rukmī the king of the Bhoja dynasty, Sūryākṣa the king of Mālava, Drupada the king of the Pāñcālas, Vinda and Anuvinda the two princes from Avantīnagara, the powerful Dantavakra, Chāgalī, Purumitra, Virāṭa, Mālava the king of Kauśāmvī, Śatadhanvā, Viduratha, Bhuriśravā, Trigarta, Vāṇa, and Pañcanada, all of who are as powerful as thunderbolts and thus are capable of destroying the enemies' fortifications, should also ascend the mountain.

Texts 34-36

ulūkaḥ kaitaveyaśca
vīraścāṁśu mataḥ sutaḥ
ekalavyo dṛḍhāśvaśca
kṣatradharmā jayadrathaḥ

uttamaujās tathā śālvaḥ
kairaleyaśca kauśikaḥ
vaidiśo vāmadevaśca
śālvaḥ suketuścāpi vīryavān

pūrva parvata nirvyūham
eteṣvāya tamastu naḥ
vidārayanto dhāvanto
vātā eva balāhakān

Uluka the son of Śakunī, Vīra the son of Aṁśumān,

Ekalavya, Dṛdhāśva, Kṣatradharmā, Jayadratha, Uttamaujā, Śālva, Kauśika the king of Kerala, Vāmadeva the king of Vidiśā, and the powerful Suketū, all of who drive away their enemies, just as the wind scatter clouds in the sky, should ascend the mountain from the east.

Text 37

ahaṁ ca daradaścaiva
cedirājaśca vīryavān
dakṣiṇaṁ śailanicayaṁ
dārayiṣyāma daṁśitāḥ

Darada and I, along with the powerful king of Cedī, Śiśupāla, will assault the mountain from the south with our invincible weapons.

Text 38

evameṣa giriḥ kṣipraṁ
samantād viṣṭito balaiḥ
vajra prapāta pratimaṁ
prāpnotu tumulaṁ bhayam

In this way, we will surround the mountain and attack from all sides, striking great fear into the hearts of our enemies, as if threatened by a thunderbolt.

Text 39

gadino vai gadābhiśca
parighaiḥ parighāyudhāḥ
apare vividhaiḥ śastrair
dārayantu nagottamam

Those who are very expert in wielding clubs should fight with clubs, those who are expert in fighting with maces should utilize that weapon and be prepared to pulverize the mountain if need be.

Text 40

eṣa bhūmidhoro'dyaiva
viṣamocca śilānvitaḥ
karyo bhūmisamaḥ sarve
bhavadbhir vasudhādhipaiḥ

Indeed, if all else fails, we should together attack the mountain, breaking it to pieces, so that the terrain becomes leveled.

Text 41

jarāsandha vacaḥ śrutvā
pārthivā rājaśāsanāt
gomantaṁ veṣṭayā māsuḥ
sāgarāḥ pṛthivīm iva

After hearing these instructions of Jarāsandha the king of Magadha, the assembled kings surrounded Gomanta Hill, just as the ocean surrounds the earth.

Text 42

uvāca rājā cedīnāṁ
devānāṁ maghavāniva
kiṁ te yuddhena durge'smin
gomante ca nagottame

At that time, Damaghoṣa the king of Cedī, who resembled Indra the king of the demigods, spoke to Jarāsandha: O King, this best of all mountains will be very difficult for us to climb. What do you hope to gain by fighting?

Texts 43-47

durārohaśca śikhare
prāṁśu pādapa kaṇṭake
kāṣṭhais tṛṇaiśca bahubhiḥ
parivārya samantataḥ

adyaiva dīpyatāṁ kṣipram
alamanyena karmaṇā
kṣatriyāḥ sukumārā hi
raṇe sāya kayodhinaḥ

niyuktāḥ parvate durge
niyoktuṁ pādayodhinaḥ
nanāma pratibandhena
na cāva skanda karmaṇā

śakya eṣa giristāta
devair apyava marditum
durgayuddhe kramaḥ śreyān
rodhayuddhena pārthivāḥ

bhaktodakendhanaiḥ kṣīṇāḥ
pātyante girisaṁśritāḥ
vayaṁ bahava ityevaṁ
nāpyeṣa nipuṇo nayaḥ

On the way to the top we will have to pass through dense jungles full of thorny bushes. Instead of going to so much trouble, let us quickly gather heaps of dry wood, as well as dry grass and leaves, and build fires all around the base of the mountain. Just consider how our soldiers are accustomed to fighting on flat plains and not in mountainous terrain. It is my opinion that our soldiers will be unable to effectively fight while attempting to climb this practically inaccessible region. Even the demigods of heaven would find such a task quite formidable. When our enemies are within a well-defended fort, we surround it, thus cutting off all supplies. However, in this case, all necessities of life can be had from the mountain itself. Let us not be so foolish as to underestimate the strength of the opposition.

Text 48

yādavau nāvamantavyau
dvāvapyetau raṇe sthitau
avijñāta balāvetau
śrūyete devasammitau

These two descendants of Yadu are certainly capable of fighting with us, and so we should not neglect them. We do not know their actual strength, but I have heard that they are as powerful as demigods.

Text 49

karmabhis tvamarau vidmo
bālāvati balānvitau
duṣkarāṇīha karmāṇi
kṛtavantau yadūttamau

I have heard that in their childhood, these two descendents of Yadu performed many wonderful activities, indicating that they are not ordinary human beings. Having superhuman strength, these two are surely not mere mortals.

Text 50

śuṣka kāṣṭhais tṛṇair veṣṭya
sarvataḥ parvatottamaḥ
angina dīpayiṣyāmo
dahyetāṁ gatacetanau

My suggestion is that we should gather heaps of dry wood, grass, and leaves, placing them all around the mountain. In this way, we can encircle the mountain with fire, so that they will fall unconscious and then be burnt to ashes.

Text 51

yadi cenniṣkram iṣyete
dahyamānā vito'ntike
sametya pātayiṣyāmas
tyakṣyato jīvitaṁ tataḥ

If the two brothers attempt to escape from the fire then we can capture Them or kill Them. In this way, we can surely rid ourselves of our enemies.

Text 52

vākyam etattu ruruce
sabalānāṁ mahīkṣitām
yaduktaṁ cedirājena
nṛpāṇāṁ hitaśaṁsinā

After hearing this plan of the King of Cedī, the assembled kings enthusiastically accepted it, considering it to be the best means for attaining their objective.

Text 53

tataḥ kāṣṭhais tṛṇair vaṁśaiḥ
śuṣka śākhaiśca pādapaiḥ
upādīpyata śailendraḥ
sūryapādair ivāmbudaḥ

Thereafter, everyone collected dry wood, grass, bushes, leaves, and branches and placed these all around Gomanta Hill. Thereafter, when the fire blazed brightly, the mountain appeared like a huge cloud surrounded by intense sunlight.

Text 54

daduste sarvatas tūrṇaṁ
pāvakaṁ tatra pārthivāḥ
yathoddeśaṁ yathāvātaṁ
śailasya laghuvikrarmaḥ

The kings fanned the fire by creating wind with their celestial weapons so that soon, the entire mountain was engulfed in flames.

Text 55

sa vāyudīpito bahnir
utpapāta samantataḥ
sadhūma jvāla mālābhir
bhābhiḥ khamiva śobhayan

Being driven by the wind, the blazing fire gradually spread upwards on all sides. The blazing fire and billows of black smoke gave the sky a pleasing aspect.

Text 56

so'nalaḥ pavanāyastaḥ
kāṣṭha saṅcaya mūlavān
dadāha śailaṁ śrīmantaṁ
gomantaṁ kāntapādapam

Because the forests surrounding the mountain were very dry, the fire soon became a great conflagration. Before long, the entire mountain, which was the resort of innumerable trees, was burning.

Text 57

sa dahyamānaḥ śailendrom
umoca vipulāḥ śilāḥ
śataśaḥ śatadhā bhūtvā
maholkākāra darśanāḥ

Indeed, because of the intense heat of the fire, the rocks on the side of the mountain began to crumble. Thus a landslide was created and the falling rocks appeared like great balls of fire.

Text 58

sa citrabhānuḥ śailendraṁ
bhābhir bhānu rivāmbudam
ālimpatīva vidhivat
samantādarci ruddhataḥ

Just as the sun covers the entire sky with the extension of its rays, that terrible fire spread everywhere, covering the entire mountain.

Text 59

dhātubhiḥ pacyamānaiśca
jvaladbhiścaiva pādapaiḥ
udbhrāntaś cāpado rauti
tudyamāna ivādrirāṭ

With its burning metal, minerals, and trees, as well as the frightened wild animals running here and there, that king of mountains, Gomanta, appeared to be crying out with severe pain.

Text 60

pratapto dahyamānastu
sa śailaḥ kṛṣṇavartmanā
rītīr nirva tayāmāsa
kāñccanāñjana rājatīḥ

Being scorched by the blazing fire, the mountain emitted streams of molten gold, silver, and black metal.

Text 61

vahninā cāpi dīptāṅgo
girirnāti virājato
dhūmāndha kāror dhvatanur
majjamāna ivāmbudaḥ

Although the mountain was illuminated by the fire, the peak appeared black because of the heavy smoke, giving it a gloomy aspect, like a cloud being consumed by the ocean.

Text 62

viśliṣṭo palasaṁghātaḥ
karkaśāṅkāra varṣaṇaḥ
girirbhātya nalodvārair
ulkāvṛṣṭir ivāmbudaḥ

As the gigantic boulders of Gomanta Hill crumbled, it appeared as if balls of fire were falling from the sky. Indeed, it was as if the mountain were showering fire upon those at the base.

Text 63

prapāta prasra gotkṣipto
dhūma saṁvarddhi todaraḥ
sa girir bhasmatāṁ yāto
yugāntāgni hatopamaḥ

The fire dried up all of the mountain streams and thick, black smoke filled the air. It appeared as if the mountain were being destroyed at the time of the dissolution of the universe.

Text 64

vihvalāstasya pārśvebhyaḥ
sarpā dagdhārdha dehinaḥ
śvasantaḥ pṛthu mūrdhāno
niścerura śivekṣaṇāḥ

The snakes residing within the mountain caves fearfully emerged from their residences. Being burnt in the conflagration, their eyes emitted poisonous glances as they spread their hoods.

Text 65

utpatyot patya gaganāt
punaḥ punara vāṅmukhāḥ
resuścodve jitāḥ siṁhāḥ
śārdūlāścā lanāvilāḥ

Being burned by the blazing fire, the lions and tigers fearfully ran here and there, screaming pathetically, finding no escape.

Text 66

mumucuḥ pādapāścaiva
dāha niryā sajaṁ jalam

The trees on the mountain side oozed sap while being burnt.

Text 67

vahatyūrdha gatirvāto
bhasmāṅgārāti piṅgalaḥ
dhūmacchāyā ca gagane
darpitāmbhoda darśanā

Strong winds blew, carrying the ashes and sparks high into the sky, which was filled with billowing smoke, making it appear as if filled with dark clouds.

Text 68

vyajyamāno mahāsānur
vihagaiḥ śvāpadair api

girirvaikalya māyāti
pragalbhyāt kṛṣṇa vartamanaḥ

All the birds and wild animals tried their best to flee the conflagration, which raged on all sides.

Text 69

sa mumoca śilāḥ śailaś
caladagra śolccayaḥ
vajreṇa puruhūtasya
yathā syād dāritas tathā

Great boulders and showers of small stones fell from the mountain, making it appear as if it had been struck by Indra's thunderbolt.

Text 70

ādīpya taṁ tu śailendraṁ
kṣatriyā vyūha daṁśitāḥ
ardhakrośam apakrāntāḥ
pāvakenābhi tāpitāḥ

After igniting the fire all around that king of mountains, Gomanta, the *kṣatriyas* retreated some distance to avoid being scorched by the intense heat.

Texts 71-72

dahyamāne nagaśreṣṭhe
sīdamānair mahādrumaiḥ
dhūmabhārair analakṣye
mule śithilatāṁ gate

saroṣaṁ hi tadā rāmo
vacanaṁ keśisūdanam
babhāṣe padmapatrākṣām
sa sākṣān madhusūdanam

As Gomanta Hill was being devastated by fire, it was very difficult to gaze upon. Being clouded by dense smoke, the mountain appeared to be on the verge of collapse. At that time, Lord Balarāma angrily addressed lotus eyed Kṛṣṇa, the origin of Lord Viṣṇu and killer of the Keśi and Madhu demons.

Text 73

dahyate'yaṁ giristāta
sasānu śikharadrumaḥ
āvayoḥ kṛṣṇa vaireṇa
balimir vasudhādhi paiḥ

My dear Kṛṣṇa, because We created enmity with these powerful kings, this glorious mountain is being consumed by a dreadful fire.

Text 74

paśya kṛṣṇā nalau ṣṇāṇāṁ
sadhūmānāṁ samantataḥ
vanānāṁ virasantīva
nagābhyāśe dvipottamāḥ

O Kṛṣṇa, look at these elephants, crying out in anguish, being unable to breath due to the dense smoke!

Text 75

ayaṁ yadyāva yorarthe
gomantastāta dahyate
ayaśasyam idaṁ loke
kaulīnaṁ ca bhaviṣyati

My dear magnanimous brother, if Gomanta Hill is burnt to ashes in Our presence, We will certainly suffer infamy so that out spotless character will be tarnished.

Text 76

tadamyā nṛṇya hetorhi
nagasya nagasaṁnibha
kṣatriyān niha niṣyāmo
dorbhyāmeva yudhāṁ vara

Therefore, O foremost of warriors who remains steadfast in battle, to give protection to this mountain, it is Our duty to kill all of the opposing *kṣatriyas*.

Text 77

ete te kṣatriyāḥ sarve
girimādīpya daṁśitāḥ
rathinas tāta dṛśyante
yathādeśaṁ yuyutsavaḥ

My dear brother, after burning the mountain to ashes, these kings will be very eager to fight with Us. Indeed, while seated upon their chariots, weapons in hand, they patiently wait for such an opportunity.

Text 78

evamuktvā gireḥ śṛṅgān
meru śṛṅgādi voḍurāṭ
nipapāta balaḥ śrī mān
vanamālā dharo yuvā

After speaking in this way, the greatly effulgent and ever-youthful Lord Balarāma, who was nicely decorated with a garland of forest flowers, jumped from the peak of Gomanta Hill, just as the moon descends from the peak of Mount Sumeru.

Text 79

kādambarī madkṣīvo
nīlavāsāḥ sitānanaḥ
sa śāradendu saṁkāśo
vanamālāñ citodaraḥ

He was somewhat intoxicated due to drinking honey from a *kadamba tree*, He was dressed in blue garments, His face was very fair, and He appeared as brilliant as the autumn moon. His chest was decorated with a flower garland.

Text 80

kāntaika kuṇḍala dharaś
cāru mauli ravāṅmukhaḥ
nipapāta narendrāṇāṁ
madhye keśava pūrvajaḥ

Lord Balarāma wore a beautiful earring in one ear and His head was bedecked with a magnificent crown. After jumping from the peak of the mountain, Kṛṣṇa's elder brother, Balarāma, landed in the midst of the enemy kings.

Text 81

avaplute tato rāme
kṛṣṇaḥ kṛṣṇāmbudo pamaḥ
gomanta śikharācchrīmān
āpluto mitavikramaḥ

Seeing how Balarāma had jumped from the peak of the mountain, the unlimitedly powerful Lord Kṛṣṇa, whose complexion was the color of a dark cloud, also jumped from the peak of Gomanta Hill.

Texts 82-84

tatastaṁ pīḍayāmāsa
padbhayāṁ girivaraṁ hariḥ
sa pīḍito giristena
nirmamajja samantataḥ

jalākulo palastatra
prasruto dvirado yathā
sa tena vāriṇā vahnis
tatkṣaṇāt praśamaṁ yayau

kalpānte vāridhārābhir
meghajālair ivāṁśumān
siṁhāra sita nirghoṣaḥ
pītavāsā ghanākṛtiḥ

As He sprang from the top of the mountain, Lord Hari pressed down on it with His lotus feet. As a result, the mountain sank within the earth and became surrounded by water. At this time, the boulders on the mountainside became drenched, so that they appeared like elephants in the monsoon, and the raging fire was extinguished. Thus, the mountain appeared like the sun when it is dimmed by incessant showers at the time of annihilation. Dark-complexioned lotus-eyed Lord Kṛṣṇa, who was dressed in yellow garments, roared like a triumphant lion.

Texts 85-87

kirīṭa mūrddhā saumyāsyaḥ
puṇḍarīka nibhekṣaṇaḥ
śrīvatsa vakṣāḥ sumukhaḥ
sahasrākṣa samadyutiḥ

rāmād anantaraṁ kṛṣṇaḥ
pluto vai vīryavāṁstataḥ
tābhyāmeva plutābhyāṁ
ca caraṇaiḥ pīḍito giriḥ

mumoca salilot pīḍāṁs
tīvra pāvaka śāntaye
salilot pīḍanaṁ dṛṣṭvā
pārthivā bhayamāviśan

His head was bedecked with a glorious crown, His face appeared unlimitedly attractive, His broad chest bore the mark of Śrīvatsa, and his luster defeated the effulgence of Indra, the king of the demigods. Following Balarāma, Kṛṣṇa jumped from the peak of the mountain and landed in the midst of the inimical kings.

Thus ends the translation of the forty-second chapter of the Viṣṇu Parva of Śrī Harivamsa.

Chapter 43

The battle fought by Kṛṣṇa and Balarāma with Jarāsandha and his allies

Text 1

vaiśampāyana uvāca
tau nagādāpluto dṛṣṭvā
vasudeva sutāvubhau
kṣubdhaṁ naravarānīkaṁ
sarvaṁ sammūḍha vāhanam

Vaiśampāyana said: When the kings saw the two sons of Vasudeva jump from the peak of Gomanta Hill, they became bewildered with fear, as did their soldiers and carriers.

Text 2

bāhu praharaṇau tautu
ceratus tatra yādavau
makarāviva saṁrabdhau
samudra kṣobhaṇā vubhau

The two descendents of Yadu then roamed through the ranks of the enemy like two powerful crocodiles moving about in the ocean.

Text 3

tābhyāṁ mṛdhe praviṣṭābhyāṁ
yādavābhyāṁ matistvabhūt
āyudhānāṁ purāṇānām
ādāna kṛta lakṣaṇā

After entering the battlefield, Kṛṣṇa and Balarāma, remembering the purpose of Their mission, invoked Their eternal weapons.

Texts 4-6

tato'mbaratalād bhūyaḥ
patanti sma mahātmanoḥ
madhye rāja sahasrasya
samaraṁ pratikāṅkṣiṇoḥ

yāni vai māthure yuddhe
prāptānyāha vaśobhinoḥ
tānyambarāt patanti sma
divyānyāhava samplave

lelihānāni dīptāni
dīptāgni sadṛśāni vai
nikṣipya yāni tatraiva
tāni prāptau sma yādavau

As soon as they were thought of by these two foremost Personalities of Godhead as They were stationed in the midst of Their enemies, the divine weapons appeared in Their hands. These weapons had been previously wielded by the Lords while fighting at Mathurā and then dismissed by Them. Now, their great effulgence lit up the entire sky.

Text 7

kravyādair anuyātāni
mūrtimanti bṛhanti ca
tṛṣitānyāhave bhoktuṁ
nṛpamāṁsāni sarvaśaḥ

Following the Lord's eternal weapons were countless ghosts and hobgoblins, desiring to eat the flesh of the slain warriors. Indeed, it appeared as if the Lord's weapons had assumed these forms just to eat the flesh and drink the blood of their enemies.

Text 8

divya sragdāma dhāriṇi
trāsayanti ca khecarān
prabhayā bhāsamānāni
daṁśitāni diśo daśa

All of the personifications of the divine weapons were decorated with flower garlands and their effulgence illuminated the ten directions, so that even the creatures that course through the sky became frightened.

Texts 9-10

halaṁ sāṁvartakaṁ nāma
saunandaṁ muṣalaṁ tathā
cakraṁ sudarśanaṁ nāma
gadāṁ kaumodakīṁ tathā

catvāryetāni tejāṁsi
viṣṇu praharaṇāni vai
tābhyāṁ samavatīr ṇāni
yādavābhyāṁ mahā mṛdhe

The four supremely powerful weapons of Lord Viṣṇu, known as the Sāṁvartaka plough, Saunanda *muṣala*, Sudarśana *cakra*, and Kaumodaki club arrived at that great battlefield to render service to the two foremost Yādavas.

Text 11

jagrāha prathamaṁ rāmo
lalāma pratimaṁ raṇe
sarpantamiva sarpendraṁ
divya mālā kulaṁ halam

Lord Balarāma took in His right hand His powerful and excellent plough weapon, which was shaped like the king of serpents and decorated with a splendid flower garland.

Text 12

savyena sātvatāṁ śreṣtho
jagrāha musalottamam
saunandaṁ nāma balavān
nirānandakaraṁ dviṣām

In His left hand, the descendent of Yadu, supremely powerful Lord Balarāma, placed His powerful *muṣala* known as Saunanda. Simply the sight of this weapon vanquishes all happiness of the enemies.

Text 13

darśanīyaṁ ca lokeṣu
cakramāditya varcasam
nāmnā sudarśanaṁ nāma
prīto jagrāha keśavaḥ

Lord Kṛṣṇa cheerfully carried His unlimitedly powerful Sudarśana *cakra*, more brilliant than many suns and most beautiful within the three worlds.

Text 14

darśanīyaṁ ca lokeṣu
dhanurjalada niḥsvanam
nāmnā śārṅgamiti khyātaṁ
prīto jagrāha vīryavān

Lord Kṛṣṇa also carried His famous Śārṅga bow, which is very beautiful to behold and which produces a sound as grave as the rumbling of clouds.

Text 15

devair nigaditārthasya
gadā tasyā pare kare
niṣaktā kumudākṣasya
nāmnā kaumodakīti sā

Thereafter, Lord Kṛṣṇa, unto whom the demigods had submitted their appeal, and whose eyes are as beautiful as fully blossomed lotus flowers, picked up His renowned Kaumodakī club.

Text 16

tau sapraharaṇau vīrau
sākṣād viṣṇotunūpamau
samara rāmagovindau
ripūṁstān pratyayuddhayatām

When the two heroic brothers, Kṛṣṇa and Balarāma, who are not in any way different from Lord Viṣṇu, were thus equipped with Their transcendental weapons, They initiated Their fight with Their enemies.

Text 17

āudhapagrahau vīrau
tāvanyonya mayāvubhau
pūrvajānuja saṁjñau tu
rāma govinda lakṣaṇau

The two brothers, Kṛṣṇa and Balarāma, while wielding Their weapons, appeared to tower over the battlefield, supporting one another.

Text 18

smara'pratirūpau tau
viṣṇureko dvidhā kṛtaḥ
dviṣatsu pratikurvāṇau
parākrāntau yatheśvarau

There was no one on that battlefield that could compare with Kṛṣṇa and Balarāma, both of whom were *viṣṇu-tattva*, who had appeared in this world to display Their supreme prowess while vanquishing the miscreants.

Text 19

halamudyamya rāmastu
sarpendramiva kopanam
cacāra samara vīro
dviṣatām antakopamaḥ

In great anger, Lord Balarāma raised His Saṁvartaka plough, which resembles the king of serpents, and roamed over the battlefield, appearing like Death personified to His enemies.

Texts 20-21

vikarṣan rathavṛndāni
kṣatriyāṇāṁ mahātmanaḥm
cakāra roṣaṁ saphalaṁ
nāgeṣu ca hayeṣu ca

kuñjarāṁṅgalot kṣiptān
musalākṣe patāḍitān
rāmo'bhirāmaḥ samara
nirmamantha yathācalān

The highly intelligent Balarāma drove back the enemy chariots while whirling His plough in the air, even as the elephant and horse warriors looked on. All-attractive Balarāma threw some of the elephants in the air and then killed them by throwing His muṣala. In this way, He created a great slaughter among the elephants as huge as mountains.

Text 22

te vadhyamānā rāmeṇa
samara kṣatriyarṣabhāḥ
jarāsandhāntikaṁ bhītā
virathāḥ pratijagmire

Being defeated and injured by Balarāma on that battlefield, the best of *kṣatriya* warriors lost their chariots and so fled on foot, fearing chastisement from King Jarāsandha.

Text 23

tānuvāca jarāsandhaḥ
kṣatradharme vyavasthitaḥ

dhigetāṁ kṣatravṛttiṁ vaḥ
samara kātarātmanām

Upon seeing this, King Jarasandha, who possessed genuine *ksātriya* character, chastised them, saying, "Shame on your *kṣatriya* status! How can one who fearfully flees from battle continue to maintain his shameful existence?"

Text 24

parākrāntasya samara
virathasya palāyataḥ
bhrūṇahatyām ivāsahyāṁ
pravadanti manīṣiṇaḥ

"According to learned authorities, such cowardice exhibited by so-called warriors who flee the battlefield after losing their chariots is inexcusable, like abortion."

Text 25

pattino bhuvi caikasya
gopasyālpa balīyasaḥ
bhītāḥ kiṁ vinivartadhvaṁ
dhigetāṁ kṣatravṛttitām

"These cowherd boys are very weak and They are on foot and without support. Why do you flee in fear of Them? I condemn your so-called *kṣatriya* status."

Text 26

kṣipraṁ samabhi vartantāṁ
mama vākyena noditāḥ

yāvadetau raṇe gopau
preṣayāmi yamakṣayam

I order you to return to the battle and attack my enemies. I am determined to send these two cowherd boys to the abode of Yamarāja this very day.

Texts 27-28

tataste kṣatriyāḥ sarve
jarāsandhena noditāḥ
kṣipantaḥ śarajālāni
dṛṣṭvā yoddhum upasthitāḥ

te hayaiḥ kāñcanāpīḍai
rathaiścendu samaprabhaiḥ
nāgaiścām modasaṁkāśair
mahāmātra praṇoditaiḥ

Being rallied by King Jarāsandha in this way, all the *kṣatriyas* regrouped and began showering their arrows upon the enemy. They cheerfully entered the battlefield, riding horses decorated with golden ornaments, chariots as bright as the moon, and elephants as dark as rain clouds that hissed like kings of serpents.

Text 29

satanutrāṇa nistriṁśāḥ
sāyudhā bharaṇāmbarāḥ
svāropita dhanuṣmantaḥ
satūṇīrāḥ sasāyakāḥ

These kings wore armor and carried tridents. They were

all gorgeously dressed and decorated with valuable ornaments. They carried bows, arrows and swords as well.

Text 30

sacchatrotsedhinaḥ sarve
cāru cāmara vījitāḥ
ranāva nigatā rejuḥ
syandanasthā mahīkṣitaḥ

The chariot warrior appeared very handsome as they were being fanned by servants with *cāmaras* as umbrellas covered their heads.

Text 31

tau yuddha raṅgā patitau
vidhāvantau mahābhujau
vasudeva sutau vīrau
yuyutsū pratyadṛśyatām

Meanwhile, the mighty-armed son of Vasudeva roamed over the battlefield at will with undeterred enthusiasm.

Text 32

tad yuddham abhavat tatra
tayosteṣāṁ tu saṁyuge
sāyakotsarga bahulaṁ
gadānirghāta dāruṇam

When the allies of Jarāsandha re-entered the battlefield, a fierce encounter ensued between them and the two brothers. There were exchanges of showers of arrows, and when they came at close quarters, they fought with clubs.

Text 33

tataḥ śara sahasrāṇī
pratīcchantau raṇeṣiṇau
tasthaturyo dhamukhyau
tāvabhivṛṣṭau yathācalau

In spite of being assailed by countless arrows, the two foremost of fighters remained fixed like two immovable mountains, receiving incessant torrents of rain.

Text 34

gadābhiścaiva gurvībhiḥ
kṣepaṇīyaiśca mugdaraiḥ
ardyamānnau maheṣvāsau
yādavau na cakampatuḥ

Despite being struck by heavy clubs, sharp spears, blazing tridents, iron maces and other weapons, the two mighty Yādava warriors did not flinch.

Text 35

tataḥ kṛṣṇo'mbudākāraḥ
śaṅkha cakra gadādharaḥ
vyavardhata mahātejā
vātayukta ivānalaḥ

Thereafter, the supremely powerful Lord Kṛṣṇa of dark complexion, carrying a conch, a disc, and a club in His hands, began to exterminate the enemy like a blazing fire.

Text 36

sa cakreṇārka tulyena
dīpyamānena tejasā
ciccheda samare vīro
nṛgajāśva mahārathān

Heroic Lord Madhusūdana slashed human beings, elephants, horses, and chariots to pieces with His Sudarśana *cakra*, which appeared as brilliant as millions of sun.

Text 37

gadānipāta vihatā
lāṅgalena ca karṣitāḥ
na śekuste raṇe sthātuṁ
pārthivā naṣṭacetasaḥ

Being struck by the club and pulled down by the plough, the kings on that battlefield swooned and fell to the ground.

Text 38

cakra kṣura nikṛttāni
vicitrāṇi mahīkṣitām
rathayuthāni bhagnāni
na śekuś calituṁ raṇe

The chariots of the enemy warriors ground to a halt after being broken by the Lord's most powerful and razor-sharp Sudarśana *cakra*.

Text 39

musalākṣepa bhagnāśca
kuñjarāḥ ṣaṣṭihāyanāḥ
ghanā eva ghanāpāye
bhagnadantā vicukruśuḥ

Being injured by the attack of the *muṣala*, countless elephants lost their tusks so that they looked like sixty-years-old men. They were thus rendered as useless as clouds in autumn as they screamed in pain.

Text 40

cakrānalajvālahatāḥ
sādinaḥ sapadātayaḥ
petuḥ parāsa vastatra
yaṭhā vajra hatāstathā

Innumerable horses, cavalry soldiers, and infantry fell to the ground after being burnt by the fiery effulgence of the Sudarśana *cakra*. They lost their lives, as if struck by a thunderbolt.

Text 41

cakra lāṅgala nirdagdhaṁ
tatsainyaṁ vidalīkṛtam
yugāntopahata prakhyaṁ
sarvaṁ patitamābabhau

Countless enemy soldiers were burned by the Sudarśana *cakra* and pierced by the plough. The dead bodies strewn all over the battlefield made it appear as if it was the time of cosmic annihilation.

Text 42

ākrīḍabhūmiṁ divyānām
āyudhānāṁ vapuṣmatām
vaiṣṇavānāṁ nṛpāste tu
duṣṛtum apyabalīyasaḥ

What to speak to fighting, the enemy kings were unable to even look at the battlefield, which had become the playground for the transcendental weapons of Lord Viṣṇu. After displaying their prowess, these weapons appeared in personified form.

Text 43

kecid rathāḥ sammṛditāḥ
kecin nihata pārthivāḥ
bhagnaika cakrāstvapare
vikīrṇā dharaṇītale

Countless chariots were strewn here and there, smashed to pieces. Many kings had been mercilessly killed, without a fight. Many chariots had lost one of their wheels so that they could no longer be driven.

Text 44

tasmin viśasane ghore
cakralāṅgala samplave
dāruṇāni pravṛttāni
rakṣāṁsyaut pātikāni ca

Having experienced a terrible defeat at the hands of the *cakra* and plough, the demoniac kings resorted to various kinds of illusion, thus creating a terrifying situation.

Text 45

ārtānāṁ kūjamānānāṁ
pāṭitānāṁ ca veṇuvat
anto na śakyate'nveṣṭuṁ
nṛnāga rathavājinām

It was impossible to estimate how many people were screaming in pain, how many soldiers were cut in two, and how many human beings, elephants, and horses had been killed in that great battle.

Text 46

sā pātita narendrāṇāṁ
rudhirā'rdrā raṇakṣitiḥ
yoṣeva candanārdrāṅgī
bhairavā pratibhāti vai

The entire battlefield became soaked with the blood of the dead and injured warriors, thus giving it the fearful appearance of a woman whose entire body had been smeared with sandalwood paste.

Text 47

narakeśāsthi majjāntraiḥ
śātitānāṁ ca dantinām
rudhiraugha plavastatra
cchādayāmāsa medinīm

The flow of blood from the wounded and slain soldiers created a river in which human hair, bones, hands, and legs, as well as the limbs of elephants were floating.

Text 48

tasmin mahābhīṣaṇake
naravāhana saṁkṣaye
śivānāma śivaiḥ śabdair
nādite ghoradarśane

The battlefield thus took on a very fearful aspect with slain warriors and their carriers strewn here and there. The howling of jackals come to feast on the flesh added to the horror.

Text 49

ārtas tanita saṁnāde
rudhirāmbuh ṛdākule
antakākrīḍa sadṛśe
nāgadehaiḥ samāvṛte

Pathetic cries for help could be heard in all directions amidst the pools of blood that flowed from the bodies of the dead soldiers and animals. The dead elephants appeared like islands in those lakes and the entire scene was like the residence for Death personified.

Text 50

apāstair bāhubhiryor
dhaisturagaiśca vidāritaiḥ
kaṅkaiśca balagṛdnraiśca
nāditaiḥ pratinādite

The battlefield was littered with severed hands and legs, the bodies of slain soldiers, and wounded and slain horses, making it a place of pilgrimage for cranes, crows, and jackals, that filled the air with their sounds.

Text 51

nipāte pṛthivīśānāṁ
mṛtyusādhāraṇe raṇe
kṛṣṇaḥ śatruvadhaṁ kartuṁ
cacārāntaka darśanaḥ

As Lord Kṛṣṇa, appearing like Death personified, roamed over the battlefield, killing His enemies, the whole scene appeared like a crematorium for many great kings.

Text 52

yugāntārka prabhaṁ cakraṁ
kālīṁ caivāyasīṁ gadām
gṛhya sainyavā nigato
babhāṣe keśavo nṛpān

Lord Kṛṣṇa, holding the effulgent Sudarśana *cakra* in one hand and a formidable black club in another, stood in the middle of the enemy soldiers and made the following announcement to the assembled kings.

Text 53

kina yuddhayat vai śūrā
hastyaśva ratha saṁyutaḥ
kimidaṁ gamyate śūrāḥ
kṛtāstrā dṛḍhaniścayāḥ
ahaṁ sapūrvajaḥ saṁkhye
padātiḥ pramukhe sthitaḥ

O warriors difficult to conquer, you have many elephants, horses, and chariots and so why are you wavering, thinking of running away from the battle? I am standing here with My brother without any other assistance.

Text 54

adṛṣṭa doṣeṇa raṇe
bhavanto yena pālitāḥ
sa idānīṁ jarāsandhaḥ
kimarthe nābhivartate

Where is Jarāsandha, who was very eager for battle, and for whose sake you are all standing here before Me? Why has he not entered the fray?

Text 55

evamukte tu nṛpatir
darado nāma vīryavān
rāmaṁ halāgrogra bhujaṁ
pratyayāt sainya madhyagam

After Lord Kṛṣṇa finished speaking, the powerful King Darada, who was standing in the midst of the assembled warriors, came and stood in front of Lord Balarāma's plough weapon.

Text 56

babhāṣe sa tu tāmrākṣam
ukṣāṇamiva sevanī
ehyehi rāma yudhyasva
mayā sārddham ariṁdam

Just as a farmer shouts at his bulls, he began to challenge Lord Balarāma, whose eyes were red with rage: O killer of the enemies, O Rāma, fight with me if You think that You are a great hero.

Text 57

tad yuddham abhavat
tābhyāṁ rāmasya daradasya ca
mṛdhe lokavariṣṭhāṁbhyāṁ
kuñjarābhyām ivaujasā

Both Balarāma and Darada were the foremost of warriors. As they began to fight, it appeared as if two giant elephants were battling.

Text 58

yojayitvā tataḥ skandhe
rāmo daradamāhave
halena balināṁ śreṣṭho
musalenā vapothayat

After a short skirmish, Balarāma, the foremost of powerful personalities, pulled King Darada by his neck with His plough and then killed him with a blow of His *muṣala*.

Text 59

svakāya gatamūrdhā vai
musalenā vapothitaḥ
papāta darado bhūmau
daritārdva ivācalaḥ

Indeed, Lord Balarāma struck King Darada's head so forcefully that it sunk into his trunk. When the dead body fell to the ground, it appeared like a large hill.

Texts 60-62

rāmeṇa nihate tasmin
darade raja sattame
jarāsandhasya rājñastu
rāmeṇāsīt samāgamaḥ

mahendrasyava vṛtreṇa
dāruṇo lomaharṣaṇaḥ
gade gṛhītvā vikrāntā
vanyonyam abhidhāvataḥ

kampayantau bhuvaṁ vīrau
tāvudyata mahāgadau
dadṛśāte mahātmānau
girī saśikharāviva

When Jarāsandha received the news of King Darada's death at the hands of Balarāma, he hurriedly launched an assault on the Lord. Thereafter, a fierce battle ensued, resembling the duel between Indra, the king of the demigods, and the demon Vṛtrāsura. Both wielded their clubs, chasing each other so that their footsteps caused the earth to shake. When they raised their clubs to strike one another, they appeared like two mountains with high peaks.

Text 63

vyapāramanta yuddhāni
prekṣya tau puruṣarṣabhau
saṁrabdhāviva dhāvantau
gadāyuddheṣu viśrutau

As Balarāma and Jarāsandha engaged in frenzied combat, all the other kings and soldiers stopped fighting to become spectators. Both were very expert fighters with clubs and so it was fascinating to watch them angrily strike one another.

Text 64

tābubhau paramācāryau
lake khyātau mahābalau
mattāviva mahānāgā
vanyonyaṁ samadhāvatām

Both supremely powerful warriors were famous as masters of fighting with the club. They attacked each other just like two maddened elephants.

Text 65

tato devāḥ sagandharvāḥ
siddhāśca paramarṣayaḥ
yakṣā ścāpsara saścaiva
samājagmuḥ sahasraśaḥ

To watch this extraordinary battle, the denizens of heaven, the demigods, Gandharvas, Siddhas, great sages, Yakṣas, and thousands of Apsarās, appeared overhead.

Text 66

taddeva yakṣa gandharva
maharṣibhir alaṅkṛtam
śuśubhe'bhya dhikaṁ rājan
nabho jyotirgaṇairiva

O King, with the appearance of the demigods, Yakṣas, Gandharvas, and great sages, who were all nicely decorated with costly ornaments, the sky appeared as if filled with innumerable stars.

Text 67

abhidudrāva rāmaṁ tu
jarāsandho narādhipaḥ
savyaṁ maṇḍalam āśritya
baladevastu dakṣiṇam

Jarāsandha then suddenly attacked Balarāma from His left side, hoping to catch Him unawares. However, Balarāma was alert and easily countered the onslaught.

Text 68

lavanyonyaṁ prajahlāte
gadāyuddha vśāradau
dantābhyāmiva mātaṅgau
nādayantau diśo daśa

Both warriors, who were very expert at fighting with the club, repeatedly struck each other just as two intoxicated elephants strike one another with their tusks. Then, as they continued to fight, fearful sounds filled the ten directions.

Text 69

gadānipāto rāmasya
śuśruve'śa niniḥsvanaḥ
jarāsandhasya ca raṇe
parvatasyeva dīryataḥ

When Balarāma struck Jarāsandha with His club, the sound

resembled that of a thunderbolt, and when Jarāsandha struck Balarāma, the sound resembled the splitting of a mountain.

Text 70

na sma kampayate rāmaṁ
jarāsandha karacyutā
gadā gadābhṛtāṁ śreṣṭhaṁ
vindhyaṁ girim ivānilaḥ

Despite his best efforts, Jarāsandha could not even slightly budge Balarāma, the foremost of all wielders of the club, just as a powerful wind cannot move the Vindhya Mountains.

Text 71

rāmasya tu gadāvegaṁ
rājā sa magadheśvaraḥ
sehe dhairyeṇa mahatā
śikṣayā ca vyapothayat

Jarāsandha, the king of Magadha, patiently tolerated the blows of Balarāma's club. Again and again he expertly dodged the Lord's terrible blows, or rendered them ineffective.

Texts 72-73

tato'ntarikṣe vāgāsīt
susvarā lokasākṣiṇī
na tvayā rāma vadhyo'
yamalaṁ khedena mānada

vihito'sya mayā mṛtyus
tasmāt sādhu vyupāram

acireṇaiva kālena
prāṇāṁstyakṣyati māgadhaḥ

As this terrible duel continued, an unembodied voice suddenly announced from the sky: O Balarāma! O worshipable Lord of everyone, Jarāsandha is not destined to be killed by You. Do not lament, for I have already made arrangement for his death. For now, abstain from further fighting. Very soon the king of Magadha will breathe his last.

Texts 74-75

jarāsandhastu tacchṛtvā
vimanāḥ samapadyata
na prāharat tatas tasmai
punareva halāyudhaḥ
tay vyupāramatāṁ yuddhād
vṛṣṇayaste ca pārthivāḥ

dīrghakālaṁ mahārāja
nijaghnuri taretaram
parājite tvapakrānte
jarāsandhe mahīpatau
viviktam abhavat sainyaṁ
parāvṛtta mahāratham

When Jarāsandha heard this divine voice in the sky, he felt disappointment. After hearing the celestial announcement, Balarāma immediately stopped fighting. Indeed, both desisted from further combat. O King, after that hard-fought battle, Jarāsandha left the battlefield feeling defeated, and his allies followed him.

Text 76

te nṛpāścoditair nāgaiḥ
syandanais turagais tathā
dudruvur bhīta manaso
vyāghrāghrātā mṛgā iva

In fact, the king of Magadha's allies were very fearful at heart, like deer that had been captured by a tiger, and so they hurriedly retreated on their horses, elephants, and chariots.

Text 77

tannarendraiḥ parityaktaṁ
bhagna darpair mahārathaiḥ
ghoraṁ kravyāda bahulaṁ
raudram āyodhanaṁ babhau

The entire battlefield looked like a mass graveyard full of dead bodies and the blood of the great warriors whose pride and heads had been smashed. Numerous jackals and other carnivorous animals and birds made a feast of those corpses, creating a ghastly scene.

Text 78

dravatsu rathamukhyeṣu
cedirājo mahādyutiḥ
smṛtvā yādava sambandhaṁ
kṛṣṇam evān vavartata

After the departure of the king of Magadha and his allies, Damaghoṣa, the king of Cedi, remembered his relationship with the Yadu dynasty and so approached Lord Kṛṣṇa.

Text 79

vṛtaḥ kāruṣa sainyena
cedisainyena cānagha
sambandha kāmo govindam
idamāha sa cedirāt

O sinless Janamejaya, surrounded by the vast army of the Karuṣa and Cedi kingdoms, Damaghoṣa spoke as follows to Lord Kṛṣṇa, hoping to establish friendly relations.

Text 80

ahaṁ pitṛṣva surbhartā
tava yādava nandana
sabalastvām upāvṛttas
tvaṁ hi me dayitaḥ prabho

O scion of the Yadu dynasty, I am the husband of your aunt. O master, I have come to You with all my soldiers because You are very dear to me.

Text 81

uktaścaiṣa mayā rājā
jarāsandho'lpa cetanaḥ
kṛṣṇād virama durbuddhe
vigrahād raṇakarmaṇi

I had warned evil-mined Jarāsandha long ago, saying: O sinful one, give up your futile aspiration to fight with Kṛṣṇa, the most exalted of illustrious personalities. However, he did not pay any heed to my words.

Text 82

tadeṣoḍya mayā tyakto
mama vākyasya dūṣakaḥ
bhagno yuddhe jarāsandhas
tvayā dravati sānugaḥ

Rather, he criticized me for giving him advice. It is for that reason I have now given up his association. He has left the battlefield, along with his army, having been soundly defeated by You.

Text 83

nirvairo naiṣa saṁyāti
svapuraṁ pṛthivīpatiḥ
tvayyeva bhūyo'pyaparaṁ
darśayiṣyati kilviṣam

It is my opinion that he will not return to his city, giving up his enmity toward You. He will certainly concoct some sinful plan and then put into action when the time is right.

Text 84

datimāṁ saṁtyajāśu tvaṁ
mahīṁ hatanarākulām
kravyād agaṇa saṅkīrṇau
sevitavyām mānuṣaiḥ

I think that You should return home without delay. Just see how the ground is littered with dead bodies being devoured by carnivorous animals. This place is only fit for those in the darkness of ignorance.

Text 85

karavīrapuraṁ kṛṣṇa
gacchāmaḥ sabalānugāḥ
śṛgālaṁ vāsudevaṁ vai
drakṣyāmas tatra pārthivam

My dear Kṛṣṇa, let us return to Karavīrapura, along with our army and servants. That glorious city is ruled by a king named Śṛgāla Vāsudeva, and we should meet him.

Text 86

imau rathavaro dagrau
yuvayoḥ kāritau mayā
yojitau śīghra turagaiḥ
svaṅga cakrākṣu kūvarau

I have two chariots that I specially prepared for You two brothers, drawn by the fastest horses available. The wheels, axle, and other moving parts are perfectly engineered.

Text 87

śīghram āruha bhadraṁ te
baladeva sahāyavān
tvarāmaḥ karavīrasthaṁ
draṣṭuṁ taṁ vasudhādhipam

May you achieve auspiciousness! Please mount Your chariot at once so we can quickly proceed to Karavīrapura and meet King Śṛgāla.

Text 88

vaiśampāyana uvāca
viprṛsvasṛ patervākyaṁ
śrutvā cedipatestadā
vākyaṁ hṛṣṭmanāḥ kṛṣṇoḥ
jagāda jagato guru

Vaiśampāyana said: O Janamejaya, after hearing the speech of His uncle, Damaghoṣa, the king of Cedi, Lord Kṛṣṇa, the spiritual master of everyone, felt pleased.

Text 89

aho yuddhābhi saṁtaptau
deśakālo citaṁ tvayā
bāndhava pratirūpeṇa
saṁsiktau vacanāmbunā

Lord Kṛṣṇa said: Alas, We had become exhausted due to the battle, but now We feel refreshed by the sweet words of our well-wishing relative.

Text 90

deśa kāla viśiṣṭasya
hitasya madhurasya ca
vākyasya durlabhā loke
vaktāraś cedi sattama

O King of Cedi, in this world it is very difficult to find someone who speaks sweet and beneficial words according to the requirement of time, place, and circumstances.

Text 91

cedinātha sanāthau svaḥ
saṁvṛtau tava darśanāt
nāvayoḥ kiṁcida prāpyaṁ
yayostvaṁ bandhur īdṛśaḥ

O lord of Cedi, We have found Our savior in You. With a friend like you, there will be nothing impossible for Us to achieve.

Text 92

jarāsandhasya nidhanaṁ
ye cānye tatsamā nṛpāḥ
paryāptau tvatsanāthau svaḥ
kartuṁ cedi kulodvaha

O ornament of the Cedi dynasty, with your guidance and shelter, We will certainly have no difficulty in sending Jarāsandha and other powerful enemies to the abode of Yamarāja.

Text 93

yadūnāṁ prathamo bandhus
tvaṁ hi sarva mahīkṣitām
ataḥ prabhṛti saṁgrāmān
drakṣyase cedisattama

O ruler of Cedi, among all the kings of the earth, you are the best friend and well-wisher of the Yadu dynasty. You will certainly witness many battles in the near future.

Text 94

cākraṁ mausalam ityevaṁ
saṁgrāmaṁ raṇavṛttayaḥ
kathayiṣyanti loke'smin
ye dhariṣyanti pārthivāḥ

Those who witness the fierce battles in store for Us will certainly glorify the wonderful accomplishments of My weapon, the Sudarśana *cakra*, and My brother's weapon, the *muṣala*.

Text 95

rājñāṁ parājayaṁ yuddhe
gomante'cala sattame
śravaṇād dhāraṇād vāpi
svargalokaṁ vrajanti hi

Simply by hearing about or remembering this battle at the foot of Gomanta Hill, and how We defeated all our enemies, one will certainly attain the heavenly planets after death.

Text 96

taducchāma mahārāja
karavīraṁ purottamam
tvayoddiṣṭena mārgeṇa
cedirāja śivāya vai

O King of Cedi, let Us do as you have advised and travel to the beautiful city of Karavīrapura.

Text 97

te syandana gatāḥ sarve
pavanotpatibhir hayaiḥ
bhejire dīrgham adhvānaṁ
mūrtimanta ivāgnayaḥ

When the Lord finished speaking, the three heroes, who appeared like fire-gods, mounted their chariots and departed. Being drawn by very swift horses, the chariots moved like the wind.

Text 98

te trirātreṣitāḥ prāptāḥ
karavīraṁ purottamam
śivāya ca śive deśe
niviṣṭāstri daśopamāḥ

These three prominent personalities passed three nights while going to Karavīrapura. Upon their arrival, they set up their camp at a beautiful place outside the city.

Thus ends the translation of the forty-third chapter of the Viṣṇu parva of Śrī Harivaṁsa.

Chapter 44

Kṛṣṇa and Balarāma defeat King Śṛgāla in battle. Coronation of Prince Śakradeva

Text 1

vaiśampāyana uvāca
tānāgatān viditvātha
śṛgālo yuddha durmadaḥ
purasya gharṣaṇaṁ matvā
nirjagāmendra vikramaḥ

Vaiśampāyana said: My dear Janamejaya, when the powerful King Śṛgāla, who was very fond of engaging in battle, received the news of Kṛṣṇa, Balarāma and Damaghoṣa's arrival, he thought that he was being attacked. In that mood, he came out from his palace.

Texts 2-7

rathenāditya varṇena
bhāsvatā raṇagāmīnā
āyudha pratipūrṇena
nemi nirghoṣa hāsinā

mandarācala kalpena
citrā bharaṇa bhūṣiṇā
akṣayya sāyakaistūṇaiḥ
pūrṇenārṇava ghoṣiṇā

haryaśvanāśu gatinā
saktena śikhareṣvapi

hema kūvara garbheṇa
dṛḍhākṣeṇāti śobhinā

subandhureṇa dīptena
patatrivara gāminā
khagateneva śakrāsya
haryaśvena rathādriṇā

sāvitre niyame pūrṇe
yaṁ dadau savitā svayam
āditya raśmi bhiriva
raśmimiyo nigṛhyate

tena syandana mukhyena
dviṣat syandana ghātinā
sa śṛgālo bhyātkṛṣṇaṁ
śalabhaḥ pāvakaṁ yathā

He mounted his best chariot, which was as brilliant as the sun. King Śṛgāla daily worshiped the sun-god and chanted the Gāyatri *mantra*. Being pleased with the king's worship, Sūrya rewarded him with the gift of this wonderful chariot, which could never be obstructed on the battlefield. Being drawn by swift green horses, this chariot moved with the speed of Garuḍa. Indeed, it rivaled the chariot of Indra, the king of heaven, which traverses through the skies and appears as big as a mountain. While going, this chariot sometimes made a sound as if it were laughing sarcastically while at other times, it sounded like the rumbling of clouds in the sky. The interior of this chariot was plated with gold, it was incredibly sturdy and beautiful to behold, and it could travel to the top of mountains if required. After mounting this celestial chariot, King Śṛgāla attacked Lord Kṛṣṇa, just like a fly rushes into a blazing fire.

Text 8

cāpapaṇīḥ sutīkṣṇeṣuḥ
kavacī hemamālikaḥ
sita prāvaraṇo ṣṇīṣaḥ
pāvakā kāralocanaḥ

Śṛgāla was dressed in armor and he wore a beautiful gold necklace. He was dressed in lovely garments and a turban bedecked his head. He held a bow in his hand and his eyes blazed like fire.

Text 9

muhurmuhur jyācapalaṁ
vikṣipan duḥsahaṁ dhanuḥ
nirvamanh roṣajñaṁ vāyuṁ
sāna lajvāla maṇḍalam

Being enraged, the king repeatedly twanged his bowstring. As he breathed heavily, it appeared as if fire issued from his gaping mouth.

Text 10

bhābhir bhūṣaṇa paṁktīnāṁ
dipto meru rivācalaḥ
rathastha iva śailendraḥ
śṛgālaḥ pratya dṛśyata

Being decorated by dazzling ornaments, King Śṛgāla appeared like a second Mount Sumeru. While seated upon his chariot, he looked like the foremost of mountains.

Text 11

tasyāra sitaśabdena
rathanemi svanena ca
gurutvena ca nābhyantī
cacālorvī bhayāturā

Upon hearing the king's ferocious roars mixed with the terrible rumbling of his chariot wheels, the earth became extremely frightened. Indeed, the king mounted upon his chariot created a great burden for her.

Text 12

tamāpatantaṁ śrī mantam
mūrtimantam ivācalam
śṛgālaṁ lokapālābhaṁ
dṛṣṭvā kṛṣṇo na vivyathe

Although King Śṛgāla was huge, like a great hill, and as powerful as one of the Lokapālas, Lord Kṛṣṇa felt not even the slightest tinge of anxiety while watching him approach for battle.

Text 13

śṛgālaścāpi saṁrabdhaḥ
syandanenāśu gāminā
samīpe vāsudevasya
yuyutsuḥ pratyadṛśyata

Within a moment, King Śṛgāla angrily approached Lord Kṛṣṇa, riding on his fast-moving chariot, and began challenging Him with great enthusiasm.

Text 14

vāsudevaṁ sthitaṁ dṛṣṭvā
śṛgālo yuddhalālasaḥ
abhidudrāva vegena
megharāśir ivācalam

Indeed, when He saw Lord Kṛṣṇa before him, the king's desire for battle increased unlimitedly. Although he sent forth showers of arrows, Kṛṣṇa felt these to be no more than showers of rain falling upon a mountain.

Text 15

vāsudevaḥ smitaṁ kṛtvā
pratiyuddhāya tasthivān
tad yuddham abhavat tābhyāṁ
samare ghoradarśanam
ubhābhyāmiva mattābhyāṁ
kuñjarābhyāṁ yathā vane

Kṛṣṇa simply smiled and prepared Himself to face the kings' challenge. A fierce battle then took place between them, so that it appeared as if two intoxicated elephants were fighting in a forest.

Text 16

śṛgālastva bravīt kṛṣṇaṁ
samare samupasthitam
yuddharāgeṇa tejasvī
mohāccalita gauravaḥ

The powerful Śṛgāla, who was bereft of all good sense due to excessive pride in his prestigious position, addressed Lord

Kṛṣṇa on that battlefield, being induced by the mode of passion to try and conquer Him.

Texts 17-18

gomante yuddhamārgeṇa
yat tvayā kṛṣṇa ceṣṭitam
anāyakānāṁ mūrkhāṇāṁ
nṛpāṇāṁ durable bale

sa me suviditaḥ kṛṣṇa
kṣatriyāṇāṁ parājayaḥ
kṛpaṇānāma sattvānāma
yuddhānāṁ raṇotsave

O Kṛṣṇa, I have heard all about Your exploits of fighting with foolish, weak, and leaderless kings at Gomanta Hill. I know that a *kṣatriya* may meet with defeat by the turn of fate, but those *kṣatriyas* were cowards who were inpatient, devoid of real prowess, an inexperienced.

Text 19

tiṣṭhedānīṁ yathākāmaṁ
sthit'haṁ pārthive pade
ka yāsyasi mayā ruddho
raṇeṣva pariniṣṭhitaḥ

I am the ruler of this grand city and if You are prepared to fight, then just stand before me for a moment. How can You imagine that You will survive a battle with me? I think that You are a neophyte who knows almost nothing of the art of fighting.

Text 20

na cāhamekaṁ sabalo
yuktastvāṁ yuddhumāhave
ahamekas tvamapyeko
dvau yudhyāva raṇe sthitau

You are alone and I have my vast army. For this reason, it is not proper for me to fight with You unconditionally. I think that a single combat between us would be suitable.

Text 21

kiṁ janena nirastena tvaṁ
vāhaṁ ca raṇe sthitaḥ
dharmayuddhena nidhanaṁ
vrajatve kataro raṇe

What is the use of killing unnecessarily? Let us fight according to the codes of combat so that only You or me perishes.

Text 22

loke'smin vāsudevo'haṁ
bhaviṣyāmi hate tvayi
hate mayi tvamapyeko
vāsudevo bhaviṣyasi

If You are killed in this battle then I will become the undisputed king of the entire world, and if I am killed, then You will be accepted as the real Lord Vāsudeva.

Text 23

śṛgālasya vacaḥ śrutvā
vāsudevaḥ kṣamāparaḥ
īrṣyantaṁ praharasveti
tamuktvā cakramādade

After hearing the speech of Śṛgāla, Lord Vāsudeva, who is forgiving by nature, spoke as follows to the envious king: You should be the first to strike. After saying this, Lord Kṛṣṇa invoked His transcendental weapon, the Sudarśana *cakra*.

Text 24

tataḥ sāyaka jālāni
śṛgālaḥ krodha mūrchitaḥ
cikṣepa kṛṣṇe ghorāṇi
yuddhāya laghuvikramaḥ

Thereafter, being very eager to exhibit his prowess, King Śṛgāla angrily showered his arrows upon Lord Kṛṣṇa.

Text 25

śastrāṇi yāni cānyāni
musalādyāni saṁyuge
pātayāmāsa govinde
sa śṛgālaḥ pratāpavān

As the battle continued, the envious king employed other weapons, such as his club, hoping to defeat Lord Govinda.

Texts 26-27

śṛgāla prahitair astraiḥ
pāvaka jvāla mālibhiḥ
nirdayābhihataḥ kṛṣṇaḥ
sthitao girir ivācalaḥ

so'stra prahārābhihataḥ
kiṁcid roṣa samanvitaḥ
cakram udyamya govindaḥ
śṛgālasya parikṣipat

Although Kṛṣṇa appeared to be injured by the fiery weapons mercilessly released by Śṛgāla, He remained unmoved, like a mountain. Becoming enraged, Lord Kṛṣṇa decided to retaliate with His *cakra*.

Text 28

taṁ rathasthaṁ pramāṇasthaṁ
śṛgālaṁ yuddha durmadaṁ
jaghāna samara cakraṁ
jātadarpaṁ mahābalam

Powerful Śṛgāla, who considered himself to be a great warrior, simply sat very proudly on his chariot and did not even make an effort to counter the *cakra*. That wonderful weapon inflicted a terrible wound on the foolish king's chest, however.

Text 29

tataḥ sudarśanaṁ cakraṁ
punarāyād guroḥ kare
cakreṇorasi nirbhinnaḥ
sa gatāsur gatotsavaḥ

papāta kṣata jasrāvī
śṛgālo'drir ivāhataḥ

After inflicting the wound, the Sudarśana *cakra* returned to the hands of Lord Kṛṣṇa, the spiritual master of the entire world. The *cakra* had split Śrgāla's chest, just as Indra's thunderbolt shatters a mountain. As blood gushed from his wound, the king fell from his chariot onto the battlefield, devoid of life.

Text 30

niśamya taṁ nipatitaṁ
vrajapātādi vācalam
tasya sainyānya payayurvi
manāṁsi hate nṛpe

When King Śṛgāla's soldiers saw him lying dead on the battlefield, like a mountain shattered by a thunderbolt, they panicked and began fleeing in all directions.

Text 31

kecit praviśya nagaraṁ
kaśmalā bhihatā bhṛśam
rurudur duḥkha saṁtaptā
bhartṛśokābhi pīḍitāḥ

Many panic-stricken soldiers returned to the city, wailing loudly. Being devoid of their master, they were bewildered and confused.

Text 32

kecit tatraiva śocantaḥ
smarantaḥ sukṛtāni ca

patitaṁ bhūpatiṁ bhūmau
na tyajanti sma duḥkhitāḥ

Some of the soldiers remained on the battlefield, lamenting the loss of their beloved king. While remembering their affectionate dealing with him, they gathered around the body that was now devoid of life.

Text 33

tato megha ninādena
svareṇāri vimardanaḥ
kṛṣṇaḥ kamala patrākṣo
janānām abhayaṁ dadau

At that time, Lord Kṛṣṇa, who is very expert at destroying His enemies and whose eyes resemble lotus petals, gave assurances to these bewildered soldiers with a voice as grave as the rumbling of clouds.

Texts 34-35

cakrocitena hastena
rājatāguṇli parvaṇā
na bhetavyaṁ na bhetavyam
iti tānabhya bhāsata

nāsya pāpasya doṣeṇa
nirābādha karaṁ janam
ghātayiṣyāmi samare
nedaṁ śūravrataṁ matam

Lord Kṛṣṇa raised His right hand, which holds the Sudarśana *cakra*, gesturing to the assembled warriors while speaking: O brave ones, do not be afraid. I will not kill innocent people in retaliation for the sins of this arrogant king. Such behavior would not befit a genuine *kṣatriya.*

Texts 36-37

aśrupūrṇa mukhā dīnāḥ
krandamānā bhṛśaṁ tadā
te sma paśyanti patitaṁ
dharaṇyāṁ dharaṇīpatim

cakra nirdārito raskaṁ
bhinna śṛṅgam ivācalam

All of these soldiers were crying pathetically while gazing at the face of their dead king. Tears of lamentation flowed from their eyes. King Śṛgāla's chest had been shattered and he lay like a mountain whose peak had been smashed.

Text 38

vilapantis ma te sarve
sacivāḥ saprajā bhṛśam
sāśrupātekṣaṇā dīnāḥ
śokasya vaśamāgatāḥ

All of King Śṛgāla's ministers and subjects were overwhelmed by grief and lamentation, shedding incessant tears.

Text 39

teṣāṁ rudita śabdena
paurāṇāṁ visvaraiḥ svaraiḥ

mahiṣyas tasya niṣpetuḥ
saputrā ruditānanāḥ

As all the people were lamenting, the queens of King Śṛgāla, fearing the worst, hastily came out from the palace along with their sons.

Text 40

tāstaṁ nipatitaṁ dṛṣṭvā
ślāghyaṁ bhūmipatiṁ patim
stanānārujya karajair
bhṛśārtāḥ paryadevayan

When they saw their beloved husband lying dead on the battlefield, the queens began to wail loudly while beating their chests.

Text 41

urāṁsyura sijāṁścaiva
śirojānyā kulānyapi
nirdyaṁ tāḍayan tyastā
visvaraṁ ruruduḥ striyaḥ

Beating their chests and foreheads again and again and pulling their hair in anguish, the queens continued to cry and could not be consoled.

Text 42

tasyorasi suduḥkhārtā
mṛditāḥ klinna locanāḥ
petur ūrdhva bhujāḥ sarvāś
chinnamūlā latā iva

In great distress, the queens cried incessantly as they raised their arms to the sky and then fell on the body of their dead husband, like trees that had been cut.

Text 43

tāsāṁ vāṣpāmbu pūrṇāni
netrāṇi nṛpayoṣitām
vāri vipra hatānīva
paṅkajāni cakāśire

The faces of these lamenting queens appeared like lotus flowers that had been uprooted and left to dry.

Text 44

tāḥ patiṁ patitaṁ bhūmau
rūdantyo hṛdi tāḍitāḥ
lālapyamānāḥ karuṇaṁ
yoṣitaḥ paryadevayan

While gazing at their dead husband lying upon the ground, the bewildered queens lamented pathetically while striking their chests.

Text 45

putraṁ cāsya puraskṛtya
bālaṁ prasruta locanaṁ
śakradevaṁ pituḥ pārsve
dviguṇaṁ ruruduḥ striyaḥ

Keeping the king's son, Śakradeva, in front, the queens continued to lament. The boy also was greatly distressed and tears flowed from his eyes.

Text 46

ayaṁ tye vīra vikṛanto
bālaḥ putro na paṇḍitaḥ
tvadvihīnaḥ kathamayaṁ
pade sthāsyāta paitṛke

The queens said: O powerful king, here is your small son, who has yet to learn many things. Without you, how will he rule the kingdom and properly maintain the subjects?

Text 47

kathameka pade tvaktvā
gat'syantā puraṁ param
atṛptāstava saukhyānāṁ
kiṁ kurso vidhavā vayam

O lord, why did you suddenly leave us in this way? Our desires for material happiness have not yet been fulfilled. Alas! We are now widows! What will we do?

Text 48

tasya padmāvatī nāma
mahiṣī pramadottamā
rudatī putramādāya
vāsudevam upasthitā

Among Śṛgāla's queens, Padmāvatī was the principle wife. She took her son, approached Lord Kṛṣṇa in great distress, and spoke as follows.

Text 49

yastvayā pātito vīra
raṇaproktena karmaṇā
tasya preta gatasyāṁyaṁ
putrastvāṁ śaraṇaṁ gataḥ

O supremely powerful one, You killed our husband in battle. This son of he who has departed this world has now come to Your shelter.

Text 50

yadi tvāṁ praṇame tāsau
kuryāda vā śāsanaṁ tava
nāyameka prahāreṇa
janastapyeta dāruṇam

If my husband had very humbly surrendered unto You and then followed Your instructions, he would not have met such a pathetic end, bringing with it great humiliation.

Text 51

yadi kuryādayaṁ mūḍhas
tvayi bāndhavakaṁ vidhim
naivaṁ parītaḥ kṛpaṇaḥ
seveta dharaṇītalam

If this ignorant king had behaved with You in a friendly manner, then today carnivorous animals and birds would not be making a feast of his dead body.

Text 52

ayamasya vipannasya
bāndhavasya tavānagha
santatī rakṣyatāṁ vīra
putraḥ putra ivātmajaḥ

O sinless, most powerful hero, this child is the son of the dead king. Please give him protection, as if he were Your own son.

Text 53

tasyāstad vacanaṁ śrutvā
mahiṣyā yadunandanaḥ
mṛdur pūrvamidaṁ vākyam
uvāca vadatāṁ varaḥ

After hearing the queens of Śṛgāla speak in this manner, the supremely eloquent speaker, the descendent of Yadu, Lord Kṛṣṇa, replied with a sweet voice.

Text 54

rājapatni garo roṣaḥ
sahānena durātmanā
prakṛtisthā vayaṁ jātā
devi sauṣo'smi bāndhavaḥ

O Queens, My anger has been satiated by the death of this sinful king. Having regained My composure, I am again your well-wishing friend.

Text 55

roṣo me vigataḥ sādhvi
tava vākyair kalmaṣaiḥ
yo'yaṁ putra śṛgālasya
mamāpyeṣa na saṁśayaḥ

My dear chaste women, your pious words have also soothed My anger. Rest assured that the son of King Śṛgāla will be treated by Me as if he were My own son. Of this there is no doubt.

Texts 56-59

abhayaṁ cābhi ṣekaṁ ca
dadāmyasmai sukhāya vai
āhūyantāṁ prakṛtayaḥ
purodhā mantriṇas tathā

pitṛpaitā mahe rājye
tava putro'bhi ṣicyatām
tataḥ prakṛtayaḥ sarvāḥ
purodhā mantrinas tathā

abhiṣekārtham ājagmur
yato vai rāmakeśavau
tataḥ siṁhāsanasthaṁ tu
rājaputraṁ janārdanaḥ

abhiṣekeṇa divyena
yojayāmāsa vīryavān
abhipicya śṛgālasya
karavīrapure sutam
kṛṣṇas tadahare vāśu
prasthāna mabhyarocayat

Rest assured that I will install this boy as the king of Karavīrapura and give him all protection. Invite all the other ladies, ministers, and priests, and all together we can perform the coronation ceremony for this boy as soon as possible.

As instructed by Lord Kṛṣṇa, all the ladies, ordinary citizens, ministers, and priests soon gathered to participate in the coronation ceremony. Thereafter, Kṛṣṇa and Balarāma duly performed the coronation ceremony according to the rules and regulations prescribed in the scriptures. Thus, the young prince became the king of Karavīrapura. After installing the boy upon the royal throne, Lord Kṛṣṇa thought it wise to depart without further delay.

Text 60

rathena hariyuktena
tena yuddhārjitena vai
keśavaḥ prasthito'dhvānaṁ
vṛtrahā tridiyaṁ yathā

As Indra returns to his abode in the heavenly planets after performing his duties, Lord Kṛṣṇa mounted the chariot He had obtained in battle and departed for Mathurā.

Texts 61-62

śakradevo'pi dharmātmā
saha mātrā paraṁtapaḥ
sabāla vṛddha yuvatī
mukhyāḥ prakṛtayas tathā

śivikāyām athāropya
śṛgālaṁ yuddhadurmadam
saṁhatā dūramārgeṇa
paścimābhi mukhā yuyuḥ

Pious King Śakradeva, who became expert in subduing his enemies, along with his mother, other children, the elderly and ladies picked up his father's dead body and placed it on a palanquin. He then proceeded away from the city on a road leading to the west.

Text 63

naidhanasya vidhānena
cakruste tasya satkriyām
satkāraṁ kārayāmāsuḥ
pitṛṇāṁ pāralaukikam

The king took his dead father to the crematorium and performed the funeral ceremony according to the prescribed rules and regulations. The priests then had him offer oblations into the sacrificial fire to his father and forefathers.

Texts 64-65

uddiśyod diśya rājānaṁ
śrāddhaṁ kṛtvā sahasraśaḥ
tataste salilaṁ dattvā
nāmagotradi kīrtanaiḥ

pitaryupa rate ghore
śoka saṁvigna mānasaḥ
kṛtvodakaṁ tadā rājā
praviveśa purottamam

King Śakradeva then gave away varieties of gifts in charity in honor of his departed father. He also offered water while chanting his father's name and lineage. In this way, after the death of his father, the king performed all the necessary rituals, although he was certainly very aggrieved, and then returned to his palace somewhat despondent.

Thus ends the translation of the forty-fourth chapter of the Viṣṇu Parva of Śrī Harivaṁsa.

Chapter 45

Kṛṣṇa and Balarāma enter Mathurā

Texts 1-2

vaiśampāyana uvāca
tau tu svalpena kālena
damaghoṣeṇa saṁgatau
athādhva vidhinā tau tu
pañcarātroṣitau pathi

damaghoṣeṇa saṁgamya
ekarātro ṣitāviva
jagmatuḥ sahitau vīrau
mudrā paramayā yutau
nagarīṁ mathurāṁ prāptau
vasudeva sutā vubhau

Vaiśampāyana said: Therefter, the two brothers, Kṛṣṇa and Balarāma, traveled with the king of Cedi, Damaghoṣa. In the course of Their travels, They spent five nights at different places. Still, due to having Damaghoṣa as a companion, They felt as if they had only passed one night on the road. Finally, the two heroic sons of Vasudeva cheerfully arrived at the city of Mathurā.

Text 3

tataḥ pratyudgatāḥ sarve
yādavā yadunandanau
sabalā hṛṣṭamanasa
ugrasena purogamāḥ

When They came to the outskirts of Mathurā, King Ugrasena and many members of Yadu dynasty, along with their soldiers, happily came out of the city to greet Them.

Text 4

śreṇyaḥ prakṛtayaścaiva
mantriṇaśca yathocitāḥ
sabālavṛddhā sā caiva
puri samabhivartata

Soon, all the inhabitants of Mathurā, including all the men, women, young and elderly, ministers, and even children, came out to greet Kṛṣṇa and Balarāma with great honor.

Text 5

nandi turyāṇya vādyanta
stūyetāṁ puruṣar ṣabhau
rathyāṁ patākā malinyo
bhāsanti sma samantataḥ

Auspicious sounds that brought everyone great happiness permeated the entire atmosphere. At that time, professional reciters glorified the two brothers and all the roads and lanes of the city were decorated with flags and other paraphernalia.

Text 6

dṛṣṭvā pramuditā sarvā
puri parama śobhitā
bhṛatrostayorāgamane
yathivendra mahe tathā

Indeed, everyone celebrated a great festival honoring the arrival of the two brothers, Kṛṣṇa and Balarāma. The people became so ecstatic that it appeared as if they were celebrating a festival in honor of Indra.

Text 7

muditāstatra gāyanti
rājamārgeṣu gāyakāḥ
stavāśīrbahulā gāthā
yādavānāṁ priyaṅkarāḥ

Lining the roads, professional singers jubilantly sang in glorification of Kṛṣṇa and Balarāma for Their pleasure and the pleasure of the members of the Yadu dynasty.

Text 8

govindarāmau samprāptau
bhrātarau lokaviśrutau
sve pare nirbhayāḥ sarve
krīḍadhvaṁ yādavāh sukham

The following announcement was made all over the city of Mathurā: O Yādavas, Kṛṣṇa and Balarāma have just arrived home to Mathurā. Now, everyone can work and enjoy life without fear.

Text 9

na tatra kaścid dīno
vā malino vā vicetanaḥ
mathurāyām abhūt kaścid
rāmakṛṣṇa samāgame

Because of the presence of Kṛṣṇa and Balarāma, there were no fallen, sinful, contaminated, or disappointed persons in the city of Mathurā.

Text 10

vayāṁsi sādhuvākyāni
prahṛṣṭā gohayadvipāḥā
naranārī gāṇāścaiva
bhejire mānasaṁ sukham

The birds in the trees sang melodiously. The cows, horses, and elephants appeared very jolly. Indeed, all the men and women of Mathurā felt great satisfaction at heart.

Text 11

śivāśca pravavurvātā
virajaskā diśo daśa
daivatānyapi sarvāṇi
hṛṣyantyāyata neṣvatha

Cool and fragrant breezes blew throughout the city. Everywhere one might look, the city of Mathurā looked spotlessly clean. The Deities of the Lord in the temples also seemed in a joyful mood.

Text 12

yāni liṅgāni lokasya
vṛttānīha kṛte yuge
tāni sarvāṇya dṛśyanta
tayorāgamane tadā

Indeed, all the symptoms of Satya-yuga became visible as soon as Kṛṣṇa and Balarāma returned to Mathurā.

Text 13

tataḥ kāle śive puṇye
syandane nāri mardanau
hariyuktena tau vīrau
praviṣṭau mathurāṁ purīm

At a very auspicious moment, the two incomparably powerful heroes, who were very expert at vanquishing Their enemies, entered through the main gate of the city on a chariot drawn by strong horses.

Text 14

praviśantaṁ puriṁ ramyāṁ
govindaṁ rāmameva ca
anujagmur yaduganāḥ
śakraṁ devagaṇā iva

When Kṛṣṇa and Balarāma entered the delightful city of Mathurā, all the members of the Yadu dynasty followed Them, just as the demigods follow Indra, the king of heaven.

Text 15

vasudevasya bhavanaṁ
pitustau yadunandanau
praviṣṭau dṛṣṭavadanau
candrādityā vivācalam

As the moon and sun enter a cave of Sumeru Mountain,

the two descendents of Yadu very joyfully entered the palace of Their illustrious father, Vasudeva.

Text 16

tatrāyudhāni sanyasya
gṛhe sve svairacāriṇau
mumudāte yaduvarau
vasudeva sutāvubhau

The two brothers, who were the ornaments of the Yadu dynasty, left Their weapons in the armory. They were very happy to return to Mathurā and so They enjoyed wandering here and there within the palace grounds.

Texts 17-18

tatastu vasudevasya
pādau samabhipīḍya ca
tatrograsenaṁ rājānam
anyāṁśca yadupuṅgavān

yathānyāyaṁ pūjayitvā
tau sarvaiścābhi nanditau
jagmatur hṛṣṭa manasau
mātureva niveśanam

Kṛṣṇa and Balarāma first offered Their obeisances at the feet of Their father, Vasudeva, and then to King Ugrasena. At that time, Kṛṣṇa and Balarāma gave due respect to all the senior members of the Yadu dynasty, who happily reciprocated in a very respectful and affectionate manner. Thereafter, the two brothers entered the ladies apartments to meet Their mother.

Text 19

evaṁ tāveka nirmāṇau
mathurāyāṁ śubhānanau
ugrasenānugau bhūtvā
kaṅcitkālaṁ mumodatuḥ

Kṛṣṇa and Balarāma, who are two manifestations of the same Supreme Personality of Godhead, appearing in this world to accomplish the mission of the demigods, continued to reside at Mathurā under the rule of King Ugrasena.

Thus ends the translation of the forty-fifth chapter of the Viṣṇu Parva of Śrī Harivaṁsa.

Chapter 46

Lord Balarāma visits Vṛndāvana. The pastime of Lord Balarāma attracting the Yamunā River

Text 1

vaiśampāyana uvāca
kasyacit tvatha kālasya
smṛtvā gopeṣu sauhṛdam
jagāmaiko vrajaṁ rāmaḥ
kṛṣṇasyānu mate sthitaḥ

Vaiśampāyana said: After some time, remembering the love and affection of the cowherd inhabitants of Vraja, Balarāma went to Vraja after taking permission from His brother, Kṛṣṇa.

Text 2

sa gatastatra ramyāṇi
dadarśa vipulāni vai
bhukta pūrvāṇya raṇyāni
sarāṁsi surabhīṇi ca

After entering Vraja, Balarlāma saw beautiful forests full of fragrant flowers, and many enchanting lakes. He had enjoyed the rural atmosphere of Vraja to His heart's content when He previously resided there.

Text 3

sa praviṣṭastu vegena
taṁ vrajaṁ kṛṣṇapūrvajaḥ
vanyena ramaṇīyena
veṣeṇālaṅkṛtaḥ prabhuḥ

When Kṛṣṇa's elder brother, Balarāma, who is also known as Saṅkarṣaṇa, entered Vraja, He was dressed and decorated as a cowherd boy.

Text 4

sa tānabhāṣata prītyā
yathāpūrvam arimdamaḥ
gopāṁstenaiva vidhinā
yathānyāyaṁ yathāvayaḥ

Balarāma, the relentless slayer of his enemies, met all the inhabitants of Vraja according to their position and relationship with Him. While greeting everyone, He spoke very sweetly in a voice laden with love.

Text 5

tathaiva prāha tān sarvāṁs
tathaiva pariharṣayan
tathaiva saha gopībhiryo
jayan madhurāḥ kathāḥ

As previously, He gave great transcendental happiness to everyone while conversing with them. Finally, He met the cowherd girls of Vraja, greeting them with great feelings of ecstasy.

Text 6

tamūcuḥ sthavirā gopāḥ
priyaṁ madhura bhāṣiṇaḥ
rāmaṁramayatāṁ śreṣṭhaṁ
pravāsāt punarāgatam

Lord Balarāma was naturally very pleasing to the cowherd residents of Vraja. Seeing that He had come after a long absence, the cowherd men spoke to Him as follows.

Text 7

svāgataṁ te mahābāho
yadūnāṁ kulanandana
adyasma nirvṛtās tāta
yat tvāṁ paśyāmahe vayam

O mighty-armed one! O giver of pleasure to the members of the Yadu dynasty! You are most welcome, my dear child. Today we are very happy because after a long time, we have received the opportunity to see You once again.

Text 8

prītāścaiva vayaṁ vīra
yat tvaṁ punarihāgataḥ
vikhyāta striṣu lokeṣu
rāmaḥ śatru bhayaṅkaraḥ

O unlimitedly powerful one, we are extremely pleased that You have returned home after such a long time. We know that You are now famous throughout the three worlds as a king that instills fear into the minds of Your enemies.

Text 9

vardhanīyā vayaṁ vīra
tvayā yādava nandana
athavā prāṇinastāta
ramante janmabhūmiṣu

O mighty one! O descendent of Yadu! By visiting us, You have certainly enhanced our prestige. Of course, You must also derive some pleasure out of visiting the place of Your childhood pastimes.

Text 10

tridaśānāṁ vayaṁ mānyā
dhruva madyā malānana
ye sma dṛṣṭāsta vayā tāta
kāṅkṣa māṇāstavāgamam

O beautiful-eyed one, by Your merciful glance upon us, we have become objects of worship even for the demigods. We have been waiting so long for Your auspicious arrival.

Text 11

diṣṭyā te nihatā mallāḥ
kaṁsaśca vinipātitaḥ
ugraseno'bhiṣiktaśca
māhātmyena janena vai

It is our good fortune that You two brothers killed the demons that were oppressing us, such as Muṣṭika, Cāṇura and Kaṁsa, and reinstated Ugrasena as the king of Mathurā. It is because of the king's saintly nature that all of us have accepted his rule without hesitation.

Text 12

samudre ca śruto'smābhis
thiminā saha vigrahaḥ
vadhaḥ pañcajanasyaiva
jarāsandhena vigrahaḥ

gomante ca śruto's mābhiḥ
kṣatriyaiḥ saha vigrahaḥ

We have heard that You two brothers fought with a demon named Pañcajana in the ocean and killed him. Thereafter, You had many fierce battles with Jarāsandha. Now we learned that recently You battled many *kṣatriyas* at the base of Gomanta Hill.

Text 13

daradasya vadhavścaiva
jarāsanḍha parājayaḥ
tatrāyudhāva taraṇaṁ
śrutaṁ naḥ paramāhave

In that recently-concluded battle, King Darada was killed by You, and King Jarāsandha was soundly defeated. We heard that during that great battle, celestial weapons descended from the sky, being invoked by You and Your brother.

Text 14

vadhaścaiva śṛgālasya
karavīrapurottame
tat sutasya abhiṣekaśca
nāgarāṇāṁ ca sāntvanam

You also killed King Śṛgāla at his city, Karavīrapura, and then installed his son as the heir apparent to the royal throne. Thereafter, You pacified the inhabitants of that city as far as possible.

Text 15

mathurāyāṁ praveśaśca
kīrtanīyaḥ surottamaiḥ
pratiṣṭhitā ca vasudhā
pārthivāśca vaśīkṛtāḥ

After concluding these pastimes, You returned to Mathurā, a city that is glorified by the demigods in the heavenly planets. In this way, You have diminished the burden of the earth on behalf of the demigods and brought the remaining kings under Your rule.

Text 16

tava cāgamanaṁ dṛṣṭvā
sabhāgyāḥ sma yathā purā
tena sā parituṣṭā vai
hṛṣitāśca sabāndhavāḥ

Now, due to Your auspicious presence, we again feel fortunate like before. Indeed, we now feel fully satisfied. Not only us, but all of our friends and relatives have become joyful.

Texts 17-18

pratyuvāca tato rāmaḥ
sarvaṁstāna bhitaḥ sthitān
yādaveṣvapi sarveṣu
bhavanto mama bāndhavāḥ

ihāvayor gataṁ bālyam
iha caivāvayo ratam
bhavadbhir varddhitāścaiva
yāsyāmo vikriyāṁ katham

After hearing these pleasing words, Balarāma turned His attention to the *gopīs*, who had surrounded Him. He said: Among all the members of the Yadu dynasty, you are Our most intimate friends. This is the place where We passed our childhood, being pampered and raised by all of you. Considering this, how could We ever forget you?

Text 19

gṛheṣu bhavatāṁ bhuktaṁ
gāvaśca parirakṣitāḥ
asmākaṁ bāndhavāḥ sarve
bhavanto baddhasauhṛdāḥ

We ate and drank in your houses. We tended your cows in the pasturing grounds. You are Our most affectionate friends and well-wishers.

Text 20

bruvatyevaṁ yathā tatvaṁ
gopamadhye halāyudhe
saṁhṛṣṭa vadanā bhūyo
babhūvur vrajayoṣitaḥ

Thus Balarāma, who carries a plough, disclosed the actual truth to the young and beautiful damsels of Vraja, making them become filled with ecstatic love.

Texts 21-22

tato vanāntara gato
reme rāmo mahābalaḥ
etasmin antare prāpte
rāmāya viditātmane

gopālair deśakālajñair
upānīyata vāruṇī
so'pivat pāṇḍurābhrābhas
tatkālaṁ jñātibhirvṛtaḥ

Thereafter, supremely powerful Balarāma entered the forest of Vraja to enjoy with His friends, the cowherd boys. Understanding the Lord's desire, the cowherd boys, who could very well analyze the time, place, and circumstances, brought some Vāruṇī beverage. Balarāma, whose complexion is very fair, drank that nectarean honey in the company of His cowherd boy friends.

Texts 23-24

vanāntara gato rāmaḥ
pānaṁ mada samīraṇam
upaninyus tatas tasmai
vanyāni vividhāni ca

pratyagrara maṇīyāni
puṣpāṇi ca phalāni ca
medhyāṁśca vividhān gandhān
bhakṣyāṁśca hṛḍayaṁgamān
saḍyo hṛtāni padmāni
vikacānyut palāni ca

After drinking honey in the forest, Balarāma became somewhat intoxicated. His cowherd boyfriends then brought many varieties of fragrant flowers and fresh fruit. They also offered the Lord different kinds of pure fragrant substances and varieties of delicious food. His friends took great pleasure in offering Him many fully blossomed lotus flowers and water lilies.

Texts 25-26

śirasā cārukeśena
kiṅcid āvṛta maulinā
śravaṇaikā valam bena
kuṇḍalena virājatā

candanārdreṇa pītena
vanamālā valambinā
vibabhāvurasā rāmaḥ
kailāseneva mandaraḥ

The hair crowning Lord Balarāma's head was exquisite. The crown on His head was placed so that it slanted stylishly. He had a charming earring in one ear and on His chest, which was smeared with sandalwood paste, a garland of forest flowers swung to and fro. The sight of Lord Balarāma's chest was enchanting and resembled the view of Mount Mandara from the Mount Kailāsa.

Text 27

nīle vasāno vasane
pratyagra jaladaprabhe
rarāja vapuṣā śubhras
timiraughe yathā śaśī

Lord Balarāma was dressed in two pieces of cloth having the color of a new monsoon cloud. His complexion was very fair so that He appeared like the full moon in the dead of night.

Text 28

lāṅgalenā vasiktena
bhujagā bhogavartinā

tathā bhujāgra śliṣṭena
muṣalena ca bhāsvatā

In one hand Balarāma held His plough, which was shaped like a serpent, and in the other hand He held His brightly-shining *muṣala.*

Text 29

sa matto balināṁ śreṣṭho
rarrājā bhūrṇi tānanaḥ
śaiśirīṣu triyāmāsu
yathā svedālasaḥ śaśī

Due to drinking honey, Balarāma, the best among all powerful personalities, appeared intoxicated as His head swayed back and forth. He appeared like the autumn moon decorated with drops of perspiration.

Text 30

rāmastu yamunā māha
snātumicche mahānadi
ehi māma bhigaccha tvaṁ
rūpiṇī sāgaraṁgame

Balarāma said to Yamunā-devī, who was flowing by His side: O exalted river, I would like to bathe. O traveler to the ocean, appear before Me in your personified form.

Text 31

saṅkarṣaṇasya mattoktāṁ
bhāratīṁ paribhūya sā

nābhyavartata taṁ deśaṁ
strī svabhāvena mohitā

The personified Yamunā considered Balarāma to be intoxicated and so she did not take His words seriously. Being bewildered by her womanly nature, she ignored the order of Lord Balarāma, refusing to come before Him.

Text 32

tataścu krodha balavān
rāmo madasamīritaḥ
cakāra sa halaṁ haste
karṣaṇādho mukhaṁ bali

Becoming offended, Lord Balarāma became furious. So that He could pull the River Yamunā to Him, He picked up His plough and struck it into the ground.

Text 33

tasyāmupari medinyāṁ
petus tāmara sasrajaḥ
mumucuḥ puṣpa kiśaiśca
vāsareṇ varuṇaṁ jalam

As Lord Balarāma was pulling the River Yamunā toward Him, the garland of lotus flowers from His neck fell into the water. As a result, the water of the Yamunā became filled with lotus petals and pollen, making it reddish.

Text 34

sa halenāna tāgreṇa
kūle gṛhya mahānadīm

cakarṣa yamunāṁ rāmo
vyutthitāṁ vanitāmiva

Lord Balarāma had inserted the tip of His plough into the bank of the River Yamunā and then forcibly pulled her towards Him, as if she were an unchaste woman.

Text 35

sā vihavala jalasrotā
hṛdaprasthita saṅcayā
vyāvartata nadī bhītā
halamārgānu sāriṇī

As a result, the flow of the river became disturbed. The water that had accumulated in a lake within the river flowed out. Becoming very fearful, the river started submissively following Baladeva.

Text 36

lāṅgalādiṣṭa vartmā sā
vegagā vakragāminī
saṅkarṣaṇa bhayatrastā
yoṣevākulatāṁ gatā

Yamunā-devī followed the Lord's plough so that the river that normally flowed on a straight course was moving in a crooked manner. Being fearful of Lord Saṅkarṣaṇa, she appeared distraught, like a young girl.

Text 37

pulina śroṇi bimbauṣṭhī
mṛditais toyatāḍitaiḥ

phena mekhala sūtraiśca
cchinnair ambuda gāminī

The two banks were her hips, the red lotus flowers were her lips, and it appeared as if her garments were being displaced by the agitation of her waves. In this way, the river appeared like a young girl about to enjoy conjugal pastimes with her ocean-like beloved.

Text 38

taraṅga viṣamāpīḍā
cakravākon mukhastanī
vegagambhīra vakrāṅgī
trastamīna vibhūṣaṇā

The waves were the crown of the Yamunā, bobbing up and down. The *cakravāka* birds were her breasts and her entire body appeared crooked due to the force of the Lord's plough. She was decorated with ornaments of fish.

Text 39

sitahaṁse kṣaṇāpāṅgī
kāśakṣau mocchritāmbarā
tīrajodbhūta keśāntā
jalaskhalita gāminī

White swans were her eyes and forehead, *kāśa* flowers were her silk cloth, the trees and plants on her banks were her hair, and the flow of water made it appear as if her movements were being obstructed.

Text 40

lāṅgalolli khitāpāṇgī
kṣubhitā sāgaraṅgamā
matteva kuṭilā nāri
rāja mārgena gacchati

It appeared as if the corner of her eyes had been injured by the sharp point of the plough. As the River Yamunā flowed towards the sea appeared disturbed, like an intoxicated unchaste woman walking on the king's highway.

Text 41

kṛṣyate sātivegena
srotaḥs khalita gāminī
unmārgā nītamārgā sā
yena vṛndāvanaṁ vanam

As the river was being forcibly directed towards the beautiful forest of Vṛndāvana, the agitation of the water was indicative of her obstructed movements.

Text 42

vṛndāvanasya madhyena
sā nītā yamunā nadī
rorūyamāṇeva khagair
anvitā toyavāsibhiḥ

Thus, the River Yamunā was forcibly brought to the interior of the Vṛndāvana forest, bringing with it many aquatic birds and animals. The sounds of those birds appeared to be the crying of the river.

Text 43

sā yadā samatikrāntā
nadī vṛndāvanaṁ vanam
tadā strīrūpiṇī bhūtvā
yamunā rāmam avravīt

When the River Yamunā reached her destination inside the Vṛndāvana forest, she appeared in her personified form and spoke to Lord Balarāma with folded hands.

Text 44

prasīda nātha bhītāsmi
pratilomena karmaṇā
viparīta midaṁ rūpaṁ
toyaṁ ca mama jāyate

My dear Lord, please be kind to me. I am greatly frightened by Your unconventional behavior. Now, my form and direction of flow have been altered.

Text 45

asatyahaṁ nadīmadhye
rauhiṇeya tvayā kṛtā
karṣaṇena mahābāho
svamārga vyabhicāriṇī

O son of Rohiṇi! O mighty-armed one! By pulling me in this manner, You have made me unchaste among rivers. You have diverted me from my prescribed path.

Text 46

prāptāṁ māṁ sāgare pūrvaṁ
sapatnyo vega garvitāḥ
phena hāsair hasiṣyanti
toyavyāvṛtta gāminīm

When I approach the ocean, my waves will joke with me by creating foam. I will be known as a misguided river that has deviated from her prescribed course.

Text 47

prasādaṁ kuru me vīra
yāce tvāṁ kṛṣṇapūrvaja
suprasanna manā nityaṁ
bhava tvaṁ surasattama

O elder brother of Lord Kṛṣṇa! O unconquerable hero! O foremost among the demigods, please be merciful to me. I beg You to excuse me and become pleased.

Text 48

karṣaṇāyudha kṛṣṭāsmi
roṣo'yaṁ vinivartyatām
mūrndhāna gacchāmi caraṇau
tavaiṣā lāṅgalāyudha
mārgam ādiṣṭam icchāmi
ka gacchāmi māhābhuja

O carrier of the plough, I have been attracted to You by Your weapon, the plough. Now, please let go of Your anger. I place my head at Your lotus feet, O mighty-armed Lord, and so kindly tell me where I should now go.

Text 49

vaiśampāyana uvāca
praṇayāvanatāṁ dṛṣṭvā
yamunāṁ lāṅgalāyudhaḥ
pratyuvācārṇa vavadhūṁ
madaklānta idaṁ vacaḥ

Vaiśampāyana said: Seeing that Yamunā, the wife of the ocean, was offering her obeisances, Lord Balarāma, who was still intoxicated by the influence of honey, replied as follows.

Text 50

lāṅgalādiṣṭa mārgā
tvamimaṁ me priyadarśane
deśam ambupradānena
plāvayasvakhilaṁ śubhe

My dear auspicious lady! O beautiful one! I have determined with My plough the path by which you should travel. You should now flow as I have ordained and thus supply water to a vast tract of land.

Texts 51-54

eṣa te subhru saṅdeśaḥ
kathitaḥ sāgaraṁgame
śāntiṁ vraja mahābhāge
gamyatāṁ ca yathāsukham

yāvat sthāsyati loko'yaṁ
tāvat tiṣṭhatu meyaśaḥ
yamunākarṣaṇaṁ dṛṣṭvā
sarve te vrajavāsinaḥ

sādhu sādhviti rāmāya
praṇāmaṁ cakrire tadā
tāṁ visṛjya mahābhāgāṁ
tāṁśca sarvān vrajaukasaḥ

tataḥ saṅcintya manasā
rāmaḥ praharatāṁ varaḥ
punaḥ pratijagāmāśu
mathurāṁ rohiṇīsutaḥ

O woman with beautiful eyebrows! O most fortunate one! O traveler to the ocean, this is My instruction to you. May you remain peaceful at all times. You may now go wherever you wish. As long as the world continues to exist, this pastime of ours will be narrated by learned men.

When the residents of Vraja saw Balarāma force the River Yamunā to alter her course, they exclaimed: "Well done! Well done!" and offered obeisances to Him. After bidding farewell to the greatly fortunate Yamunā, as well as to all the Vrajavāsīs, Lord Balarāma, the son of Rohiṇī, and the foremost of all warriors, considered something within His mind and then quickly left for Mathurā.

Text 55

sa gatvā mathurāṁ rāmo
bhavane madhusūdanam
parivartamānaṁ dadṛśe
pṛthivyāḥ sāram avyayam

When He arrived at Mathurā, Balarāma saw Lord Madhusūdana, the indestructible Lord and original cause of the cosmic manifestation, turning over while sleeping on an opulent couch.

Text 56

tathaivādhvanya veṣeṇa
sopaśliṣṭo janārdanam
pratyagra vanamālena
vakṣa sābhi virājatā

Without even changing His clothes, Lord Balarāma embraced Lord Janārdana, whose chest was adorned with a beautiful garland made of fresh and fragrant forest flowers.

Text 57

sa dṛṣṭvā tūrṇa māyāntaṁ
rāmaṁ lāṅgala dhāriṇam
sahasotthāya govindo
dadāvāsanam uttamam

As soon as Lord Govinda saw Balarāma, the carrier of the plough, He quickly stood up and offered Him a comfortable seat.

Text 58

upaviṣṭaṁ tadā rāmaṁ
papraccha kuśalaṁ braje
bāndhaveṣu ca sarveṣu
goṣu caiva janārdanaḥ

After Balarāma was comfortably seated, Lord Kṛṣṇa inquired from Him about the welfare of the residents of Vraja. It was obvious that He was very concerned about His friends and relatives, as well as the cows.

Text 59

pratyuvāca tato rāmo
bhrātaraṁ sādhubhāṣiṇam
sarvatra kuśalaṁ kṛṣṇa
yeṣāṁ kuśalam icchasi

In reply, Balarāma informed His brother, Lord Kṛṣṇa the foremost of eloquent speakers: My dear Kṛṣṇa, everyone in Vṛndāvana enjoys good fortune because they are the objects of Your mercy.

Text 60

tatastayor vicitrārthāḥ
paurāṇyaścā bhavan kathāḥ
vasudevāgrataḥ puṇyā
rāmakeśa vayostadā

Thereafter, when They entered the royal assembly, Kṛṣṇa and Balarāma described Their pastimes away from Mathurā before an eager audience, headed by Vasudeva. Such discussions invariably award one transcendental bliss, and are filled with confidential understandings unknown even to the *Vedas*.

Thus ends the translation of the forty-sixth chapter of the Viṣṇu Parva of Śri Harivaṁsa.

Chapter 47

Lord Kṛṣṇa travels to Kundinapura to attend the svayamvara of Princess Rukminī

Text 1

vaiśampāyana uvāca
etasmin antare prāptā
loka prāvṛttikā narāḥ
cakrāyudha gṛhaṁ sarve
lokapāla gṛhopamam

Vaiśampāyana said: All the residents of Mathurā, being very eager to inform Him of all that was happening, and also advise Him as to what the future might hold in store, gathered at the palace of Lord Kṛṣṇa, who carries the *cakra* in His hand.

Text 2

teṣvātyayika śaṁsīṣu
lokaprāvṛtti keṣviha
kṛtasaṁjñā yaduśreṣṭhāḥ
sametāḥ kṛṣṇa saṁsadi

Having received the news of Lord Kṛṣṇa's arrival, the Yādavas hurried to His palace, being very eager to inform Him of all that had happened in His absence.

Text 3

samāgateṣu sarveṣu
yadumukhyeṣu saṁsadi

prāvṛttikā narāḥ prāhuḥ
pārthivātya yikaṁ vacaḥ

The leaders of the Yādavas entered Lord Kṛṣṇa's royal assembly, being intent on discussing how the demoniac kings that burdened the earth could be eliminated. For that end, they spoke as follows.

Text 4

janārdana narendrāṇāṁ
pārthivānāṁ samāgamaḥ
bhaviṣyati kṣitiśānām
samuḍhānāṁ anekasaḥ

My dear Lord Janārdana, very soon innumerable princes and kings from all over the world will gather at the *svayamvara* of princess Rukminī, hoping to obtain her hand in marriage.

Text 5

tvaritāstatra gacchanti
nānājanā padeśvarāḥ
kuṇḍine puṇḍarīkākṣa
bhojaputrasya śāsanāt

O lotus-eyed Lord, being invited by, Rukmī, the son of the Vidarbha king, many powerful kings of from far-off lands have already set out for the city of Kuṇḍinapura to attend the *svayamvara*.

Texts 6-7

prakāśaṁ sma kathāstatra
śrūyante manujeritāḥ

rukmiṇī kila nāmāsti
rukmiṇaḥ prathamā svasā

bhāvī svayaṁvarastatra
tasyāḥ kila janārdana
ityartham ete sabalā
gacchanti manujādhipāḥ

O Janārdana, Rukmiṇī is Rukmī's younger sister, and their father, King Bhīṣmaka, has arranged her *svayamvara* at Kuṇḍinapura, his capital. All the rulers of the earth are going there, hoping to marry the princess.

Text 8

tasyāstrai lokya sundaryās
tṛtīye'hani yādava
rukma bhūṣaṇa bhūṣiṇyā
bhaviṣyati svayaṁvarāḥ

O descendent of Yadu, on the third day from today, the *svayambara* of Princess Rukmiṇī will be held. She is considered to be the most beautiful girl within the three worlds and she will be decorated with the finest golden ornaments.

Text 9

rājñāṁ tatra sametānāṁ
hastyaśva rathagāminām
drakṣyāmaḥ śataśas tatra
śivirāṇi mahātmanām

Many intelligent and strongly-built kings have already arrived on their horses, elephants and chariots, and are setting up their camps around the city.

Texts 10-11

siṁha śārdūla dṛptānāṁ
mattadvirada gāminām
sadā yuddha priyāṇāṁ hi
parasparam amarṣiṇām

jayāya śīghraṁ sahitā
balaughena samanvitāḥ
niruddhāḥ pṛthivīpālāḥ
kimekānta carā vayam
nirutsāhā bhaviṣyāmo
gacchāmo yadunandana

Many rulers of the earth have arrived there, exhibiting their great pride. Some are strutting like lions and tigers and others are moving about like intoxicated elephants. It appears that there might be a great fight because all of these kings are certainly envious of one another and they have come fully armed and surrounded by their armies. Each and every king harbors the desire to marry Rukmiṇī. Why should we sit here idly? My dear Lord, don't You want to go and take part in Rukmiṇī's *svayamvara?*

Text 12

śrutvaitat keśavo vākyaṁ
hṛdi śalyam ivārpitam
nirjagāma yaduśreṣṭho
yadūnāṁ sahito balaiḥ

After hearing about Rukmiṇī's *svayamvara*, Kṛṣṇa felt His heart being pierced by Cupid's arrows. Govinda, the best of all the Yadavas, quickly assembled an army and set out for Kuṇḍinapura.

Text 13

yādavāste balodagrāḥ
sarve saṁgrāma lālasāḥ
niryayuḥ syandana varair
garvitā stridaśā iva

Thus, the very powerful Yādavas, who were always very eager to fight with their enemies, mounted their chariots and departed, appearing as formidable as the demigods of heaven, who are all very proud of their prowess.

Text 14

balāgreṇa niyuktena
haririīśāna sammataḥ
cakrodyata karaḥ kṛṣṇo
gadāpāṇir vyarocata

As He proceeded with His army, Lord Kṛṣṇa, who is very dear to Śiva, appeared astonishingly attractive, carrying His *cakra* in one hand and His club in another.

Text 15

yādavāścā pare tatra
vāsudevānu yāyinaḥ
rathairāditya saṁkāśaiḥ
kiṅkiṇī pratināditaiḥ

Many powerful Yādavas warriors, as brilliant as the sun, mounted their chariots decorated with tinkling bells and followed Lord Kṛṣṇa.

Text 16

ugrasenaṁ tu govindaḥ
prāha niścita darśanaḥ
tiṣṭhatvaṁ nṛpaśārdula
bhrātrā me sahito'nagha

Lord Govinda, the knower of past, present, and future, first approached King Ugrasena and said: O foremost ruler of men, You should stay here and protect the city, along with My elder brother, Balarāma.

Text 17

kṣatriyā vikṛti prajñāḥ
śāstra niścita darśanāḥ
purīṁ śūnyamimāṁ vīra
jaghanye'bhi patanti ha

O greatly powerful one, *kṣatriyas* are very cunning by nature, their minds being immersed in political intrigue. I suspect that after I leave, My enemies will take the opportunity to attack Mathurā, considering it to be unprotected.

Text 18

asmākaṁ śaṅkitāḥ sarve
jarāsandha vaśānugāḥ
modante sukhinas tatra
devaloke yathāmarāḥ

Many kings are flourishing under the shelter of Jarāsandha, being afraid of us. Under his protection, they now live very freely, thinking that they can do as they please, like the demigods in the heavenly planets.

Text 19

vaiṣampāyana uvāca
tasya tadvacanaṁ śrutvā
bhojarājo mahāyaśāḥ
kṛṣṇa snehena vikṛtaṁ
babhāṣe vacanāmṛtam

Vaiśampāyana said: After hearing the words of Lord Kṛṣṇa, King Ugrasena, the ruler of the Bhojas, replied in a choked voice with speech that was affectionate and as sweet as nectar.

Text 20

kṛṣṇa kṛṣṇa mahābāho
yadūnāṁ nandivarddhana
śrūyatāṁ yadahaṁ tvadya
vakṣyāmi ripusūdana

O mighty-armed Kṛṣṇa, vanquisher of the enemies who brings great happiness to the Yādavas, please listen attentively to my words.

Text 21

tvayā vihīnāḥ sarve sma
na śaktāḥ sukhamāsitum
pure'smin viṣayānte vā
patihīnā iva striyaḥ

We cannot remain here contentedly and peacefully without You, just as a wife cannot live happily without her husband.

Text 22

tvatsanāthā vayaṁ tāta
tvad bāhu balaprāśritāḥ
vibhīmo na narendrāṇāṁ
sendrāṇāmapi mānada

My dear Lord, who is like my grandson, You are our only shelter and master. Being protected by You, we do not fear even the demigods of heaven, and so what to speak of ordinary rulers of the earth.

Text 23

vijayāya yaduśreṣṭha
yatra yatra gamiṣyasi
tatra tvaṁ sahit'smābhir
gacchethā yādavarṣabha

O leader of the Yādavas, wherever You may go to carry out Your mission, You should always take us with You.

Text 24

tasya rājño vacaḥ śrutvā
sasmitaṁ devakīsutaḥ
yatheṣṭaṁ bhavatāmadya
tathā kartāsmya saṁśayam

Upon hearing the speech of King Ugrasena, Lord Kṛṣṇa, the son of Devakī, smiled and said: O King, rest assured that I will always do that which you desire.

Text 25

vaiṣampāyana uvāca
evamuktvā tu vai kṛṣṇo
jagāmāśu rathena vai
bhīṣmakasya gṛhaṁ prāpto
lohitāyati bhāskare

Vaiśampāyana said: After saying this, Lord Kṛṣṇa quickly mounted his chariot and set out. Before the sun had set in the west, He arrived within sight of the palace of King Bhīṣmaka.

Text 26

prāpte rājasamāje tu
śivirā kīrṇa bhūtale
raṅgaṁ suvipulaṁ dṛṣṭvā
rājasīṁ tanumāviśat

The entire area surrounding the city of Kuṇḍinapura was completely occupied by the camps of the visiting kings. The arena of the *svayamvara* had been constructed in a very grand manner. After seeing all this from a great distance, Lord Kṛṣṇa decided to firmly establish His supremacy.

Text 27

vitrāsanārthaṁ bhūpānāṁ
prakāśārthaṁ purātanam
manasā cintayāmāsa
vainateyaṁ mahābalam

To instill fear in the hearts of the assembled kings and princes, and exhibit His superior influence, Lord Kṛṣṇa summoned His carrier, the powerful son of Vinatā, Garuḍa.

Text 28

tataścintita mātrastu
viditvā vinatātmajaḥ
sukhalakṣyaṁ vapuḥ kṛtvā
nililye keśavāntike

As soon as he was thought of by the Lord, Garuḍa, who very well understands the intention of the Lord, assumed an attractive and pleasing form and came before Him incognito.

Text 29

tasya pakṣa nipātena
pavanodbhrānta kāriṇā
kampitā manujāḥ sarve
nyubjāśca patitā bhuvi

By moving at great speed while flapping his wings, Garuḍa can bewilder even the wind-god. Upon his arrival, everyone trembled and then fell to the ground, being pushed by the force of the air from his wings.

Texts 30-36

garuḍā bhitāḥ sarve
praceṣṭanto yathoragāḥ
tān saṁnipatitān dṛṣṭvā
kṛṣṇo giri rivācalaḥ

sa tadā pakṣavātena
mene pataga sattamam
dadarśa garuḍaṁ prāptaṁ
divyasraganu lepanam

pakṣavātena pṛthivīṁ
cālayantaṁ muhurmuhuḥ
pṛṣṭhāsaktaiḥ praharaṇair
lelihyantam ivoragaiḥ

vaiṣṇavaṁ hasta saṁśleṣaṁ
manyamānam avāṁḍukham
caraṇābhyāṁ prakarṣantaṁ
pāṇḍuraṁ bhogināṁ varam

hemapatrair upacitaṁ
dhātumantam ivācalam
amṛtārambha hartāraṁ
dvijihvendra vināśanam

trāsanaṁ daitya saṅghānāṁ
vāhanaṁ dhvaja lakṣaṇam
taṁ dṛṣṭvā sa dhvajaṁ prāptaṁ
sacivaṁ sāmparāyikam

dhṛtimantaṁ garutmantaṁ
jagāda madhusūdanaḥ
dṛṣṭvā parama saṅhṛṣṭaḥ
sthitaṁ devam ivāparam
tulyasām arthyayā vācā
garutmantam avasthitam

After falling to the ground, these people writhed like serpents. Seeing how they were rolling on the ground, Lord Kṛṣṇa, who stood like an immovable mountain, understood that the king of birds, Garuḍa, had arrived. When Garuḍa came and stood before the Lord, He saw that he was decorated with a flower garland and smeared with sandalwood paste. He carried formidable weapons on his back that made him appear as if he were being embraced by serpents. With His lotus-like hand, Lord

Kṛṣṇa touched Garuḍa, offering His benediction. Garuḍa, who had stolen nectar from the demigods, was so powerful that the flapping of his wings made the earth tremble. He thus instilled fear within the hearts of the demons and could kill even the most powerful serpents. In his claws, he held a gigantic white serpent. With his golden wings, Garuḍa appeared like a mountain decorated with colorful minerals. With very pleasing words, the Lord spoke as follows.

Text 37

śrī kṛṣṇa uvāca
svāgataṁ khecara śreṣṭha
surasenāri mardana
vinatā hṛdayānanda
svāgataṁ keśavapriya

Lord Kṛṣṇa said: O Garuḍa, best among those who fly through the sky, you are most welcome. O killer of the enemies of the demigods, O son of Vinatā who is very dear to Lord Keśava, you are most welcome.

Text 38

braja patra rathaśreṣtha
kaiśikasya niveśanam
vayaṁ tatraiva gatvādya
pratīkṣāma svayaṁ varam

O best of winged creatures, let us go to the residence of King Bhīṣmaka without delay, for today the *svayamvara* will be held.

Text 39

rājñāṁ tatra sametānāṁ
hastyaśva rathagāminām
drakṣyāmaḥ śataśas tatra
sametānāṁ mahātmanām

Already many thousands of powerful and intelligent kings have arrived, riding upon their elephants, horses and chariots. Let us see them from a good vantage point.

Texts 40-42

evamuktvā mahābāhur
vainateyaṁ mahābalam
jagāmātha purīṁ kṛṣṇaḥ
kaiśikasya mahātmanaḥ

vainateya sakhaḥ śrīmān
yādavaiśca mahārathaiḥ
vidarbha nagarīṁ prāpte
kṛṣṇe devakinandane

dṛṣṭāḥ pramuditāḥ sarve
nivāsāyopa cakramuḥ
sarve śastrāyudha dharā
rājāno balaśālinaḥ

After issuing this order to Vinatā's son, the greatly powerful Garuḍa, mighty-armed Kṛṣṇa sat on his back and departed, along with the other members of the Yadu dynasty, who were all very powerful warriors. Soon they came to Kundinapura, the capital of the exalted King Bhīṣmaka. When Devakī's son, Kṛṣṇa, arrived at the city within the kingdom of Vidarbha, everyone was very pleased to see Him. Immediately, the Lord's entourage began setting up their camp.

Texts 43-44

vaiśampāyana uvāca
etasmin neva kāle tu
rājā naya viśāradaḥ
kaiśikas tata utthāya
prahṛṣṭenantara ātmanā

arghyam ācamanaṁ dattvā
sa rājā kaiśikaḥ svayam
satkṛtya vidhivat kṛṣṇaṁ
svapurām sampraveścayat

Vaiśampāyana said: King Bhīṣmaka, who knew very well how to display proper etiquette, hurriedly came to greet the Lord. Indeed, he worshiped Lord Kṛṣṇa with offerings of *arghya* and *ācamanīya* before escorting Him to his palace.

Text 45

pūrvameva tu kṛṣṇāya
kāritaṁ divya mandiram
veveśa sabalaḥ śrīmān
kailāsaṁ śaṅkaro yathā

Even before Lord Kṛṣṇa's arrival, King Bhīṣmaka had constructed a wonderful residence for Him. As Śiva enters his abode, Kailāsa, Lord Kṛṣṇa, accompanied by His army, went inside the residence built by the king of Vidarbha.

Text 46

khādya pānādi ratnaughair
arcito vāsa vānujaḥ
sukhena ūṣitaḥ kṛṣṇas
tasya rājño niveśane
pūjito bahumānena
snehapūrṇena cetasā

Indra's younger brother, Lord Kṛṣṇa, was then served delicious food and refreshing drinks, and offered varieties of jewels and ornaments. The Lord remained there in a very happy mood. In this way, King Bhīṣmaka worshiped the Lord with great respect and affection.

Thus ends the translation of the forty-seventh chapter of the Viṣṇu Parva of Śri Harivaṁsa.

Chapter 48

Jarāsandha's speech to the assembled kings at Kundinapura

Text 1

vaiśampāyana uvāca
te kṛṣṇam āgataṁ dṛṣṭvā
vainateya sahācyutam
babhūvuś cintayāviṣṭāḥ
sarve nṛpati sattamāḥ

Vaiśampāyana said: After seeing the infallible Lord Kṛṣṇa arrive on the back of Garuḍa, the foremost of kings became filled with anxiety.

Text 2

te sametya sabhāṁ rājan
rājāno bhīma vikramāḥ
mantrāya mantrakuśalā
nīti śāstrārtha vittamāḥ

O King, all these kings were very formidable and powerful, expert in the art of diplomacy, and military strategy. To plan their course of action, they decided to hold a conference.

Text 3

bhīṣmakasya sabhāṁ gatvā
ramyāṁ hema pariṣkṛtām
siṁhāsaneṣu citreṣu
vicitrās taraṇeṣu ca

niṣeduste nṛpavarā
devā deva sabhāmiva

As the demigods meet in their assembly hall in the heavenly planets, these foremost kings gathered at the assembly hall of King Bhīṣmaka, which was decorated with gold and contained beautiful and comfortable seating arrangements, and sat on their assigned thrones.

Text 4

teṣāṁ madhye mahābāhur
jarāsandho mahābalaḥ
babhāṣe sa mahātejā
devān deveśvaro yathā

In that meeting, the greatly powerful and influential Jarāsandha was the first to speak, just as Indra, the king of heaven, addresses the demigods.

Text 5

jarāsandho uvāca
śrūyatāṁ bho nṛpaśreṣṭhā
bhīṣmakaśca mahāmatiḥ
kathyamānaṁ mayā buddhyā
vacanaṁ vadatāṁ varāḥ

Jarāsandha said: My dear kings present here, who are all very eloquent speakers, I request you, and especially King Bhīṣmaka, to hear me with attention for I have carefully deliberated over the present situation as far as my intelligence goes.

Texts 6-7

yo'sau kṛṣṇa iti khyāto
vasudeva suto bali
vainateya sahāyena
samprāptaḥ kuṇḍinaṁ tviha

kanyāhetor mahātejā
yādavair abhi saṁvṛtaḥ
avaśyaṁ kurute yatnaṁ
kanyā vāptir yathā bhavet

You must know that Kṛṣṇa, the son of the powerful king, Vasudeva, has arrived at Kuṇḍinapura with Garuḍa. He is certainly a formidable opponent. He has come here with His Yādava associates, hoping to win the hand of the princess and no doubt He will not ṣtop at anything to get what He wants.

Text 8

yadatra kāraṇaṁ kāryaṁ
sunayo petaṁ ṛddhitam
kurudhvaṁ nṛpaśārdūlā
viniścitya balābalam

O respectable rulers of men, you are all conversant with what is to be done and what is not to be done while advancing the cause of prosperity and enjoyment. I am confident that we can come to a consensus after carefully considering the matter.

Text 9

padātinau mahāvīryau
vasudeva sutābubhau

vainateyaṁ vinā tasmin
gomante parvatottame
kṛtavantau mahāghoraṁ
bhavadbhir viditaṁ hi tat

The two sons of Vasudeva are supremely powerful. They climbed Gomanta Hill, the best of mountains, without the help of Their carrier, Garuḍa. I am sure that you have heard about how fiercely They fought in the battle that took place there.

Text 10

vṛṣṇibhir yādavaiścaiva
bhojāndhaka mahārathaiḥ
sametya yuddhaya mānasya
kīdṛśo vigraho bhavet

Now They have the support of all the powerful kings of the Yadu, Vṛṣṇi, Bhoja, and Andhaka dynasties and so you can just imagine how fiercely They will fight if we oppose Them.

Text 11

kanyārthe yatatānena
garuḍasthena viṣṇunā
kaḥ sthāsyati raṇe tasmin
napi śakraḥ suraiḥ saha

When Lord Viṣṇu attacks us while riding on the back of Garuḍa, determined to gain the hand of the princess, who will be able to stand in front of Him? I think that not even Indra, the king of heaven, would be able to do so.

Text 12

yadā cāsmai nāpi sutā
kadācit sampradīyate
tato hyaṁ balādenāṁ
netuṁ śaktaḥ suraiḥ saha

If by some means He is denied the princess, He will certainly enter the *svayamvara* by force, along with all the demigods, and take her as His wife.

Texts 13-14

purā ekārṇave ghore
śrūyate medinī tviyam
pātāla tala sammagnā
viṣṇunā prabhaviṣṇunā

vārāhaṁ rūpam āsthāya
uddhṛtā jagadādinā
hiraṇyākṣaśca daityendro
varāheṇa nipātitaḥ

We have heard that long ago, in a previous millennium, the earth had been pushed down into the Garbhodaka Ocean, sinking all the way to Rasātala. At that time, Lord Viṣṇu, who is the original cause of the universe, assumed the form of the Boar Incarnation, Varāha, delivered the earth, and then killed the king of the demons, Hiraṇyākṣa.

Texts 15-16

hiraṇyakaśipuś caiva
mahābala parākramaḥ

avadhyo'mara daityānām
ṛṣi gandharva kinnaraiḥ

yakṣa rākṣasa nāgānāṁ
nākāśe nāvanisthale
na cābhyantara rātrya
horna śuṣkeṇārdrakeṇa ca

The King of the demons, Hiraṇyakaśipu, possessed incomparable strength and influence. He could not be killed by any demigod or demon. The sages, Gandharvas, and Kinnaras were incapable of killing Him. He was unconquerable by the Yakṣas, Rākṣasas, and Nāgas as well. He could not be killed in the sky, on the earth, during the day, nor at night. He could not be killed by any dry or wet weapon.

Text 17

avadhya striṣu lokeṣu
daityendras tva parājitaḥ
narasiṁhena rūpeṇa
nihato viṣṇunā purā

Indeed, Hiraṇyakaśipu could not be defeated by anyone within the universe but still, Lord Viṣṇu assumed the form of Nṛsiṁhadeva and killed him.

Texts 18-21

vāmanena tu rūpeṇa
kaśyapasyātmajo bali
ādityā garbha saṁbhuto
balir baddho'surottama

satyarajju mayaiḥ pāśaiḥ
kṛtaḥ pātāla saṁśrayaḥ
kārtavīryo mahāvīryaḥ
sahasrabhuja vigrahaḥ

dattātreya prasādena
matto rājya madena ca
jāmadagnyo mahātejā
reṇukā garbha saṁbhavaḥ

tretā dvāparayoḥ saṅdhau
rāmaḥ śastra bhṛtāṁ varaḥ
paśunā vajrakalpena
sapta dvīpeśvaro nṛpaḥ
viṣṇunā nihato bhūyaḥ
chadmarūpeṇa haihayaḥ

Later on, the incomparably powerful Lord Viṣṇu took birth from the womb of Aditi as the son of the great sage, Kaśyapa. In this way, He assumed the form of a dwarf *brāhmana* named Vāmanadeva and arrested Bali, the king of the demons, and sent him to Pātālaloka. The greatly powerful Kārtavīryārjuna received one thousand arms by the mercy of Lord Dattātreya, but unfortunately he became blinded by pride. To bring about his destruction, Lord Viṣṇu appeared from the womb of Reṇuka at the junction of Tretā and Dvāpara *yugas* and received the name Paraśurāma. This son of the sage Jamadagni was supremely powerful and the foremost among those who know the art of discharging weapons in battle.

Text 22

ikṣvāku kula sambhūto
rāmo dāśarathiḥ purā

triloka vijayaṁ vīraṁ
rāvaṇaṁ saṅyapātayat

Thereafter He appeared in the Ikṣvāku dynasty as the son of King Daśaratha. He was known as Rāmacandra and He killed the heroic king, Rāvana, who had conquered the three worlds.

Texts 23-24

purā kṛtayuge viṣṇuḥ
saṅgrāme tārakāmaye
ṣoḍaśārddha bhujo bhūtvā
garuḍastho hi vīryavān

nijadhānā surān yuddhe
varadānena garvitān
kālanemiśca daiteyo
devānāṁ ca bhayapradaḥ

Long ago, during Satya-yuga, when there was a fierce battle between the demigods and demons, Lord Viṣṇu entered the battlefield, riding on the back of Garuḍa. At that time, He appeared in an eight-arm form and killed innumerable demons that had become very proud due to receiving benedictions. During that battle, the Lord killed Kālanemi, eliminating the great fear within the minds of the demigods.

Text 25

sahasra kiraṇābhena
cakreṇa nihato yudhi
mahāyoga balenājau
viśvarūpeṇa viṣṇunā

Lord Viṣṇu, who manifests the universal form, killed Kālanemi with His Sudarśana *cakra*, which is as brilliant as many suns.

Text 26-35

anena prāpta kālāste
nihatā vahavo'surāḥ
vane vanacarā daityā
mahābala parākramāḥ

nihatā bāla bhāvena
pralāmbāriṣṭa dhenukāḥ
śakunīṁ keśinaṁ caiva
yamalārjuna kāvapi

nāgaṁ kuvalayāpīḍaṁ
cāṇūraṁ muṣṭikaṁ tathā
kaṁsaṁ ca balināṁ śreṣṭhaṁ
sagaṇaṁ devakīsutaḥ

nyahanad gopaveṣeṇa
krīḍamāno hi keśavaḥ
evam ādīni divyāni
chadmarūpāṇi cakriṇā

kṛtāni divya rūpāṇi
viṣṇunā prabhaviṣṇunā
tenāhaṁ vaḥ pravakṣyāmi
bhavatāṁ hita kāmyayā

taṁ manye keśavaṁ viṣṇuṁ
surādyam asurāntakam
nārāyaṇāṁ jagadyoniṁ
purāṇaṁ puruṣaṁ dhruvam

sraṣṭāraṁ sarvabhūtānāṁ
vyaktā vyaktaṁ sanātanam
adhṛṣyaṁ sarvalokānāṁ
sarvaloka namaskṛtam

anādi madhya nidhanaṁ
kṣaram akṣaram avyayam
svayambhuvam ajaṁ sthāṇum
ajeyaṁ sacarācaraiḥ

trivikramaṁ trilokeśaṁ
tridaśendrāri nāśanam
iti me niścitā buddhir
jāto'yaṁ mathurāmadhi

kule mahati vai rājñāṁ
vipule cakravartinām
kathamanyasya martyasya
garuḍo vāhanaṁ bhavet

Thus, in the distant past, Kṛṣṇa killed many demons. In this incarnation, when He was only a small child, He effortlessly killed the greatly powerful demons Pralambāsura and Dhenukāsura. This son of Devakī, who is also called Keśava, while playing in the forest as a cowherd boy, easily killed many demons and their followers, such as Putanā and Keśi. He delivered the sons of Kuvera, who were known as Yamalārjuna, and he later on killed the elephant Kuvalayāpiḍha, the wrestlers Cāṇura and Muṣṭika, and the supremely powerful King Kaṁsa.

This Kṛṣṇa is none other than Lord Viṣṇu, the wielder of the *cakra*, who killed innumerable demons while assuming various transcendental forms in all the previous *yugas*. Thus it should be understood that Kṛṣṇa is the origin of all the demigods, and the original cause of this universe and the Supreme Personality of

Godhead. He is the original Lord Nārāyaṇa, the eternal master of all living entities. Although He is eternal, sometimes He appears before the conditioned souls and sometimes He remains unmanifest. He is the Supersoul residing within the hearts of all living beings.

Considering all this, it must be concluded that He could not be defeated even by the combined effort of everyone within the universe. Indeed, He is the beginning, middle, and end of all existence. He is unborn, unchanging, and beyond the perception of the blunt material senses or the materially-conditioned mind. He is none other than Lord Viṣṇu, who had previously assumed the form of Trivikrama. This is my final opinion. Now, Lord Viṣṇu has appeared in the Yadu dynasty at Mathurā. Please consider—how could Garuḍa become the carrier of an ordinary human being?

Text 36

viśeṣeṇa tu kanyārthe
vikramasthe janārdane
kaḥ sthāsyati pumānadya
garuḍasya agrato bali

When Lord Janārdana becomes eager to display His unlimited prowess to secure the hand of the princess, who is that man that will dare to stand in front of Him as He rides on Garuḍa?

Texts 37-40

svayaṁvara kṛtenāsau
viṣṇuḥ svayam ihāgataḥ
viṣṇor āgamane caiva
mahān doṣaḥ prakīrtitaḥ

bhavadbhir anucintyedaṁ
kriyatāṁ yadanantaram

vaiśampāyana uvāca
evaṁ vibruva māṇetu
magadhānāṁ janeśvare
sunītho'tha mahāprājño
vacanaṁ cedam abravīt

sunītha uvāca
samyagāha mahābāhur
magadhādhi patir nṛpaḥ
samakṣaṁ naradevānāṁ
yathāvṛttaṁ mahāhave

gomante rāma kṛṣṇābhyaṁ
kṛtaṁ karma suduṣkaram

You should understand that it is Lord Viṣṇu who has come to this *svayaṁvara*. Thus I have dutifully warned you about what to expect and so you should carefully consider the matter and then do what is beneficial.

Vaiśampāyana said: When the King of Magadha finished speaking, the greatly intelligent Sunītha spoke in reply.

Sunītha said: Whatever the mighty-armed King of Magadha has said is certainly correct. All that took place at Gomanta Hill recently, as well as the wonderful pastimes that Kṛṣṇa and Balarāma performed previously, many of which were witnessed by you, are ample proof of Their inconceivable potency.

Text 41

gajāśva ratha sambādhā
pattidhvaja samākulā

nirdagdhā mahatī senā
cakra lāṅgala vahninā

In that great battle at Gomanta Hill, countless elephant, horse, chariot, and infantry soldiers were burnt to ashes by the blazing effulgence of Lord Kṛṣṇa's *cakra* and Balarāma's plough.

Texts 42-43

tenāyaṁ māgadhaḥ śrīmāna
nāgatama cintayat
bruvate rājasenāyām
anusmṛtya sudāruṇam

padātyor yudhyatos tatra
balakeśavayor yudhi
durnivārya taro ghoro
hyabhavad vāhinīkṣayaḥ

The king of Magadha has correctly understood the future consequences of opposing Lord Kṛṣṇa. He has spoken as one who has had personal experience of Kṛṣṇa and Balarāma's incomparable prowess. Even thought They fought without assistance, and on foot, the two brothers easily defeated our vast army.

Text 44

viditaṁ vaḥ suparṇasya
svāgatasya nṛpottamāḥ
pakṣavegā niloddhūtā
babhramurga ganecarāḥ

O noble kings, just consider the havoc that was created

by the arrival of Garūḍa. The wind created by the flapping of his wings was so strong that the birds in the sky were seen spinning out of control.

Text 45

samudrāḥ kṣubhitāḥ sarve
cacālādrir mahī muhuḥ
vayaṁ sarve susaṁtrastāḥ
kimutpāteti viklavāḥ

The water of the ocean became agitated, the hills shook, and the earth trembled violently. We were all very frightened, wondering what calamity awaited us.

Text 46

yadā saṁnahya yudhyeta
ārūḍhaḥ keśavaḥ khagam
kathamasma dvidhaḥ śaktaḥ
pratisthātuṁ raṇājire

When Lord Keśava takes up His weapons and begins fighting on the back of Garuḍa, how will we be able to stand before Him and counter His attack?

Text 47

rājñāṁ svayaṁvaro nāma
sumahān harṣavardhanaḥ
kṛto narovarai rādyair
yaśo dharmasya vai vidhiḥ

The *svayambara* is meant to be a joyful occasion for the

pleasure of the rulers of the earth. This system of marriage was arranged long ago for increasing the prestige of righteous kings.

Text 48

idaṁ tu kuṅḍina nagaram
āsādya manujeśvarāḥ
punare vaiṣyate kṣipraṁ
mahāpuruṣa vigraham

O rulers of men, here at Kuṇḍinapur we will soon find ourselves facing the wrath of a great personality who is eager for battle.

Text 49

yadi sā varaye danyaṁ
rājñāṁ madhye nṛpātmajā
kṛṣṇasya bhujayor vīryaṁ
kaḥ pumān prasahiṣyati

If Princess Rukmiṇī chooses one of us as her husband, then who among us can dare to stand up to the might of Kṛṣṇa's arms ?

Text 50

vijñāpitam idaṁ doṣaṁ
svayaṁvara mahotsave
tadartham āgataḥ kṛṣno
vayaṁ caiva narādhipāḥ

There is every possibility that this *svayambara* will turn into a great massacre. After all, Lord Kṛṣṇa has come here and He will certainly not accept defeat at our hands.

Text 51

kṛṣṇamyāgamanaṁ caiva
nṛpāṇām atigarhitam
kanyāhetor narendrāṇāṁ
yathā vadati māgadhaḥ

It is my opinion that Kṛṣṇa's attendance of this *svayambara* is a very inauspicious omen for all of us. This is also the opinion of the King of Magadha.

Thus ends the translation of the forty-eighth chapter of the Viṣṇu Parva of Śri Harivaṁsa.

Chapter 49

Speeches made by Dantavakra, Śālva, and Bhīṣmaka

Text 1

vaiśampāyana uvāca
ityevam ukte vacane
sunīrthena mahātmanā
karūṣādhi patirvīro
dantavaktro'bhyabhāṣata

Vaiśampāyana said: After hearing these statements of the very learned Sunītha, the king of Karūṣa, Dantavakra, was next to speak.

Text 2

dantavakra uvāca
yaduktaṁ māgadhenātra
sunīthena narādhipāḥ
yukta pūrvam ahaṁ manye
yadasmākaṁ vaco hitam

Dantavakra said: My dear kings, I think that everything the king of Magadha and King Sunītha said is reasonable and meant for our welfare.

Text 3

na ca vidveṣa ṇenāhaṁ
na cāhaṁ kāravādinā
na cātma vijigīṣutvāda
dūṣayāmi vaco'mṛtam

I am not envious of anyone, nor am I puffed up with false pride, nor do I have any desire to defeat anyone. I am not impelled by any of these to find fault with anyone.

Text 4

vākyārṇavaṁ mahāgādhaṁ
nīti śāstrārtha vṛṁhitam
ka eṣa nikhilaṁ vaktuṁ
śakto vai rājasaṁsadi

Who is that great personality among us who can perfectly speak meaningful and beneficial words that are in agreement with the literature that prescribe the codes of good conduct?

Text 5

kiṁ tvanusmaraṇārthe'haṁ
yad vravīmi śṛṇuṣva me
āgato vāsudeveti
kimāścaryaṁ narādhipāḥ

At this crucial time, I would like to point out something to you and so kindly listen attentively. O kings, why are you so alarmed that Vasudeva's son, Kṛṣṇa, has come here?

Text 6

yathā'gatā vayaṁ sarve
kṛṣṇo'pīha tathā"gataḥ
kimatra doṣo gauṇyo vā
kanyāhetoḥ samāgatāḥ

Just as we have all come here in the hopes of attaining the

beautiful princess of Vidarbha, so has Kṛṣṇa. What is surprising about that?

Text 7

yadasmābhiḥ sametyaikyāt
kṛtaṁ gomantarodhanam
tatra yuddhakṛtaṁ doṣaṁ
kathaṁ vai vaktumrahatha

It was us who united to surrounded Gomanta Hill in an attempt to kill Kṛṣṇa, and this was the cause of the great battle that followed. What blame can be placed upon Kṛṣṇa?

Texts 8-11

vanavāse sthitau vīrau
kaṁsavyāmoha hetunā
devarṣi vacanād rājan
vṛndāvana taṭe sthitau

tāvāhūya vadhārthena
ubhau rāmajanārdanau
nāgena dīpitau vīrau
gatvā nāgaṁ viveśatuḥ

tataḥ svavīryam āśritya
nihato raṅgasāgare
gatāsuriva cāsīno
mathureśaḥ sahānugaḥ

kimatra vihito doṣo
yenāsmābhir vage'dhikaiḥ
uparodha parā rājan
vayaṁ sarve samāgatāḥ

O kings, Kṛṣṇa and Balarāma intentionally resided in the forest of Vṛndāvana just to bewilder Kaṁsa. They were peacefully residing in Vṛndāvana, but on the advice of Nārada, Kaṁsa invited Them to Mathurā for his own destruction. Kaṁsa then aroused Their anger by having the elephant Kuvalayāpīḍa attack Them. The two brothers killed the elephant and then entered the wrestling arena. What fault can be attributed to Kṛṣṇa for killing the inimical king of Mathurā, along with his followers? Similarly, what was His fault in vanquishing all the other inimical kings that attacked Him after the death of Kaṁsa?

Text 12

senāti bala mālokya
vitrastau rāmakeśavau
puraṁ balaṁ samutsṛjya
gomante ca gatāmante

Kṛṣṇa and Balarāma became so fearful after seeing the strength of our vast army that They left Mathurā and took shelter on top of Gomanta Hill.

Texts 13-14

tatrāpi gatamasmābhir
hantuṁ samarayo dhibhiḥ
aprāptaya yauvanābhyaṁ ca
padātibhyāṁ raṇajire

rathāśva nara nāgena
nāsmābhir vigrahaḥ kṛtaḥ
kṛtvopa rodhaṁ śailasya
kṣatradharmeṇa kīpitaḥ

We had chased Him, hoping to kill Him. Kṛṣṇa and Balarāma are barely adults and fought with us on foot. Observing the rules governing *kṣatriya* behavior, we did not oppose Him with our four divisions of warriors but rather surrounded Gomanta Hill and set it on fire.

Text 15

dāvāgni mukhamāviśya
durvinīta tapasvinau
vinīta iti manyāmaḥ
sarve kṣatriya puṅgavāḥ
pratiyuddhe kṛte tvevaṁ
dūṣayāma janārdanam

Being experienced *kṣatriyas*, were under the impression that the two arrogant brothers would perish in the blazing forest fire. Considering all that, when Janārdana fought with us in self-defense, how can He be at fault?

Text 16

yatra yatra prayāsyāmo
vayaṁ tatra bhavet kaliḥ
prītyarthaṁ prayatiṣyāmaḥ
kṛṣṇena saha bhūmipāḥ

As long as we maintain this inimical mentality towards Him, we will be harassed by His superior strength. Therefore, O kings, let us make peace with Kṛṣṇa.

Text 17

idaṁ kuṇḍīnapuraṁ kṛṣṇo
nāgataḥ kalihetunā

kanyā nimittāgamane
kasya yuddhaṁ prayacchati

Kṛṣṇa has not come to Kuṇḍinapur to fight. He has certainly come seeking the hand of the fair princess and so what is the question of fighting?

Text 18

martye'smin puruṣendro'sau
nakaścit prākṛto naraḥ
devalokeṣu deveṣu
pravaraḥ puruṣottamaḥ

Kṛṣṇa is not an ordinary human being. He is the foremost personality on earth. He is the master of the demigods as well.

Text 19

devānāmapi kartāsau
lokānāṁ ca viṣeṣataḥ
na caiva bāliśā buddhirna
cerṣyā nāpi matsaraḥ

He is the creator of the universe and the origin of the demigods and great sages. Don't think that this supremely intelligent person is a mere village boy! Nor should you think that he is envious of you.

Text 20

na stabdho na kṛśo nārtaḥ
praṇatārti haraḥ sadā
eṣa viṣṇuḥ prabhurdevo
devānāmapi daivatam

Kṛṣṇa is not harsh in His behavior, nor is He weak. He never suffers from a disease or lamentation. Indeed, He always ready to remove the distresses of the surrendered souls.

Texts 21-22

āgato garuḍe nehaś
cchadmas prākāśya hetunā
nānāstra sahito yāti
kṛṣṇaḥ śatruvināśane

imāṁ yātrāṁ vijānīdhvaṁ
prītyarthaṁ hyagato hariḥ
sahito yādavendraiśca
bhoja vṛṣṇyandhakair iha

In my opinion, Kṛṣṇa has come here with Garuda to reveal His true identity. Generally, He incarnates within the material world, along with His transcendental weapons, to destroy the miscreants. However, His coming here is not like that. I believe that He has come here along with the members of the Bhoja, Vṛṣṇi, Andhaka, and Yadu dynasties to enhance our love and affection for Him.

Text 23

arghyam ācamanaṁ dattvā
ātithyaṁ ca narādhipāḥ
kariṣyāmo vigatodvegā
nirghayā vigatajvarāḥ

Therefore, my dear kings, we should go and greet this exalted Keśava, offering Him *arghya, ācamanīya* and other articles of worship.

Text 24

evaṁ saṁdhānataḥ kṛtvā
kṛṣṇena sahitā vayam
vasāmo vigatodvegā
nirbhayā vigatajvarāḥ

In this way we should make peace with Kṛṣṇa so that we can all live together without fear, anxiety, or antagonism.

Text 25

tasya tad vacanaṁ śrutvā
dantavaktrasya dhīmataḥ
śālvaḥ pravadatāṁ śreṣṭhās
tānuvāca narādhipān

After the wise Dantavakra finished speaking, the best of speakers, Śālva, addressed the assembled kings.

Text 26

śālva uvāca
kiṁ bheyanāsya naḥ sarve
nyasta śastrā bhavāmahe
saṁghāna karaṇāddhetoḥ
kṛṣṇasya bhayakampitāḥ

Śālva said: If we do as you say and lay down our weapons to make peace with Kṛṣṇa, then it will appear as if we are afraid of Him.

Text 27

parastavena kiṁ kāryaṁ
vinindya balamātmanaḥ
naiṣa dharmo narendrāṇāṁ
kṣātre dharma ca tiṣṭhatām

What is the use of condemning one's own strength and glorifying another's prowess? This is not the duty of a *kṣatriya.*

Text 28

mahatsu rājavaṁśeṣu
sambhūtāḥ kulavarddhanāḥ
teṣāṁ kāpuruṣā buddhiḥ
kathaṁ bhavitum arhati

How did this cowardly mentality arise in the minds of members of royal families? Instead of bringing shame to your dynasties, you should be enhancing the fame of your family by your heroic deeds.

Text 29

ahaṁ jānāmi vai kṛṣṇam
ādidevaṁ sanātanam
prabhuṁ sarvā marendrāṇāṁ
nārāyaṇa parāyaṇam

I know that Kṛṣṇa is the master of the demigods, the primeval Lord, and the original Personality of Godhead, the shelter of Lord Nārāyaṇa.

Texts 30-35

vaikuṇṭhm ajayaṁ loke
carācara guruṁ harim
sambhūtaṁ devakīgarbhe
viṣṇuṁ lokanamaskṛtam

kaṁsarājava dhārthāya
bhārāva taraṇāya ca
asmākaṁ ca vināśāya
loka saṁrakṣaṇāya ca

aṁśāvataraṇe kṛtsnaṁ
jāne viṣṇor viceṣṭitam
saṁgrāmam atulaṁ kṛtvā
viṣṇunā saha bhūmipāḥ

cakrānala vinirdagdhā
yāsyāmo yamasādanam
tattvaṁ jānāmi rājendrāḥ
kālenāyuḥ kṣayo bhavet

nākāle miryate kaścit
prāpte kāle na jīvati
evaṁ viniścayaṁ kṛtvā
na kuryāt kasyacid bhayam

sa eva bhagavān viṣṇur
ālokya tapasaḥ kṣayam
nihantā ditijendrāṇāṁ
yathākālena yogavit

I know that Lord Viṣṇu, the unconquerable Lord of Vaikuṇṭha, the master of all moving and non-moving living entities, the destroyer of all sins, and the Lord who is worshiped by all, has appeared from the womb of Devakī to diminish the burden of the earth, to kill King Kaṁsa, to destroy all the demoniac kings like us, and to protect those who are pious. I know very well all the pastimes He will perform in this present incarnation. Therefore, O kings, if we put up a spirited fight against Him, he will send us to the abode of Yamarāja, burning us with the fire of His *cakra*. O kings, I am well aware of how time takes away one's duration of life. Until one's time is ripe, he does not relinquish his material body, and when death arrives, nobody survives. By understanding this, one should give up all fear. Lord Viṣṇu possesses knowledge of past, present and future and so He kills demoniac kings just when their prowess attained by previous penance has become practically exhausted.

Text 36

baliṁ vairocaniṁ caivaṁ
baddhvā vadhyaṁ mahābalam
kṛtavān devadeveśaḥ
pātāla tala vāsinam

Long ago, this Lord of the demigods bound King Bali, the son of Virocana, who could not be killed by anyone, and sent him to Pātālaloka.

Text 37

evam ādīni vai viṣṇoś
ceṣṭāni ca narādhipāḥ
tasmād ayuktaṁ bhavatāṁ
vigrahārthaṁ vicāraṇam

O rulers of men, such is the behavior of Lord Viṣṇu. My advice is that we should not even think of fighting with Him.

Text 38

na ca saṁgrāma hetorhi
kṛṣṇasyā gamanaṁ tviha
yasya vā kasya vā kanyā
varayiṣyati tasya sā
kimatra vigraho rājñāṁ
prītir bhavatu vai dhruvam

Kṛṣṇa has not come here to fight. The princess will become the queen of the person she chooses. Where is the question of quarreling? Let there be harmony among all the kings.

Text 39

vaiśampāyana uvāca
evaṁ kathaya mānānāṁ
nṛpāṇāṁ buddhiśālinām
na kiṁcid vravīd rājā
bhīṣmakaḥ putrakāraṇāt

Vaiśampāyana said: After hearing the intelligent kings speak in this manner, King Bhīṣmaka remained silent for some time, being afraid of offending his dear son.

Text 40

mahāvīrya madotsiktaṁ
bhārgavāstrābhi rakṣitam
raṇapracaṇḍātir athaṁ
vicintya manasā sutam

King Bhīṣmaka was very proud of his great strength, his powerful weapons, and his heroic deeds performed on the battlefield. After thinking about his son for some time, he began to speak to the assembly of kings.

Text 41

bhīṣmaka uvāca
kṛṣṇaṁ na sahate nityaṁ
putro me baladarpitaḥ
nityābhimānīca raṇe
bhibheti ca kasyati

Bhīṣmaka said: My son is very proud of his great strength. Thinking very highly of himself, he cannot tolerate talk of Kṛṣṇa's unlimited prowess. He doesn't fear anyone when he stands upon the battlefield.

Text 42

kṛṣṇasya bhujavīryeṇa
hriyate nātra saṁśayaḥ
bhaviṣyati tato yuddhaṁ
mahāpuruṣa vigraham

My fear is that my daughter may be kidnapped by mighty-armed Kṛṣṇa. If this were to happen, a fierce battle between Kṛṣṇa and the other kings would be inevitable.

Text 43

dveṣī caivābhi mānī ca
kuto jīvati me sutaḥ
jīvitaṁ nātra paśyāmi
mama putrasya keśavāt

If this were to happen, how would my proud son, who is envious of Kṛṣṇa, be able to save himself? It appears to me that this otherwise joyful occasion simply heralds the death of my son at the hands of Keśava.

Text 44

kanyāhetoḥ sutaṁ jyeṣṭhaṁ
pitṛṇāṁ nandi varddhanam
kārayiṣye kathaṁ yuddhaṁ
putreṇa saha keśavam

How can I, for the sake of my daughter, allow my eldest son, who must act for the welfare of our forefathers, fight against Kṛṣṇa?

Text 45

na ca nārāyaṇaṁ devaṁ
varamicchati rukmavān
mūḍhabhāvo madonmattaḥ
saṁgrāmeṣva nivartakaḥ
niyataṁ bhasmasād yāti
tūlarāśir yathānalāt

My son, Rukmī is very foolish. He cannot tolerate the thought of Rukmiṇi marrying Kṛṣṇa, and he is very fond of fighting with others. As a mound of cotton is burned to ashes by fire, my son will certainly be vanquished if there is a quarrel with Kṛṣṇa.

Text 46

karavīreśvaraḥ śūraḥ
śṛgālaś citrayodhinā

kṣaṇena bhasma sānnītaḥ
keśavena balīyasā

Just remember how the unlimitedly powerful Lord Keśava smashed the heroic king of Karavīrapur within a moment.

Texts 47-48

vṛndāvane'vasacchrīmān
keśavo balināṁ varaḥ
uddhṛtyai kena hastena
saptāhaṁ dhṛtavān girim

duṣkaraṁ karma saṁsmṛtya
manaḥ sedate me bhṛśam

When Lord Keśava, the foremost among all powerful personalities, resided at Vṛndāvana, He picked up Govardhana Hill with one hand and held it for seven days. When I remember all His superhuman feats, my heart becomes depressed.

Text 49

nagendre sahasā'gamya
daivataiḥ saha vṛtrahā
abhiṣicyā bravīt kṛṣṇam
upendreti śacīpatiḥ

At that time, Indra, the slayer of Vṛtāsura and husband of Śacī, came along with the demigods and performed *abhiṣeka* to Kṛṣṇa. Knowing Kṛṣṇa to be the Supreme Personality of Godhead, Indra addressed Him as Upendra and other transcendental names.

Text 50

yathā vai damito nāgaḥ
kāliyo yamunā
viṣāgni jvalito ghoraḥ
kālāntaka samaprabhaḥ

The Kāliya serpent, who lived within a lake of the Yamunā, appeared as formidable as death personified. By his presence, the entire area was poisoned and yet Kṛṣṇa effortlessly chastised him. Everyone has heard about this wonderful pastimes of the Lord.

Text 51

keśī cāpi mahāvīryo
dānavo hayavigrahaḥ
nihato vāsudevena
devairapi durāsadaḥ

There was a powerful demon named Keśi, who wandered over the earth, having assumed the form of a gigantic horse. He was unconquerable even by the demigods, but he was killed by Lord Vāsudeva.

Text 52

sāndīpani sutaścaiva
ciranaṣṭo hi sāgare
daityaṁ pañcajanaṁ hatvā
ānīto yama mandirāt

Kṛṣṇa brought back the dead son of his teacher, Sāndipani Muni, from the abode of Yamarāja after killing the demon Pañcajana within the sea.

Texts 53-54

gomante sumahad yuddhaṁ
bahubhir veṣṭitā bhubhau
kṛtvā vidhāsa jananaṁ
nāgāśva rathasaṁkṣayam

gajena gajavṛndāni
rathena rathayodhinaḥ
sādinaścāśva yodhena
nareṇa ca padātinaḥ
jagna tustau mahāvīryau
vasudeva sutābubhau

During the battle that took place at Gomanta Hill, He and His brother, Balarāma, were besieged by innumerable kings. Still, the two sons of Vasudeva demonstrated Their superior prowess by destroying innumerable elephant, horse, and chariot warriors. They killed elephants with elephants, smashed chariots with chariots, and killed the cavalry and others while fighting on foot.

Texts 55-56

na devāsura gandharvā
na yakṣoraga rākṣasāḥ
na nāgā na ca daityendrā
na piśācā na guhyakāḥ

kṛtavantas tathā ghoraṁ
jagāśva rathasāṁkṣayam
tamanus mṛtyaṁ saṁgrāmaṁ
bhṛśaṁ sedatī me manaḥ

Never had the demigods, *asuras*, Gandharvas, Yakṣas, Rākṣasas, Nāgas, Daityas, *piśācas*, or Guyhakas destroyed so many elephants, horses, and chariots in this manner. The more I think about that formidable battle, the more my heart becomes aches.

Text 57

na mayā śrutapūrvo vā
dṛṣṭvapūrvaḥ kuto'pi vā
tādṛśobhuvi martyo'nyo
vāsudevāt surottamāt

I think that on this earth, there is no one to compare with Vāsudeva, the Lord of the demigods. At least I have never heard of such a person.

Text 58

samyagāha mahābāhur
dantavaktro mahīpatiḥ
sāntvayitvā mahāvīryaṁ
saṁvidhā syāma yatkṣamam

Mighty-armed King Dantavakra is right. Whatever the consequences, we should try and satisfy Lord Kṛṣṇa in all regards.

Text 59

vaiśampāyana uvāca
iti saṁcintya manasā
balābala viniścayam
gamanāya matiṁ cakre
prasādayitum acyutam

Vaiśampāyana said: Finally, after contemplating all the pros and cons, King Bhīṣmaka made up his mind to approach Kṛṣṇa and please Him in all respects.

Text 60

cintayāno narendrastu
bahubhir nayaśālibhiḥ
sūtamāgadha vandibhyo
bodhitaḥ stuti maṅgalaiḥ

After discussing the matter with his ministers, all of whom were very learned strategists, King Bhīṣmaka retired for the night. The next morning, he woke up to the auspicious recitations of the bards.

Text 61

prabhātāyāṁ rajanyāṁ tu
kṛta pūrvāhṇika kriyāḥ
upaviṣṭā nṛpāḥ sarve
sveṣu viśrāma veśmasu

As was their regular practice, all the kings rose from their beds early in the morning and then performed their religious duties. After completing the performance of their morning duties, they sat down to conduct other business.

Text 62

ye visṛṣṭāstu rājāno
vidarbhāyāṁ narādhipaiḥ
tairāgamya sva bhūpeṣu
raho gatvā niveditam

At that time, the kings sent their young sons into the city. They soon returned, one by one, and informed their fathers of the news.

Text 63

śrutvā kṛṣṇābhiṣekaṁ tu
kecid dhṛṣṭā narādhipāḥ
kecid dīnatarā bhītā
udāsīnās tathā pare

When they heard that an *abhiṣeka* was being performed for Lord Kṛṣṇa, some of the kings became jubilant, others became frightened, some became morose, and still others simply felt indifference.

Text 64

tridhā prabhinnā sā senā
naranāgāśva mālinī
mahārṇava iva kṣubdhā
abhilṣekeṇa cālitā

Because of this development, the kings and their armies became divided into three groups as their minds became agitated like the waves of the ocean during a storm.

Texts 65-66

nṛpāṇāṁ bhedamālokya
bhīṣmako rājasattamaḥ
vyatikramam acintyaṁ ca
kṛtaṁ nṛpatinā svayam

vicintya manasā rājā
dahyamānena cetasā
jagāma naradevānāṁ
samāje pratibodhitum

That foremost of kings, Bhīṣmaka, observed these differences among the assembled rulers. Thinking that he might have committed a great offense, his mind became very troubled. Finally, he approached the kings, just to pacify them.

Text 67

etasmitrantare dūtāḥ
samprāptāḥ kratha kaiśikau
lekham uddhṛtya śirasā
viviśuste nṛpārṇavam

Meanwhile, a messenger from Indra, the king of heaven, came and delivered a letter to Bhīṣmaka's younger brother, Kratha. After doing so, he seemed to disappear, merging into the ocean of kings.

Thus ends the translation of the forty-ninth chapter of the Viṣṇu Parva of Śri Harivaṁsa.

Chapter 50

Kauśika and Kratha decide to perform the coronation of Lord Kṛṣṇa. The message of Devadūta and the appearance of the celestial assembly hall

Text 1

janamejaya uvāca
havtvā kaṁsaṁ mahāvīryaṁ
devairapi durāsadam
nābhiṣiktaḥ svayaṁ rājye
nopaviṣṭo nṛpāsane

Janamejaya said: O sage, even after killing Kaṁsa, who was unconquerable by the demigods, Kṛṣṇa didn't accept the royal throne for Himself. What was the reason for this?

Text 2

kanyārthe cāgataḥ kṛṣṇas
tatrāpi na kṛto'tithiḥ
amānam atulaṁ prāpya
kṣāntavān kena hetunā

When Lord Kṛṣṇa came to Kuṇḍinapur to win the hand of the princess, He came there uninvited and so was not treated as a distinguished guest. How could He tolerate such negligence?

Text 3

vinatāyāḥ sutaścaiva
mahābala parākramaḥ

sa cāpi kṣamayā yuktaḥ
kāraṇaṁ kimapekṣitaḥ
etadākhyāhi bhagavat
paraṁ kautūhalaṁ hi me

Vinatā's son, Garuḍa, is a greatly powerful personality. How could he forgive such offensive behavior toward his master? My lord, kindly enlighten me in this regard.

Text 4

vaiśampāyana uvāca
vidarbhanagarīṁ prāpte
vainateye sahācyute
manasā cintayāmāsa
vāsudevāya kauśikaḥ

Vaiśampāyana said: As Lord Kṛṣṇa remained at Vidarbha along with Vinatā's son, Garuḍa, Kauśika contemplated as follows.

Texts 5-10

dṛṣṭvā'ścaryaṁ hi naḥ sarvān
rājanyān pravadāmyaham
vasudevasute dṛṣṭe
dhruvaṁ pāpakṣayo bhavet

viśuddhabhāvaḥ kṛṣṇasya
āvayor dṛṣṭa tatvataḥ
ataḥ pātrataraḥ ko'nya
striṣu lokeṣu vidyate

kṛṣṇāṭ kamala patrākṣād
deva devā janārdanāt

tasyāvāṁ kiṁ pradāsyāva
ātithya karaṇe nṛpa

pātramāsādya vai rājan
yathā dharmo na lupyate
evamanyonyaṁ saṁcintya
bhrātarau kratha kauśikau

svaṁrājyaṁ dātu kāmautu
jagmatuḥ keśavāntikam
devamāsādya tau vīrau
vidarbha nagarādhipau

ūca tustau mahābhāgau
praṇamya śirasā harim
adyāvāṁ saphalaṁ janma
adyāvāṁ saphalaṁ yaśaḥ
adyāvāṁ pitarastṛptāḥ
deve cava gṛhāgate

With Kratha I can perform the *abhiṣeka* of Lord Kṛṣṇa so that all those who witness it will become freed from all sins so that their minds will be purified. Indeed, I will make a proclamation to the kings that just by seeing Lord Kṛṣṇa, all of their sins will be vanquished. We two have understood the actual truth about Lord Kṛṣṇa. Who within the three worlds is more fit to be worshiped than lotus-eyed Janārdana, the master of the demigods? We should offer the Lord many valuable gifts. If we were to fail to do this, we would certainly become degraded in the near future, for He is the actual recipient of charity.

Kauśika and Kratha were younger brothers of Bhīṣmaka, the king of Vidarbha. After contemplating in this way, they approached Lord Keśava, and they were prepared to give Him their kingdom if necessary. After coming before Lord Kṛṣṇa, they very humbly offered their obeisances and spoke: O Supreme Lord, today we are blessed because You have come to our kingdom. This in itself has made our lives successful. Indeed, our fame has been enhanced and our forefathers have become joyful.

Text 11

cāmaraṁ vyajanaṁ chatraṁ
dhvajaṁ siṁhāsanaṁ balam
sphītakośā pure ceyam
āvābhyāṁ sahitā tava

We now offer these *cāmaras*, umbrellas, fans, thrones, armies, wealth, and this prosperous city, as well as our very selves for Your service. Now all of this belongs to You alone.

Text 12

upendrastvaṁ mahābāho
devendreṇābhi ṣiktavān
āvāmiha hi rājye
tvāmabhiṣiktaṁ dadāmi te

O mighty-armed Lord, You formerly appeared as Upendra. The king of the demigods, Indra, had performed Your *abhiṣeka*. We now hand over this kingdom to You.

Text 13

āvayor yatkṛtaṁ kāryaṁ
bahubhiḥ pārthivair api
na śakyate'nyathā kartuṁ
jarāsaṅdhena vā svayam

We have dedicated our kingdom to You. No one, not even Jarāsandha, can make us change our minds in this regard.

Text 14

śatruste māgadho rājā
jarāsaṅdho mahādyutiḥ
kathāṁ te bruvate nityaṁ
nṛpāṇām abhayapradaḥ

The greatly powerful King Jarāsandha is Your avowed enemy. He has turned the minds of many other kings against You. Every day he takes the opportunity to criticize You in so many ways.

Text 15

siṁhāsanam anadhyāsyaṁ
puraṁ cāsya na vidyate
kathaṁ rājasamāje'smin
nāsyate devakīsutaḥ

He said to the kings assembled here: Kṛṣṇa is not qualified to rule a kingdom. After all, he grew up tending cows in the forest. This is not the training of a *kṣatriya*. How can the son of Devakī dare sit on a royal throne meant only for genuine kings?

Text 16

kṛṣṇo'pi sumahāvīryo
hyabhimānī mahādyutiḥ
na cāgamiṣyate vāsmin
kanyārthe ca svayaṁvare

It is true that Lord Kṛṣṇa is a supremely powerful, proud, and influential personality. It is my opinion that He has not come here merely to accept the hand of Rukminī in this *svayambara.*

Text 17

pārthiveṣū paviṣṭṣeṣū
sveṣu siṁhāsaneṣu vai
kathamāsyati nīceṣu
āsaneṣu mahādyutiḥ

When all the kings are seated upon the royal thrones allotted to them, how will the incomparably powerful Kṛṣṇa accept an inferior seat?

Texts 18-20

iti saṁcodya mānastu
śrutvāsau bhīṣmako nṛpaḥ
āvayoḥ saha sammantrya
vigrahopa śamāya ca

tava viśrāma hetorhi
kāritedaṁ gṛhottamam
devānām ādidevo'si
sarvaloka namaskṛtaḥ

mānuṣye martyaloke'smin
rājendratvaṁ samācara
samāje manujendrāṇāṁ
mā bhūdāsana saṁkaṭam

After Jarāsandha had spoken in this challenging way, King Bhīṣmaka consulted us as to how we could maintain peace.

O Supreme Lord, You are the origin of all the demigods. The entire world offers respect unto Your lotus feet. You remain in this material world not as an ordinary king, but as the emperor. There is no doubt that Your presence will soon dispel all doubts about Your eligibility to sit on the best of royal thrones.

Text 21

vidarbhanagare vaiṣāṁ
rājendratvaṁ viceṣṭaya
āsyatā māsane śubhre
śvaḥ prabhāte mahādyute

O supremely powerful Lord Govinda, You are fully capable of destroying the kings of Vidarbha, and so what to speak of others. Therefore, You should subdue the pride of all these kings and occupy the most prominent throne in the assembly tomorrow morning.

Text 22

adhivāsyādya cātmānaṁ
vidhidṛṣṭena karmaṇā
yathā gamiṣyanti nṛpāḥ
kariṣye devaśāsanāt

Complete all the required formalities today, the day before the coronation ceremony. I will insure that tomorrow all of the assembled kings will perform your *abhiṣeka*.

Text 23

evamuktvā suraśreṣṭhaṁ
praṇipatya kṛtāñjalī

preṣayāmāsa tuvīrau
raṅgamadhye nṛpaivṛte

After saying this, the two brothers, Kratha and Kauśika, offered obeisances to the leader of the demigods, Lord Kṛṣṇa, with folded hands and then sent a message to all the kings, who were seated in the *svayamvara* arena.

Text 24

devadūtasya vacanaṁ
yathoktaṁ vajrapāṇinā
likhitvā sumahā tejāḥ
kauśikaḥ prāha śāsanam

In that message, Kauśika first conveyed the words of Indra, the king of heaven, the wielder of the thunderbolt, so that they could be heard by the assembled kings.

Text 25

kauśika uvāca
viditaṁ vo nṛpāḥ sarve
vainateya sahācyutaḥ
āgato'tithi rūpeṇa
vidarbha nagarīṁ hariḥ

Kauśika said: O kings, you know very well that Lord Acyuta has arrived with Garuda at Vidarbha, and thus is one of our honored guests.

Texts 26-27

prāptām ālokya pātro'yām
iti saṁcintya bhūpatiḥ

pradadau vāsudevāya
svaṁ rājyaṁ dharmahetunā

idamāsanam āsveti
bhrātrā me codite tataḥ
vāguktā cāsa rīreṇa
kenapi vyomacāriṇāḥ

Understanding that Lord Vāsudeva is the Supreme Person, King Kratha has surrendered his entire kingdom unto Him. My brother, Kratha, had requested: O Lord, this throne belongs to You and so kindly sit upon it.

As soon as my brother spoke these words, an unembodied voice made an announcement from the sky.

Texts 28-30

devadūta uvāca
na yuktam āsanaṁ dātuṁ
tvayāsīnaṁ narādhipa
idamasyāsanaṁ divyaṁ
sarvaratna vibhūṣitam

jāmbūnada mayaṁ śubhraṁ
racitaṁ viśvakarmaṇā
preṣitaṁ devarājena
siṁhalakṣaṇa lakṣitam

atropaviṣṭaṁ deveśaṁ
carācara namaskṛtam
abhiṣiñcantu rājendraṁ
bahubhiḥ pārthivaiḥ saha

Devadūta said: O ruler of men, it is not proper to offer a

throne to Lord Kṛṣṇa that has already been occupied by others. There is a lion throne called Jāmbunada that is decorated with celestial jewels and gold that was built by Viśvakarmā. This throne was specially made for the Lord and has been sent by Indra, the king of heaven. When Lord Kṛṣṇa, the master of the demigods and Lord of all moving and non-moving living entities, sits upon that throne, all of you should perform the coronation ceremony.

Text 31

āgatāḥ kuṇḍinagare
kanyāhetor narādhipāḥ
nāgamiṣyati yaḥ kaścit
so'sya vadhyo bhaviṣyati

Any king who has come to the city of Kuṇḍinapura hoping to obtain the princess as a wife that does not participate in the Lord's *abhiśeka* will certainly be killed by Him.

Texts 32-33

ime caivāṣṭa kaḷaśā
nidhī nāmaṁśa sambhavāḥ
akṣayā rājarājasya
dhaneśasya mahātmanaḥ

divyā kāñcana ratnāḍhyā
divyābharaṇayo nayaḥ
rājendrasya abhiṣekārtham
āgacchanti nṛpair vṛtāḥ

There are also eight inexhaustible pitchers that were produced from the ocean. These pitchers are filled with gold and jewels that were supplied by Kuvera, the treasurer of the demigods. We have also brought transcendental ornaments for the Lord. These pitchers and ornaments are to be used for the *abhiśeka* of Lord Kṛṣṇa.

Text 34

eṣa śakrasya saṁdeśaḥ
kathito vo narādhipāḥ
lekhenāhūya tān sarvān
abhiṣiñcantu keśavam

O rulers of men, I have thus conveyed the message of Indra to you. In accordance with his order, all of you should prepare to perform Lord Kṛṣṇa's *abhiśeka* with great pomp.

Text 35

kauśika uvāca
iti saṁcodya svastho'sau
devadūto gato divaṁ
dattvā 'sanaṁ ca kṛṣṇāya
bālārka sadṛśa prabham

Kauiśika said: After delivering these instructions of the king of heaven and handing over the throne as brilliant as the morning sun, which was specifically intended for Lord Kṛṣṇa, the Devadūta departed for the heavenly planets.

Text 36

tenāhaṁ nodayiṣyāmi
bhavadbhirye samāgatāḥ
durnivārya taraṁ ghoraṁ
śakrasya svayamī ritam

Now you can understand why I am urging all of you to perform Kṛṣṇa's *abhiṣeka*. It will be your great misfortune, bringing about many miseries, if you transgress this order of Indra, the king of heaven.

Texts 37-40

yuṣmābhir darśane yuktam
adbhutaṁ bhuvi durlabham
kalaśair abhiṣicyantaṁ
svayameva nabhastalāt

dṛṣṭvā'ścaryaṁ hi naḥ sarvān
dhruvaṁ pāpakṣayo bhavet
snāpanārthaṁ ca kṛṣṇāya
devadevāya viṣṇave

āgacchadhvaṁ nṛpaśreṣṭhā
na bhayaṁ kartumarhatha
āvayoḥ kṛtasandhāno
yuṣmadarthe janārdanaḥ

sarveṣāṁ majujendrāṇām
abhayaṁ kurute hariḥ
viśuddhabhāvaḥ kṛṣṇastu
āvayor dṛṣṭa tattvataḥ

Lord Kṛṣṇa's *abhiṣeka* will be performed with eight celestial pitchers pouring water from the heavens. This wonderful ceremony is extremely rarely seen on this earth. You should all take part in this ceremony, for by witnessing it, all of your sinful reactions will be vanquished. O exalted kings, it is my humble request that you all take part in the bathing ceremony of Lord Kṛṣṇa, the master of the demigods, understanding that He is non-different from Lord Viṣṇu. There is no need to be fearful. We will make peace with Kṛṣṇa for our own benefit, and in return He will certainly give us all protection. I have understood the transcendental qualities of the Lord and am convinced that He bears no enmity toward any of us.

Text 41

māgadhasya viśeṣeṇa
na vairaṁ hṛdi dṛśyate
yadatra kāraṇaṁ kāryaṁ
tad bhavadbhir vicintyatām

I am convinced that the Lord doesn't have even a tinge of enmity toward the king of Magadha, although he was His avowed enemy. Think over what I have said and then act as you wish.

Text 42

vaiśampāyana uvāca
evaṁ saṁcintayāmāsur
nṛpāḥ śāpa bhayārditāḥ
bhūyaḥ śuśruvu rājendrāḥ
keśavāya mahātmane

Vaiśampāyana said: After hearing this speech, the kings contemplated the matter in various ways, being fearful of becoming the object of a curse. Just then, a voice from the sky spoke to Kṛṣṇa within the hearing of all these kings.

Text 43

megha gambhīra nādena
svareṇā pūrayan nābhaḥ
vāguvācāsa rīreṇa
devarājasya śāsanāt

Conveying the order of the king of heaven, an unembodied voice spoke gravely, like the rumbling of clouds, filling all directions.

Text 44

citrāṅgada uvāca
trailokyādhi patiḥ śakraḥ
prajāpālana hetunā
ājñāpayati yuṣmākaṁ
nṛpāṇāṁ hitakāmyayā

Citrāṅgada said: For insuring the welfare of the inhabitants of the three worlds, Indra, the king of the demigods, has issued this order.

Text 45

na yuktaṁ vasatānyonyaṁ
kṛṣṇena saha vairiṇā
vasadhvaṁ prītim utpādya
svarāṣṭreṣu nṛpottamāḥ

O foremost kings, it is not suitable for you to maintain an inimical attitude toward Lord Kṛṣṇa. You should never be envious of Him. Indeed, you should give up all feelings of enmity towards one another and thus live peacefully in your kingdoms, without encroaching upon that which has been allotted to others.

Text 46

praṇatārti haraḥ kṛṣṇaḥ
pratisenāntako'nalaḥ
anena saha samprītyā
modadhvaṁ vigatajvarāḥ

Lord Kṛṣṇa is the destroyer of the distress of all those who take shelter of Him. On the other hand, for His enemies, He is as fearful as death personified or a blazing fire. You can all live peacefully if you simply cultivate friendship with Him.

Text 47

mānuṣāṇāṁ nṛpā devā
nṛpāṇāṁ devatāḥ surāḥ
surāṇāṁ devatā śakraḥ
śakrasyāpi janārdanaḥ

For his subjects, the king is like a demigod. For kings, the demigod are their objects of worship. Indra is the king of the demigods, and Lord Kṛṣṇa is the worshipable Lord of Indra.

Text 48

eṣa viṣṇuḥ prabhurdevo
devānāmapi daivatam
jāto'yaṁ mānuṣe loke
nararūpeṇa keśavaḥ

The Supreme Lord Viṣṇu is the worshipible Lord of all the demigods. Lord Keśava is Lord Viṣṇu, appearing in this mortal world in the form of a human being.

Text 49

ajeyaḥ sarvalokeṣū
devadānava mānavaiḥ
kārtikeya sahāyasya
api śūlabhṛtaḥ svayam

No demigod, demon, or human being within the three worlds can conquer Him. What to speak of others, even Śaṅkara, who carries a trident in his hand, or his son Kārtikeya, can conquer Him.

Text 50

tasmai devādhi devāya
keśavāya mahātmane
abhiṣektuṁ suraiḥ sārddhaṁ
kimiccheya mataḥ param

Therefore it is my desire, as well as the desire of all the demigods, that the Supreme Personality of Godhead, Lord Keśava, the master of the demigods, be installed as the king of Vidarbha. What could be more pleasing than this?

Text 51

na cādhikāro devānāṁ
rājendrasyābhi ṣecane
tenāhaṁ nābhiṣiñcāmi
sarvaloka namaskṛtam

However, no demigod or ordinary human being is allowed to perform the *abhiṣeka* to install Kṛṣṇa as the king of kings. Indeed, even I cannot perform the *abhiṣeka* of Lord Kṛṣṇa, the worshipable Lord of everyone.

Texts 52-56

nṛpāṇām adhikāro'yaṁ
rājendrasya niveśane
gatvā yūyaṁ vidarbhāyāṁ
krathakauśi kayoḥ saha

saṁcintya vidhidṛṣṭena
kurudhvaṁ nṛpasattamāḥ
prītisandhāna kālo'yam
iti saṁcintya vāsavaḥ

bodhanārthaṁ visṛṣṭo'haṁ
yusmākaṁ manujeśvarā
vidarbha nagare kṛṣṇaḥ
śrāvito'syādhi vāsanam

rājendratvabhi ṣekārthaṁ
rājānau krathakauśikau
tābhyāṁ saha nṛpaśreṣṭhaḥ
kṛtvā sumahad utsavam

abhiṣekeṇa satkṛtya
pratigṛhyāsya dakṣiṇam
āgamiṣyatha saṁdṛṣṭāḥ
punareva svayaṁvaram

O foremost kings, only a king is qualified to install another king as emperor. Therefore, you should all cooperate with the rulers of Vidarbha, Kratha and Kauśika, and perform the *abhiṣeka* of Lord Kṛṣṇa in accordance with the scriptural rules and regulations.

O kings, now is the time for you to make peace among yourselves. It is for this purpose that I had dispatched my messenger. Lord Kṛṣṇa is now within the kingdom of Vidarbha and all preparations for His *abhiṣeka* have been completed by Kratha and Kauśika. All of you should assist them and then circumambulate the Lord before entering the *svayamvara* arena.

Texts 57-59

jarāsandhaṁ sunīthaśca
rukmī caiva mahārathaḥ
śālvaḥ saubha patiścaiva
catvāro rājasattamāḥ
raṅgasyā śūnya hetorhi
tiṣṭhantu iha pārthivāḥ

vaiśampāyana uvāca
evamājñāṁ sureśasya
śrutvā citrāṅga deritām

gamanāya matiṁ cakruḥ
sarva eva nṛpottamāḥ
anujñātā narendreṇa
jarāsaṅdhena dhīmatā

So that the city may not be vacant, let these four principal kings—Jarāsaṅdha, Sunītha, Rukmī, and Śālva, the proprietor of the Saubha airplane—remain here.

Vaiśampāyana said: After hearing Citrāṅgada's announcement conveying the order of Indra, all the assembled kings agreed to participate in Lord Kṛṣṇa's *abhiṣeka.* The intelligent King Jarāsandha gave them permission to do so.

Texts 60-61

bhīṣmakaṁ purataḥ kṛtvā
prayātāḥ svabalair vṛtāḥ
bhīṣmakaśca mahābāhuḥ
svabalena samanvitaḥ

jagāma pārthivaiḥ sārddhaṁ
dahyamānena cetasā

yatra kṛṣṇo mahābāhuḥ
kauśikasya niveśane

Thereafter, all the kings led by Bhiṣmaka, along with their armies, went to the sacrificial arena. Mighty-armed Bhiṣmaka first went to the palace of Kauśika, where Lord Kṛṣṇa had set up camp. King Bhiṣmaka's heart was burning with anxiety due to thinking about his son's envious nature.

Text 62

dūrādeva prakāśantī
patākā dhvaja mālinī
śubhā deva sabhā ramyā
snāna hetor ihāgatā

At that time, the enchanting beautiful assembly hall of the demigods appeared on the earth for the *abhiṣeka* of Lord Kṛṣṇa. It was self-illuminating and decorated with colorful flags and varieties of auspicious articles.

Text 63

divyaratna prabhākīrṇā
divyadhvaja samākulā
divyāmbara patākāḍhyā
divyābharaṇa bhūṣitā

That celestial hall shone brilliantly because of the precious jewels that were everywhere to be seen. Many beautiful colorful flags flapped in the breeze. The entire arena was decorated as gorgeously as possible.

Text 64

divyasrag dāma kalilā
divya gandhādhi vāsitā
vimānayānaiḥ śrī madbhiḥ
samantāt parivāritā

Flower garlands had been hung, practically covering the entire place. The atmosphere at assembly hall thus carried a very sweet fragrance. Everywhere demigods could be seen in their celestial airplanes.

Texts 65-66

divyāpsaro gaṇāścaiva
vidyādhara gaṇāstathā
gandharvā manuyaścaiva
kinnarāśca samantataḥ

upagāyanti deveśam
ambarāntaram āśritāḥ
stuvanti munayaścaiva
siddhāśca paramarṣayaḥ

Apsarās, Vidyādharas, Gandharvas, Siddhas, great sages, and Kinnaras sang the glories of Lord Kṛṣṇa, the master of the demigods, while traveling in their airplanes.

Texts 67-83

devadundu bhayaścaiva
svayamevā nadan divi
pañcayoni samutthāni
gandhacūrṇānya nekaśaḥ

samantāt pātyamānāni
cākāśasthair divaukasaiḥ
svayamāgatya devendro
devaiḥ saha śacīpatiḥ

vimāna varam āruhya
saprakāśaḥ sthito'mbare
aṣṭau ye loka pālāste
svāsu dikṣu samāsthitāḥ

upagāyanti nṛtyanti
stuvanti ca samantataḥ
śrutvā sutu mulaṁ nādaṁ
sarva eva narādhipāḥ

vismayot phulla nayanā
viviśuste sabhāṁ śubhām
kauśikaśca mahābāhu
rupagamya narādhipān

praveśayā māsa balī
pratipūjya yathāvidhi
nivedite suraśreṣṭhe
pārthivānāṁ samāgame

nirjagāma hariḥ śrīmān
sarvamaṅgala pūjitaḥ
tato'mbara sthāste divyāḥ
kalaśāścaila kāṇṭhinaḥ

sahakāra samāyuktā
vavarṣur jaladā iva
divya kāñcana ratnaughair
divyapuṣpa samanvitaiḥ

gandhacūrṇa vimiśraiśca
rājendrasya abhiṣecane
yathokta vidhi pūrveṇa
abhiṣicya janārdanam

darśayitvā narendrāṇāṁ
divyair āvaraṇaiḥ śubhaiḥ
divyāmvara vicitraiśca
divyamālyānu lepanaiḥ

satkṛtya vidhivadrājña
upaviṣṭo janārdanaḥ
śubhe devasabhe ramye
snānahetor ihāgate

upāsyamāno yadubhir
vidarbhaiśca narādhipaiḥ
vainateyaśca balavān
kāmarūpī narākṛtiḥ

dakṣiṇaṁ pārśva māśritya
āsanasyo mahābalaḥ
krathaśca kāuśiko vīro
vāmapārśve tathāsane

upaviṣṭau mahātmānau
devasyānu mate nṛpau
tathaiva vāma pārśve tu
vṛṣṇyandhaka mahārathāḥ

sātyaki pramukhā vīrā
upaviṣṭā mahābalāḥ
bhāskara pratime divye
divyāstarana vistṛte

sukhopaviṣṭaṁ śrīmantaṁ
devairiva śacīpatim
sacivaiḥ śrāvitāḥ sarve
praviṣṭāste narādhipāḥ

yathārheṇa ca sampūjya
rājānaḥ sarva eva te
sukhopaviṣṭāste sveṣu
āsaneṣu narādhipāḥ

In the sky was heard the sound of drums. From their airplanes, the demigods showered fragrant powder. Indra then appeared overhead, along with Śacī, surrounded by all the demigods so that everyone could see him. The eight *loka-pālas* danced in the different directions while offering prayers to the Supreme Lord. Upon hearing the sound of the celestial singing with musical accompaniment, the eyes of the assembled kings blossomed with wonder.

Thereafter, all the kings entered the celestial assembly hall, being greeted by King Kauśika. When news of kings' arrival was conveyed to the Supreme Lord, He also made His entrance. After He was worshiped by the assembled kings, the eight inexhaustible pitchers, which were decorated with fine cloth, gold and jeweled ornaments, fragrant flowers, and mango twigs, began pouring scented water upon the Supreme Lord Hari. Thus, the *abhiṣeka* ceremony of the Supreme Lord was performed with great pomp, in accordance with the rules and regulations prescribed in the scriptures.

After being bathed, the Lord was dressed in attractive garments and valuable ornaments. He was then smeared with sandalwood paste and offered a garland of forest flowers. At the conclusion of the *abhiṣeka*, all the assembled kings were also worshiped with due respect. Finally, Lord Kṛṣṇa was comfortably seated upon a brightly shining throne, surrounded by the members of the Yadu dynasty and the kings of Vidarbha. The Lord's carrier, the greatly powerful Garuḍa, who is capable of assuming any form at will, also came there and sat on an *āsana* placed to the right of the Lord.

By the order of the Lord, the two kings, Kratha and Kauśika, took their seats to the left of the Lord, as did many powerful warriors of the Vṛṣṇi and Andhaka dynasties, headed by Satyakī. Thus the greatly effulgent Lord Kṛṣṇa appeared like Indra, the husband of Śacī, surrounded by all the demigods. After worshiping Lord Kṛṣṇa once again, all of the assembled kings took their seats.

Text 84

kaiśikastu mahāprajñaḥ
sarvaśāstrārtha vittamaḥ
pūjayitvā yathānyāyam
uvāca vadatāṁ varaḥ

After the worship of Lord Kṛṣṇa, when everyone was seated, the saintly King Kauśika, foremost of eloquent speakers well-versed in all the scriptures, began to speak.

Text 85

kauśika uvāca
avijñātā nṛpāḥ sarve
mānuṣo'yamiti prabho
bhavantam uparuddhānāṁ
deva tvaṁ kṣantum arhasi

Kauśika said: O almighty Lord, until recently all these kings were under the misconception that You are an ordinary human being. Because of this, they have certainly committed a grave offense. Now that they have rectified their mistake, however, I request You to kindly forgive them.

Texts 86-88

śrī kṛṣṇa uvāca
na me vairaṁ pravasati
ekāham api kauśika
viśeṣeṇa narendrāṇāṁ
kṣatradharme'vatiṣṭhatām

yoddhavyam iti dharmeṇa
adharme tu parāṅmukhe
teṣāṁ kiṁhetunā kopaḥ
kartavyas tvavanīśvarāḥ

yadgataṁ tadati kṛantaṁ
ye mṛtāste divaṁ gatāḥ
eṣa dharmo nṛloke'smiñ
jāyante ca mriyanti ca

Lord Kṛṣṇa said: My dear Kauśika, I do not feel enmity towards anyone, not even for a moment. Why should I be displeased with kings who are fixed in the principles of *kṣatriya* dharma, who engage in battle as a religious duty, and who are very careful to avoid sinful activities. O rulers of the earth, whatever has happened cannot be reversed. Those who have died on the battlefield have gone to the heavenly planets. This is the law of *karma* in this mortal world, where all living entities are subject to birth and death.

Text 89

tasmād aśocyaṁ bhavatāṁ
mṛtārthe ca narādhipāḥ

kṣantavyaṁ rocate'smākaṁ
vītavairā bhavantu te

O kings, there is no need to lament for those who have died on the battlefield. As for enmity, you should know that forgiveness is the finest ornament for an intelligent person. Therefore, give up your envious nature and try to live with one another in harmony.

Text 90

vaiśampāya uvāca
evamuktvā narendrāṁstān
āśvāsya madhusūdanaḥ
kaiśikasya mukhaṁ vīkṣya
virarāma mahādyutiḥ

Vaiśampāyana said: After giving assurances to all the kings present in that assembly, Lord Madhusūdana finished speaking while looking at King Kauśika.

Text 91

etasmin neva kāle tu
bhīṣmako nayakovidaḥ
pūjayitvā yathanyāyam
uvāca vadatāṁ varaḥ

Taking this opportunity, King Bhīṣmaka, who was a foremost political strategist and very convincing orator, began speaking after mentally offering obeisances to Lord Kṛṣṇa.

Thus ends the translation of the fiftieth chapter of the Viṣṇu Parva of Śrī Harivaṁsa.

Chapter 51

Conversation between Lord Kṛṣṇa and King Bhīṣmaka. Departure of Lord Kṛṣṇa for Mathurā.

Text 1

bhīṣmaka uvāca
putro me bālabhāvena
bhaginīṁ dātum icchati
svayaṁvare narendrāṇaṁ
ca cāhaṁ dātum utsahe

Bhiṣmaka said: My dear Lord, my foolish and restless son, Rukmī, insists that his sister marry one of the kings who are present in this *svayamvara* arena.

Text 2

atīva bāla bhāvatvād
dātumicchen matirmama
ekāhi ekaṁ samālokya
varayiṣyati me matiḥ

This is not at all my desire. It is my conviction that You alone are the suitable husband for my beloved daughter.

Text 3

ataḥ prasādayiṣye tvāṁ
putradur nayahetunā
prasādaṁ kuru deveśa
kṣantum arhasi me prabho

My dear Lord, master of the demigods, I consider myself to be an offender because of my son's misbehavior. My only desire is to please You and so kindly be merciful to me and forgive my offenses.

Text 4

śrī kṛṣṇa uvāca
bālabhāvena putreṇa
cālitaṁ nṛpamaṇḍalam
yadā bhavati vaiu prauḍhaḥ
kīḍṛśo'vinayo bhavet

Lord Kṛṣṇa said: Your son is still quite young and yet he has created a lot of mischief. Just imagine how troublesome he will become when he is a fully mature ruler of men.

Texts 5-6

sūryendu sadṛśāṁ lokāṁs
tapaso pārjitaśriyaḥ
loke'smin naradevānāṁ
mahākula samudbhavān

ekasyāpi nṛpasyāgre
mohād yo vitathaṁ badet
na sa tiṣṭhati loke'smin
nirdahed daṇḍavahninā

One who purposely speaks untruthfully in the presence of a king will never be able to attain the heavenly planets, which are effulgent like the sun and moon and which are achieved by performing severe austerities. Such an untruthful person has uselessly taken birth in a noble family, a birth that is generally attained by the performance of sacrifice. Even in this life, he will not be able to live peacefully.

Text 7

eṣa dharmo narendrāṇām
iti te viditaṁ prabho
lokadharmaṁ puraskṛtya
purā gītaṁ svayambhuvā

It is the duty of a king to always speak the truth and all of you know this very well. This is the principle that was laid down by Lord Brahmā at the beginning of creation.

Text 8

kathaṁ tava sutasteṣām
agrato majujeśvara
vaktum arhati rājendra
vitathaṁ rājasaṁsadi

O foremost ruler of men, how could your son dare to speak falsely in this assembly of learned kings? How could your son dare to act in a way that does not have your approval?

Text 9

tādṛśaṁ raṅgam atulaṁ
kārayaṁs tanayas tava
kathaṁ tvaya hyavijñāta
iti me saṁśayo mahān

Your son is preparing to do something extraordinary during this *svayamvara* of Your daughter. How can you say that you don't know what he intends to do? This is the great doubt I have in My mind.

Text 10

āgatānāṁ narerndrāṇām
analokendu varcasām
yathārheṇa tu sampūjya
ātithyaṁ kṛtavānasi

Many kings as powerful as the fire, sun, and moon have arrived here, and you have welcomed them all with great respect. How can you claim to be ignorant of what your son is planning?

Text 11

rathāśva naranāgānāṁ
vimardam atulaṁ tathā
kathaṇ na jñātavān rājaṁs
tava putrasya ceṣṭitam

Many chariots, horses, elephants and infantry soldiers have recently been destroyed. Know for certain that this is due to the evil motive of your son. How can you say that you don't know of this?

Text 12

viṣādo na bhaved atra
caturaṅga balāgame
kathaṁ na jñāte rājann
iti me buddhi saṁśayaḥ

O King, wherever there are soldiers, weapons, and enmity,

there will certainly be war and ultimately, great lamentation. Do you not know this? For this reason, My intelligence is filled with doubt.

Text 13

mamāgamanam eveha
prāyeṇa na hitaṁ tava
ato na kṛtamātithyam
apātrāya nareśvara

O master of human society, You thought that My presence here would not benefit you in any way. That is why you did not properly greet Me, thinking Me to be an unsuitable husband for your daughter.

Text 14

pātrebhyo dīyatāṁ kanyā
māmapāsya nareśvara
mamāgamana doṣeṇa
kathaṁ kanyāṁ na dāsyase

If it is your desire, you can give your daughter in charity to any of the kings present here. Just because of My presence here, you need not hesitate to give your daughter to whoever you find most suitable.

Text 15

kanyāvighnaṁ ca kurvāṇo
narake paripacyate
iti dharma vidair gītaṁ
manvādibhir narottamaiḥ

It is said that a person who puts obstacles on the path of a girl's marriage will be burnt by fire in hell. This is the verdict of great personalities like Manu, who are the best knowers of religious principles.

Text 16

ator'thaṁ na praviṣṭo'haṁ
raṅgamadhye viśāmpate
viditvā nakṛtā tithyaṁ
naradeva tavālayam

It is for this reason that I didn't enter the *svayamvara* arena until invited. I had understood that your family is not very conversant with the etiquette for honoring guests.

Text 17

hiyābhi bhūto rājendra
pārthivo'haṁ narādhipa
vidarbha nagare rājan
balaviśrāma hetunā

My dear King, I hesitated to set up camp for My army near your capital of Vidarbha. I was sure that if I came uninvited, all that I would have received was insults.

Text 18

āvābhyāṁ kṛtamātithyaṁ
kauśikastu priyātithiḥ
uṣitau ca yathā svarge
purā garuḍa keśavau

And yet, My carrier, Garuḍa, and I have been nicely welcomed and worshiped by King Kauśika, who is very expert in honoring guests. We reside at his palace very happily, just as we do in the abode of Vaikuṇṭha.

Text 19

vaiśampāyana uvāca
evameva bruvāṇaṁ tu
kṛṣṇaṁ vāgvajra coditam
ślakṣṇa vācāmbunā'sicya
śamito'gnir iva jvalan

Vaiśampāyana said: After Lord Kṛṣṇa finished speaking these thundering words, thus revealing His mind, King Bhīṣmaka spoke to pacify Him with a shower of nectar.

Text 20

bhīṣmaka uvāca
prasīda devalokeśa
pāhi māṁ lokaścāsana
ajñāna tama sāviṣṭaṁ
jñānacakṣuḥ prado bhava

Bhīṣmaka said: O Lord of the demigods, please be kind to me, who has fallen into the dark well of material existence. Kindly dispel my darkness with the torchlight of knowledge so that I can see things as they are.

Text 21

mānuṣye māṁsa cakṣuṣ ṭvāda
samyag viditā vayam

na prasiddhayanti karmāṇi
kriyatāma avicāraṇāt

Although I have attained the rare human form of life, my vision is clouded by the material conception of life so that my intelligence is not pure. It is for this reason that I am always baffled in my attempts to rise above the darkness of ignorance.

Text 22

bhavantaṁ śaraṇaṁ prāpya
devānāmapi daivatam
samyag bhavatu me dṛṣṭiḥ
sampaśyantu ca me kriyāḥ

I have taken shelter of You, the Lord of creation, and so kindly award me transcendental knowledge and the perfection of all my activities.

Text 23

aniṣpannām api kriyāṁ
nayopetāṁ vicakṣaṇāḥ
phaladāṁ hi prakurvanti
mahāsenā patiryathā

Just as the commander-in-chief can train a neophyte soldier to become a valiant warrior, one who is expert can instruct anyone how to make all of his activities glorious and beneficial.

Text 24

bhavantaṁ śaraṇaṁ prāpya
nāti bādhati me bhayam

yanmayā cintitaṁ kārayaṁ
tad bhavācchrotum arhati

Because I have taken shelter at Your lotus feet, I no longer have anything to fear. Kindly hear my proposal, which I think You will approve of.

Text 25

na dātum icche kanyāṁ vai
pārthivebhyaḥ svayaṁvare
prasādaṁ kuru deveśa
na kopaṁ kartum arhasi

I do not want to give my daughter in charity to any of the kings present in this *svayamvara* arena. Please be merciful to me and withdraw Your anger.

Text 26

śrī kṛṣṇa uvāca
vacanena kimuktena
tvayā rājan mahāmate
svakanyāṁ dāsyase neti
ko'tra netā tavānagha

Lord Kṛṣṇa said: O sinless king, I think you have spoken to camouflage the actual truth. Why speak in a duplicitous manner? Who can stop you from giving your daughter to whoever you please?

Text 27

mā dehīti na cākhyeyaṁ
dadasveti na me vacaḥ

rukmiṇyā divyamūrtitvaṁ
sambandhe kāraṇaṁ mama

Still, if you understand the truth, you will see that it would be improper to give your daughter to anyone other than Me. Rukmiṇī is not an ordinary girl, she is a celestial goddess. That exalted qualification is what makes her obliged to become My consort.

Texts 28-29

merukūṭe purā devaiḥ
kṛtamaṁśāva tāraṇam
tadā nisṛṣṭā śrīḥ pūrvaṁ
gaccha tvaṁ patinā saha

mānuṣye kuṇḍinagare
bhīṣmakasyāṅga nodare
jāyasva vipulaśroṇi
pratyavekṣya ca vāsavam

Long ago, as the demigods were assembled on the peak of Mount Sumeru, they were ordered to appear as plenary portions upon the earth, to assist Me in My incarnation. At that time Brahmā instructed Lakṣmī: O Devī, you should accompany your husband by taking birth at Kuṇḍinapura from the womb of King Bhiṣmaka's wife.

Texts 30-31

tenāhaṁ vaḥ pravakṣyāmi
rājanna kṛtakaṁ vacaḥ
śrutvā svayaṁ viniścitya
yad yuktaṁ tat kariṣyati

rukmiṇī nāma te kanyā
na sā prākṛta mānuṣī
śrī reṣā brahma vākyena
jātā kenapi hetunā

O King, rest assured that I speak truthfully and without any tinge of duplicity. You should convey My message to your daughter, Rukmiṇī, informing her that she in non-different from Lakṣmī-devī, and not an ordinary human being, having appeared in your family at the request of Brahmā. Then she can do what she feels is best.

Text 32

na ca sā manujendrāṇāṁ
svayaṁvara vidhikṣamā
ekā tvekāya dātavyā
iti dharmo vyavasthitaḥ

With this understanding, you can see that it is not proper for you to give your daughter to any of the kings that have assembled at this *svayamvara* arena. It is the injunction of the scriptures that it is the duty of a father to give his daughter in marriage to a suitable husband.

Text 33

na ca tāṁ śakyase rājaṁ
lakṣmīṁ dātuṁ svayaṁvare
sadṛśaṁ varamālokya
dātum arhasi dharmataḥ

How could you have the audacity to give Lakṣmī-devī in marriage to an ordinary human being at this *svayambara*?

Consider the matter carefully and then give your daughter to an actually suitable husband, according to the prescribed rules and regulations governing marriage.

Text 34

ato'rthaṁ vainateyo'yaṁ
vighnakāraṇa hetunā
āgataḥ kuṇḍī nagare
devarājena coditaḥ

You should also know that Indra, the king of the demigods, dispatched Garuḍa, the son of Vinatā, to the city of Kuṇḍinapura to obstruct any injustice done at this *svayamvara.*

Text 35

ahaṁ caivāgato rājñāṁ
draṣṭukāmo mahotsavam
tāṁ ca kanyāṁ varārohāṁ
padmena rahitāṁ śriyam

As for Me, I have come here simply to take part in this great festival, witness the great assembly of kings, and gaze upon the beautiful lotus-like face of your daughter, Rukmiṇī.

Text 36

kṣantavyam iti yat proktaṁ
tvayā rājan mamāgrataḥ
yukti pūrvamahaṁ manye
kaluṣāya na pārthiva

O King, if you feel that you have been an offender, then it

is appropriate that you have begged for forgiveness. Rest assured that you have nothing to lament over.

Text 37

pūrvameva mayā'khyātaṁ
yenāsmi viṣaye tava
āgataḥ saumya rūpeṇa
tenaiva kṣāntavān vibho

As I had assured you earlier, I have not come here as an enemy. As your eternal well-wisher, I have certainly forgiven you for any offense you may have committed.

Text 38

kṣānteṣu guṇābāhulyaṁ
doṣāpa haraṇaṁ kṣamā
kathamasma dvidhe rājan
kuluṣo vavsate hṛdi

Elevated souls possess all good qualities, headed by forgiveness. Indeed, one who is forgiving has certainly nullified all of his faults. How can enviousness remain in the mind of a forgiving person?

Text 39

kulaje sattva sampanne
dharmajñe satyavādini
bhavādṛśe kathaṁ rājan
kuluṣo bhuvi vartate

My dear king, you were born in an exalted family, you

possess all good qualities, you very well know the principles of religion, and you are fixed in truthfulness. Considering this, how can any tinge of enviousness remain in your heart?

Text 40

kṣānto'yam iti mantavyaṁ
mama senā sahāgatam
na cāhaṁ senayā sārddhaṁ
yāsyāmi ripu vāhinīm

I have not come here with my army and so you should understand that My intentions are not inimical. When I approach My enemies to fight, I am always accompanied by My vast army.

Text 41

akṣāntaś cārisenāyāṁ
yāsyāmi dvijavāhane
sthitaḥ somārka saṁkāśān
āyudhāni karair vahan

Whenever I attack My enemies on the battlefield, being enraged, I sit on the back of my carrier, Garuḍa, carrying My effulgent weapons, such as the *cakra*.

Text 42

mānyo'smākaṁ tvayā rājan
vayasā ca pitā samaḥ
pālayasva purīṁ samyak
kṣatreṣu pitṛvad vasa

O King, I consider the father to be most worshipable, and

I am just like your son. Like a good father, maintain your subjects, for by doing so, you will earn the respect of all the *kṣatriyas*.

Text 43

kaluṣo nāma rājendra
vaset kāpuruṣeṣu vai
śūreṣu śuddhabhāveṣu
kaluṣo vasate katham

O foremost of kings, only cowards are possessed of sinful and envious mentalities. How can such debased qualities remain in the magnanimous heart of a great personality?

Text 44

jānīdhvameṣā me vṛttiḥ
putreṣu pitṛvad vayam
imāvapi ca rājānau
vidarbha nagarādhipau

As the Supreme Personality of Godhead, I am neutral toward all, without favoritism or malice. Whether one is a child or a father, My behavior toward him is the same. You should understand this very well. King Kratha and Kauśika, as My sincere devotees, are conversant with this understanding.

Text 45

ātithya kareṇe'smākaṁ
svarājyaṁ dadatābubhau
tena dāna phalenāsya
daśapūrvā divaṁ gatāḥ

They have not only treated Me as a guest of honor, but they have surrendered their portions of the kingdom to Me. Because of this gift of charity, seven generations of their families are now residing in the heavenly planets.

Text 46

bhaviṣyāścaiva rājānaḥ
putrapautrā daśāvarāḥ
te'pi tatraiva yāsyanti
devalokaṁ narādhipāḥ

Ten future generations of their families, including their sons and grandsons, will also attain heavenly destinations after death as a result of this perfect distribution of charity.

Text 47

anayoḥ suciraṁ kālaṁ
bhuktvā rājyam akaṇṭakam
yadābhilāṣo mokṣasya
yāsyete nirvṛtiṁ sukham

King Kratha and Kauśika will continue to enjoy their kingdom without any hindrance. Later on, when they desire liberation from material existence, they will attain the supremely blissful abode of the Supreme Lord.

Text 48

narendrāśca mahābhāgā
ye'bhi ṣecitum āgatāḥ
kālena te'pi yāsyanti
devalokaṁ triviṣṭapam

All of these fortunate kings who assembled to participate in My *abhiṣeka* will attain the abodes of the demigods in due course of time.

Text 49

svasti vo'stu gamiṣyāmi
vainateya sahāyavān
ṇagarīṁ mathurāṁ ramyāṁ
bhojarājena pālitām

May you achieve auspiciousness. I will soon return to the beautiful city of Mathurā, which is ruled by the king of the Bhojas, Ugrasena, riding upon the back of Garuda.

Texts 50-58

vaiśampāyana uvāca
evamuktvā tu rājānaṁ
bhīṣmakaṁ yadunandanaḥ
rājñaścaivam upāmantrya
vaidarbhābhyāṁ veśeṣataḥ

sabhānniṣkamya deveśa
jagāma rathamantikam
tataḥ prahṛṣṭo rājarṣir
bhīṣmakaḥ kila keśavam

te sarve ca mahīpālā
viṣaṇṇa vadanā bhavan
ādyaṁ svāyam bhuvaṁ
rūpaṁ surāsura namaskṛtam

sahasrapāt sāhasrākṣaṁ
sahasrabhuja vigraham

sahasraśirasaṁ devaṁ
sahasra mukuṭojjvalam

divyamālyāmbara dharaṁ
divyagandhānu lepanam
divyābharaṇa saṁyuktaṁ
divya anekodyatā yudham

kṛṣṇaṁ raktāra vindākṣaṁ
candrasūryāgni locanam
dṛṣṭvā sa rājā rājendraṁ
praṇipatya kṛtāñjaliḥ

vāḍmanaḥ kāya saṁyuktaṁ
stotumārabdha vāṁstadā

bhīṣmaka uvāca
devadeva namastubhyam
anādinidhayāna vai
śāśvatāyādidevāya
nārāyaṇa parāyaṇa
svayambhuve ca viśvāya
sthāṇave vedhasāya ca

padmanābhāya jaṭine
daṇḍine piṅgalāya ca
haṁsaprabhāya haṁsāya
cakrarūpāya vai namaḥ

Vaiśampāyana said: After speaking to Bhiṣmaka and taking permission to depart from the assembled kings, Lord Kṛṣṇa, the descendent of Yadu, left the assembly hall, accompanied by Kratha and Kauśika. King Bhīṣmaka then hurriedly came and fell at the lotus feet of lotus-eyed Lord Kṛṣṇa, the original cause of all causes, the worshipable Lord of the demigods and demons, who has thousands of arms, legs, and eyes, and whose form is all-attractive, being decorated with a beautiful garland of forest flowers and smeared with sandalwood paste. His eyes are the sun and moon, and He holds in His hands His transcendental weapons.

King Bhīṣmaka, having surrendered his body, mind, and speech unto the Supreme Lord, stood up and with folded hands began to glorify Him, saying: O Lord, please accept my obeisances. You are the original Lord Nārāyaṇa, without beginning or end, and thus You are the shelter of this cosmic manifestation. You are the original Supreme Personality of Godhead. You are Brahmā, You are the universal form, You are Mahādeva, and You are Lord Padmanābha. Sometimes You wear matted hair, carrying a stick in Your hand, having a golden complexion. You are the swan-like personality, the Haṁsa incarnation, and You are the wielder of the *cakra*. I offer my obeisances unto you.

Text 59

vaikuṇṭhāya namastasmai
ajāya paramātmane
sadasad bhāva yuktāya
purāṇa puruṣāya ca

You are the Lord of Vaikuṇṭha, the Supersoul of all living entities. I offer my obeisances unto You. You do not entertain the duality of matter and spirit. You are the primeval Lord. I offer my obeisances unto You.

Texts 60-65

puruṣottamāya yuktāya
nirguṇāya namo'stu te

varado bhava me nityaṁ
tvadbhaktāya surottama

lokanātho'si nātha tvaṁ
viṣṇustvaṁ viditātmanām
vaiśampāyana uvāca
evaṁ stutvā mahādevaṁ
nṛpāṇām agrato nṛpaḥ

ṃahārha maṇimuktābhir
vajra vaidūrya hāsinam
śāta kumbhasya nicayaṁ
kṛṣṇāya pradadau nṛpaḥ

punaścakre namaskāraṁ
vainateye mahābale

bhīṣmaka uvāca
namastasmai khagendrāya
namo māruta raṁhase
kāmarūpāya divyāya
kāśyapāya ca vai namaḥ

vaiśampāyana uvāca
iti saṁkṣepataḥ stutvā
satkṛtya varabhūṣaṇaiḥ
tato visarjayāmāsa
kṛṣṇaṁ kamala locanam
anujagmur nṛpāścaiva
prasthitaṁ vāsavānujam

You are the master of all mystic powers and the Supreme Lord, residing within the hearts of all living entities. My dear Supreme Lord, I am Your surrendered soul and I pray for Your mercy. You are the protector of the universe and You are the all-pervading Brahman sought by empiric philosophers.

Vaiśampāyana said: After offering these prayers to Lord Kṛṣṇa, whose effulgence defeats the luster of precious jewels, pearls, and coral, in the presence of the assembled kings, Bhīṣmaka offered the Lord a vast quantity of gold. He then offered his obeisances to the son of Vinatā.

Bhīṣmaka said: I offer my repeated obeisances unto the son of Kaśyapa, the king of birds, Garuḍa, who travels through the sky faster than the wind, who can assume any form at will, and whose form is transcendental.

Vaiśampāyana said: After glorifying Garuda, King Bhīṣmaka pleased him with gifts of many valuable ornaments. Finally, he bade farewell to lotus-eyed Lord Kṛṣṇa. After the departure of Lord Kṛṣṇa, many kings also prepared to return to their abodes.

Texts 66-69

pratigṛhya ca satkāraṁ
nṛpānāmantrya vīryavān
jagāma mathurāṁ kṛṣṇo
dyotayāno diśo daśa

vainateyaṁ puraskṛtya
saumyarūpaṁ khagottamam
mahatā rathavṛndena
parivārya samantataḥ

bherī paṭaha nādena
śaṅkha dundubhi niḥsvanaiḥ
vṛṁhitena ca nāgānāṁ
hayānāṁ heṣitena ca

siṁhanādena śūrāṇāṁ
rathanemi svanena ca

tumulaḥ sumahā nāsīn
mahāmeghara vopamaḥ

Supremely powerful Lord Kṛṣṇa bade farewell to all the kings after being worshiped by them. Then He proceeded towards the city of Mathurā, along with Garuḍa, the son of Vinatā, whose form is very beautiful to behold, riding upon a chariot. Lord Kṛṣṇa was surrounded by many chariots, and His presence was heralded by the sounds of drums, horns and conch shells. The combined tumultuous sound made by the elephants and horses, the roaring of the warriors, and the rumbling of the chariot wheels, was like the thundering of clouds.

Text 70

gate kṛṣṇe mahāvīrye
ādāya varamāsanam
sabhāmādāya devāśca
prayayustri daśālayam

After Lord Kṛṣṇa left Kuṇḍīnapura, the demigods returned to their heavenly abodes, along with the wonderful assembly hall they had brought.

Texts 71 & 72

mahatā caturaṅgeṇa
balena parivāritāḥ
krośamātram upavrajya
anujñāte janārdane

prayuste nṛpāḥ sarve
punarave svayaṁvaram

All the assembled kings, taking with them their four divisions of soldiers, followed Lord Kṛṣṇa for about two miles and then returned to the arena of the *svayamvara* after receiving the Lord's permission.

Thus ends the translation of the fifty-first chapter of the Viṣṇu Parva of Śri Harivaṁsa.

Chapter 52

Bhiṣmaka's glorification of Lord Kṛṣṇa and replies by Śālva and Jarāsandha

Text 1

vaiśampāyana uvāca
tataḥ prayāte vasudevaputre
narādhipā bhūṣaṇa bhūṣitāṅgāḥ
sabhāṁ samājgmuḥ surendrakalpāḥ
prabhodhanārthaṁ gamanotsavāste

Vaiśampāyana said: After the departure of Lord Kṛṣṇa, all the kings decorated themselves very gorgeously so that they appeared like Indra, the king of heaven. Coming before King Bhiṣmaka, who was morose on account of Kṛṣṇa's absence, they spoke in an attempt to console him.

Text 2

sabhāgatān somaravi prakāśān
sukhopaviṣṭān rucirāsaneṣu
samīkṣya rājā sunayārthavādī
jagāda vākyaṁ nararāja siṁhaḥ

All the kings, who were as brilliant as the sun or moon, went and sat down comfortably in the arena of the *svayamvara.* At that time, King Bhiṣmaka, who was powerful like a lion and a very expert logician, addressed them as follows.

Text 3

svayaṁvara kṛtaṁ doṣaṁ
viditvā vo narādhipāḥ
kṣantavyo mama vṛddasya
durdagdhasya phalodayam

O rulers of men, I had tried my best to dispel any doubts regarding the motives for Lord Kṛṣṇa's coming here. I hope that you will forgive me for any offenses I may have committed. How could one expect to get fruit from a tree that was burnt by a forest fire? How could this *svayamvara* be successful if it is performed in a mood of aversion to the Supreme Lord?

Text 4

vaiśampāyana uvāca
evamābhāṣya tān sarvān
satkṛtya ca yathāvidhi
tato visarjayāmāsa
nṛpāṁstān madhyadeśajān

Vaiśampāyana said: When he finished speaking, Bhiṣmaka very respectfully bid farewell to the assembled kings, some of whom resided toward the east, some toward the west, and some in the middle provinces.

Text 5

pūrvapaścima jāṁścaiva
uttarā pathikānapi
ye'pi sarve maheṣvāsāḥ
prahṛṣṭa manaso narāḥ

All of the great kings were very pleased by the hospitality provided them by Bhiṣmaka. They exchange greetings with each other and then departed for their respective kingdoms.

Texts 6-12

yathārheṇa ca sampūjya
jagmuste narapuṅgavāḥ
jarāsandhaḥ sunīthaśca
dantavaktraśca vīryavān

śālvaḥ saubha patiścaiva
mahākūrmaśca pārthivaḥ
kratha kaiśika mukhyāśca
nṛpāḥ pravaravaṁśajāḥ

veṇudāriśca rājarṣiḥ
kāśmīrādhi patistathā
ete cānye ca bahavo
dakṣiṇā pathikā nṛpāḥ

śrotukāmā raho vākyaṁ
sthitā vai bhīṣmakāntike
tān vai samīkṣya rājendraḥ
sa rājā bhīṣmako bale

snehapūrṇena manasā
sthitāṁs tāna vanīśvarān
trivargashitaṁ ślakṣṇaṁ
ṣaḍguṇālaṁ kṛtaṁ śubham
uvāca nayasampannaṁ
snigdha gambhīrayā girā

bhīṣmaka uvāca
bhavatām avanīśānāṁ
samālokya nayānvitam

vacanaṁ vyāhṛtaṁ śrutvā
kṛtavān kāryamīḍṛśam
sadbhir bhavadbhiḥ kṣantavyaṁ
vayaṁ nityā parādhinaḥ

However, some of the kings, including Jarāsandha, Sunītha, Dantavakra, Śālva who commands the Saubha airplane, Mahākurma, Kratha, Kauśika, Veṇudārī, the king of Kaśmira, and many others from South India, remained at Kuṇḍīnapura, desiring to hear Bhiṣmaka speak on confidential subject matters.

One day, Bhiṣmaka, the foremost of saintly kings, began speaking in a sweet yet grave voice about religiosity, economic development, and sense gratification, as well as the six methods of diplomacy.

Bhiṣmaka said: My dear kings, I greatly respect all of you, as well your opinions. I find that your words are always most reasonable. All of you are very pious kings, and so I hope that you tolerated my recent behavior without feeling hatred toward me. I considered myself to be a great offender.

Text 13

vaiśampāya uvāca
evamuktvā tu rājā sa
bhīṣmako nayakovidaḥ
uvāca sutam uddiśya
vacanaṁ rājasaṁsadi

Vaiśampāyana said: As he continued to speak at great length, the very expert and intelligent Bhiṣmaka continuously remembered the behavior of his son.

Text 14

bhīṣmaka uvāca
putrasya ceṣṭām ālokya
trāsā kulita locanaḥ
manye bālā nimāṁ lokān
sa eṣā puruṣaḥ paraḥ

Bhiṣmaka said: My dear kings, my eyes become filled with fear when they see the foolish endeavors of my son. I still consider Rukmī to still be a child, devoid of any proper sense of discrimination. In my estimation, Lord Kṛṣṇa is the Supreme Personality of Godhead.

Text 15

kīrtiḥ kīrtimatāṁ śreṣṭho
yaśaśca vipulaṁ tathā
sthāpitaṁ bhuvi martye'smin
svabāhu balamūrjitam

Lord Kṛṣṇa is the most glorious of all exalted personalities. He has firmly established Himself as the most worshipable person in this world by exhibiting His inconceivable potency.

Texts 16-17

dhanyā khalu mahābhāgā
devakī yoṣitāṁ varā
putraṁ tribhuvana śreṣṭhaṁ
kṛtvā garbheṇa keśavam

kṛṣṇaṁ kamala patrākṣām
śrīpuñjam amarārcitam

netrābhyāṁ sneha pūrṇābhyāṁ
vīkṣate mukhapaṅkajam

Glorious is mother Devakī, the best among all women, because she gave birth to lotus-eyed Lord Keśava, the supreme personality within the three worlds, the embodiment of beauty, who is worshiped by the demigods. She is certainly most fortunate to be able to gaze upon the supremely attractive face of her son with great affection.

Text 18

vaiśampāya uvāca
evaṁ lālapyamānaṁ tu
rājānaṁ rajasaṁsadi
uvāca śṛlakṣṇayā vācā
śālvarājo mahādyutiḥ

Vaiśampāyana said: As King Bhiṣmaka continued to speak about Lord Kṛṣṇa with great affection in that assembly hall, the powerful King Śālva interrupted to say some words of solace.

Text 19

śālva uvāca
alaṁ khedena rājendra
sutāya ripumardine
kṣatriyasya raṇe rājan
dhruvaṁ jaya parājayau

Śālva said: O foremost king, why are you lamenting? Your son is capable of subduing all your enemies. Besides this, for a *kṣatriya*, victory and defeat on the battlefield are arranged by destiny, and so there is never cause for despondency.

Texts 20-28

niyatā gati martyānām
eṣa dharmaḥ sanātanaḥ
balakeśa vayoranyas
tṛtīyaḥ kaḥ pumāniha

raṇe yodhayituṁ śaktas
tava putraṁ mahābalam
rathāti ratha vṛṇdānām
eka eva raṇājire

ripūn bādhāyituṁ śakto
dhanurgṛhya mahābhujaḥ
bhārgavāstraṁ mahāraudraṁ
devairapi durāsadam

sṛjoto bāhuvīryeṇa
kaḥ pumān prasahiṣyati
ayaṁ tu puruṣaḥ kṛṣṇo
hyanādi nidhano'bayaḥ

taṁ vijetā nṛloke'smin
nāpiśūla dharaḥ svayam
tava putro mahārāja
sarvaśāstrārtha tattvavit

viditvā devam īśānaṁ
na yodhayati keśavam
adya tasya raṇe jetā
yavanādhi patirnṛpa

sa kāla yavano nāma
avadhyaḥ keśavasya ha

taptvā sudāruṇaṁ ghoraṁ
tapaḥ parama duścaram

rudram ārādhayāmāsa
dvādaśābdā nayo'śanaḥ
putrakāmena muninā
toṣya rudrātsuto vṛtaḥ

māthurāṇām avadhyo'yaṁ
bhavediti ca śaṅkarāt
evamastvati rudro'pi
pradadau munaye sutam

The rule of *karma* eternally applies to everyone within the material world. My dear king, except Kṛṣṇa and Balarāma, who else would dare challenge your son? With bow in hand, your mighty-armed son is capable of fighting with the greatest warriors without assistance. He is a master of military science, knowing very well how to defend himself and how to vanquish his enemies. When he invokes his ultimate weapon, the Bhārgava-astra which is incapable of being counteracted, even the earth will be unable to tolerate it. Kṛṣṇa is the unlimited and indestructible Personality of Godhead, whom even Śiva, the wielder of the trident, cannot defeat.

O King, your son is also well-versed in the scriptures. He does not wish to fight with Kṛṣṇa because he considers Him to be the Supreme Controller. I think that only Kālayavana has the capability of defeating Kṛṣṇa in battle. He is the king of the Yavanas and he is destined not to be killed by Kṛṣṇa. The great sage Garga had performed severe austerities for twelve years to get a son. He worshiped Lord Śiva with great love and devotion. During that period, he ate only iron powder. When Lord Śiva became pleased with him, Garga prayed for a son that could not be killed by anyone who takes birth in the city of Mathurā. Lord

Śiva agreed to the sage's request and awarded him the son he desired.

Text 29

evaṁ gārgyasya tanayaḥ
śrīmān rudra varodbhavaḥ
māthurāṇām avadhyo'yaṁ
mathurāyāṁ viśeṣataḥ

Thus, by the mercy of Lord Śiva, Gargamunī begot a son who could not be killed by anyone within the boundaries of Mathurā, or by anyone who had been born there.

Text 30

kṛṣṇo'pi balavāneṣu
māthuro jātavānayam
sa jeṣyati raṇe kṛṣṇaṁ
mathurāyāṁ samāgataḥ

Although Kṛṣṇa is supremely powerful, He appeared at Mathurā. Therefore, when Kālayavana goes to attack Mathurā and challenges Kṛṣṇa to fight, I am sure that the Yavana king will come out victorious.

Text 31

manyadhvaṁ yadi vā yuktā
nṛpā vācaṁ mayeritām
tatra dūtaṁ visṛjadhvaṁ
yavanendra puraṁ prati

O kings, if you think that I have spoken reasonably, then immediately send a messenger to Kālayavana, the king of the Yavanas.

Text 32

vaiśampāyana uvāca
śrutvā saubha patervākyaṁ
sarve te nṛpasattamāḥ
kurma itya bruvan hṛṣtvā
jarāsandhaṁ mahābalam

Vaiśampāyana said: After hearing the speech of King Śalva, all the kings became very enthusiastic and addressed Jarāsandha, saying, "We will certainly do this."

Text 33

sa teṣāṁ vacanaṁ śrutvā
jarāsandho mahīpatiḥ
babhūva vimanā rājan
brahmaṇo vacanaṁ smaran

However, Jarāsandha became very aggrieved by this turn of events while remembering the predictions made by the unembodied voice in the sky.

Text 34

jarāsaṅdha uvāca
māṁ samāścritya pūrvasmin
nṛpā nṛpa bhayārditāḥ
prāpnuvanti hṛtaṁ rājyaṁ
sabhṛtya balavāhanam

Jarāsandha said: Up until now, all kings of the earth took shelter of me whenever they were in danger or attacked by their enemies. They thus remained in control of their kingdoms by my grace alone.

Text 35

iha saṁcodyate bhūpaiḥ
parasaṁśraya hetunā
kanyeva svapati dveṣād
anyaṁ rati parāyaṇā

Now you are inducing me to take shelter of someone else, like an unchaste and lusty lady who rejects her husband and seeks the association of another man.

Text 36

aho subalāvad daivam
aśakyaṁ vinivartitum
yadahaṁ kṛṣṇabhīto'nyaṁ
saṁśrayāmi balādhikam

Alas! Destiny is very powerful and cannot be reversed. Today, out of fear of Lord Kṛṣṇa, I have to take shelter of a supposedly more powerful king.

Text 37

nūnaṁ yoṣavihīno'haṁ
kārayiṣye parāśrayam
śreyo hi maraṇaṁ mahyaṁ
na cānyaṁ saṁśraye nṛpāḥ

I am certainly helpless and thus must seek the help of others. Truthfully, I consider it better to die than live such a dependent life. My dear kings, I will never be subordinate to anyone!

Text 38

kṛṣṇo vā baladevo vā
yo vāsau vā narādhipaḥ
hantāraṁ pratiyotsyāmi
yathā brāhma pracoditaḥ

Whether it is Kṛṣṇa, Balarāma, or anyone else, I will bravely face whoever challenges me. According to the celestial voice, I am destined to be killed in battle.

Text 39

eṣā me niścitā buddhir
etat sat puruṣavratam
ato'nyathā na śakto'haṁ
kartuṁ para samāśrayam

This is my firm conviction, and it is the vow of all true warriors to die in battle rather than become a coward and flee. Considering this, I am unwilling to take shelter of anyone.

Text 40

bhavatāṁ sādhuvṛttānām
ābādhaṁ na karoti saḥ
tena dūtaṁ pradāsyāmi
nṛpāṇāṁ rakṣaṇāya vai

Just so that fear of Kṛṣṇa does not jeopardize your righteousness, I will send a messenger for the purpose of giving you all protection.

Text 41

vyomamārgeṇa yātavyaṁ
yathā kṛṣṇo nabādhate
gacchantam anucintyaivaṁ
preṣayadhvaṁ nṛpottamāḥ

My dear kings, let this messenger travel through the sky so that Kṛṣṇa cannot impede him.

Text 42

ayaṁ saubhapatiḥ śrīmān
analārkendu vikramaḥ
rathenāditya varṇena
prayāti svapuraṁ bali

The powerful King Śālva, the master of the Saubha airplane, is as influential as fire, the sun, and the moon. He can traverse the sky in his effulgent airplane.

Text 43

yavanendro yathābhyeti
narendrāṇāṁ samāgamam
vacanaṁ ca tathāsmabhir
dūtye naḥ kṛṣṇavigrahe

The messenger should convey whatever we have resolved in this conference. If there must be a battle between ourselves and Kṛṣṇa, it must be insured that King Kālayavana takes our side.

Text 44

vaiśampāyana uvāca
punarevā bravīd rājā
saubhasya pati mūrjitam
gaccha sarva narendrāṇāṁ
sāhāyyaṁ kuru mānada

Vaiśampāyana said: King Jarāsandha then turned towards Śālva, the master of the Saubha airplane, and said: Approach all the kings and relay our message.

Text 45

yavanendro yathā yāti
yathā kṛṣṇaṁ vijeṣyati
yathā vayaṁ ca tuṣyāmas
tathā nītir vidhīyatām

Speak in such a way that the king of the Yavanas becomes eager to attack Kṛṣṇa and kill him. This would make us all very happy.

Text 46

evaṁ saṁdiśya sarvāṁstān
bhīṣmakaṁ pūjya dharmataḥ
prayayau svapuraṁ rājā
svena sainyena saṁvṛtaḥ

After saying this and offering respect to King Bhīṣmaka, Jarāsandha departed for home, taking his army.

Text 47

śālvo'pi nṛpati śreṣṭha
stāṁśca sampūjya dharmataḥ
jagāmākāśa mārgeṇa
rathenānila raṁhasā

King Śālva made gestures of respect to all the kings and then departed in his airplane, which travels through the sky faster than the wind..

Text 48

te'pi sarve mahīpālā
dakṣiṇā pathavāsinaḥ
anuvrajya jarāsandhaṁ
gatāḥ svanagaraṁ prati

All the kings from the South followed Jarāsandha some distance and then departed one by one for their respective kingdoms.

Text 49

bhīṣmakaḥ saha putreṇa
tābubhau cintya durnayam
sve gṛhe nyavasad dīnaḥ
kṛṣṇamevānu cintayan

King Bhīṣmaka and his son, Rukmī, carefully contemplated the unkind words of Jarāsandha and Śālva before returning to their residence in a somber mood, all the while remembering Lord Kṛṣṇa.

Texts 50-51

viditā rukmiṇī sādhvī
svayaṁvara nivartanam
kṛṣṇasyā gamanāddhetor
nṛpāṇāṁ doṣadarśanam

gatvā tu sā sakhīmadhye
uvāca vrīḍitānanā
na cānyeṣāṁ narendrāṇāṁ
patnī bhavitum utsahe
kṛṣṇāt kamala patrākṣāt
satyame tad vaco mama

When the chaste girl, Rukminī, came to know that her *svayamvara* had been suspended because of Kṛṣṇa's arrival, and that all the kings were against Kṛṣṇa's participation, she lowered her head in the midst of her companions and said: My dear friends, I cannot become the wife of any king other than lotus-eyed Lord Kṛṣṇa. This is my firm resolution.

Thus ends the translation of the fifty-second chapter of the Viṣṇu Parva of Śri Harivaṁsa.

Chapter 53

Śālva relays Jarāsandha's message to Kālayavana

Text 1

vaiśampāyana uvāca
yavanānāṁ balodagraḥ
sa kālayavano nṛpaḥ
babhūva rājā dharmeṇa
rakṣitā puravāsinām

Vaiśampāyana said: The great demon, Kālayavana, the king of the Yavanas, was incomparably powerful and he ruled his subjects according to the injunctions of the scriptures.

Text 2

trivarga viditaḥ prājñaḥ
ṣaḍguṇān upajīvakaḥ
sapta vyasana sammūḍho
guṇeṣva bhirataḥ sadā

He had a good understanding of the three objectives of human life—religiosity, economic development, and sense gratification—and he was a master of the six principles of diplomacy. He strictly avoided the seven classes of intoxication and his character was decorated with many good qualities.

Text 3

śrutimān dharmaśīlaśca
satyavādī jitendriyaḥ

sāṁgrāmika vidhijñāśca
durgalābhānu sāraṇaḥ

He was well educated, a follower of religious principles, truthful, self-controlled, a master of the arts of warfare, and he desired to attain the supreme goal of life.

Texts 4-6

śūro'prati balaścaiva
mantri pravara sevakaḥ
sukhāsīnaḥ sabhāṁ ramyāṁ
sacivaiḥ parivāritaḥ
upāsyamāno yavanair
ātmavid bhirvi paścitaiḥ
vividhāśca kathā divyāḥ
kathyamānāḥ parasparam

etasmin neva kāle tu
divyagandha vaho'nilaḥ
pravavau madanābodhaṁ
cakāra sukhaśitalaḥ

There was no one more powerful than Kālayavana. He was highly regarded by the greatest of warriors and surrounded by very intelligent ministers. One day, as he was seated in the midst of his ministers in his assembly hall, discussing various topics, a cool fragrant breeze began to blow, arousing everyone's lusty desires.

Text 7

kiṁsvi dityeka manasaḥ
sabhāyāṁ ye samāgatāḥ

utphullanayanāḥ sarve
rājā caivāv alokya saḥ

Everyone pondered the cause of this extraordinary occurrence, their eyes filled with wonder. Indeed, even King Kālayavana could not hide his astonishment.

Texts 8-9

apaśyanta ratham divyam
āyāntaṁ bhāskaropamam
śātakumbha mayaiḥ śubhraṁ
rathāṅgair upaśobhitam
divyaratna prabhākīrṇaṁ
divyadhvaja patākinam
vāhitaṁ divya turagair
manomāruta raṁhasaiḥ

Suddenly a brilliantly effulgent golden airplane bedecked with innumerable jewels descended from the sky. It was a celestial chariot decorated with nice flags that was drawn by horse that ran faster than the speed of mind or wind.

Text 10

candra bhāskara bimbāni
kṛtvā jāmbūnadena tam
racitaṁ vai viśvakṛtā
vaiyāghra varabhūṣitam

This chariot had been specially constructed by Viśvakarmā with the gold known as *jāmbūnada*, which is more brilliant than the sun. This airplane was covered with tiger skin all around.

Text 11

ripūṇāṁ trāsa jananaṁ
mitrāṇāṁ harṣavarddhanam
dakṣiṇādi guṇāyāntaṁ
rathaṁ pararathārujam

This chariot of Śālva created great fear in the minds of his enemies and bestowed great pleasure upon his friends. It had approached from the south and appeared prepared to smash the enemy chariots.

Texts 12-18

tatropaviṣṭaṁ śrī mantam
saubhasya patimūrjitam
dṛṣṭvā parama saṁhṛṣṭaś
cārghyaṁ pādyeti cāsakṛtam

uvāca yavanendrasya
mantrī mantra vidāṁ varaḥ
tatrotthāya mahābāhuḥ
svayameva nṛpāsanāt

pratyudgam ārghyam ādāya
rathā vataraṇe sthitaḥ
śālvo'pi ca mahātejā
dṛṣṭvā rājānam āgatam

mudā paramayā yuktaṁ
śakrapratima tejasam
avatīrya suviśrabdha
eka eva rathottamāt

viveśa paramaṁ prīto
mitradarśana lālasaḥ
dṛṣṭvārgham udyataṁ rājā
śālvo rājarṣi sattamaḥ

uvāca ślakṣṇayā vācā
nārghārho'smi mahādyute
dūt'haṁ majujendrāṇāṁ
sakāśad bhavato'ntikam

preṣito bahubhiḥ sārddhaṁ
jarāsaṅdhena dhīmatā
tena manye mahārāja
nārghārho'smīti rājasu

When the Yavana king's chief minister, who was very expert in the art of chanting *mantras*, saw Śālva seated in his Sauba airplane, he joyfully exclaimed, again and again: Look who has come! Quickly, bring *pādya* and *arghya*!

Mighty-armed Kālayavana got down from his throne and approached the airplane with *pādya* and *arghya* in his hands. When the powerful King Śālva saw Kālayavana, who was as influential as Indra, standing before him in a happy mood, he gave up his fear and descended from his celestial chariot. Thereafter, the two kings entered the palace. Śālva, who was very pleased to meet Kālayavana, spoke very sweetly: O greatly effulgent personality, I am not qualified to accept *arghya* from you. I have come as a messenger on behalf of an assembly of prominent kings, headed by the greatly intelligent Jarāsandha. O King, considering this, I don't consider myself qualified to accept your offering of *arghya*.

Text 19

kālayavana uvāca
jānāmyahaṁ mahābāho

dautyena tvām ihāgatam
sāhitye naradevānāṁ
preṣito māgadhena vai

Kālayavana said: O mighty-armed one, I know that you have come here as a messenger, sent by an assembly of kings, headed by the ruler of Magadha, Jarāsandha.

Texts 20-21

tena tvāmarcaye rājan
viśeṣeṇa mahāmate
arghya pādyādi satkārair
āsanena yathāvidhi

bhavatyabhyarcite rājñāṁ
sarveṣām arcitaṁ bhavet
āsyatām āsane śubhre
mayā sārddhaṁ janeśvara

My dear king, it is for this very reason I would like to worship you. If I satisfy you with offerings of *pādya*, *arghya*, *āsana*, and so on, then I will certainly please all the kings. Therefore, O ruler of men, please be seated on this excellent throne.

Text 22

vaiśampāyana uvāca
sa hastā liṅganaṁ kṛtvā
pṛṣṭvā ca kuśalāmayam
sukhopaviṣṭau sahitau
śubhe siṁhāsane sthitau

Vaiśampāyana said: Thereafter, Kālayavana inquired about

the welfare of Śālva and others. The two kings sat comfortably on beautiful thrones and engaged in pleasant conversation.

Texts 23-24

kālayavana uvāca
yadvāhu balamāśritya
vayaṁ sarve narādhipāḥ
vavsāmo vigatod vignā
devā iva śacīpatim

kimasādhyaṁ bhavedasya
yenāsi preṣito mayi
vada satyaṁ vacastasya
kimājñā payati prabhuḥ
karṣye vacanaṁ tasya
api karma suduṣkaram

Kālayavana said: What is impossible for Jarāsandha, under the shelter of whose mighty arms all of us live fearlessly in this world, just as the demigods live free from fear under the shelter of Indra, the husband of Śacī? What has happened that Jarāsandha has sent you to me? Tell me frankly what is on his mind. What order has my master given? I will definitely accomplish whatever he desires.

Text 25

śālva uvāca
yathā vadati rājendra
magadhādhi patistava
tathāhaṁ sampravakṣyāmi
śrūyatāṁ yavanādhipa

Śālva said: O ruler of the Yavanas, please listen attentively as I relate to you exactly what the king of Magadha said.

Text 26

jarāsandha uvāca
jāto'yaṁ jagatāṁ bādhī
kṛṣṇaḥ parama durjayaḥ
viditvā tasya durvṛttam
ahaṁ hantuṁ samudyataḥ

Jarāsandha said: Unconquerable Lord Kṛṣṇa, who has now appeared within this world, is harassing the rulers of the earth who do not accept His supremacy. Having experienced His arrogance, I have decided that He must be eliminated at all costs.

Texts 27-28

pārthivair bahubhiḥ sārddhaṁ
samagra balavāhanaiḥ
uparudhya mahāsainyair
gomantam acalottamam

cedirājasya vacanaṁ
mahārthaṁ śrutavānaham
tadā tayor vināśāya
hutaśana mayojayam

Many kings, accompanied by their vast armies, are ready to sacrifice their lives for my sake. With their support, I had surrounded Gomanta Hill in the hopes of killing Kṛṣṇa and Balarāma. After surrounding the hill, when I heard the advice of the king of Cedi, Damaghoṣa, I set fire all around the mountain, certain that I would burn the two brothers.

Texts 29-30

jvālāśata sahasrāḍhyaṁ
yugāntāgni samaprabham
dṛṣṭvā rāmo gireḥ kūṭāda
apluto hematāladhṛk

viniṣpatya mahāsenāṁ
madhye sāgara saṁnibhām
ājaghāna durādharṣo
narāśva rathadantinām

Soon the entire mountain was afire, so that it appeared like the Samvartaka fire that burns everything at the time of devastation. When Balarāma saw everything engulfed in flames, He jumped from the peak of the mountain, landing in the midst of our powerful army, which was as vast as the ocean. He mercilessly began to destroy all our elephants, horses, chariots, and infantry soldiers, and it was impossible for us to check Him.

Text 31

sarpantamiva sarpendraṁ
vikṛṣyā kṛṣya lāṅgalam
naranāgāśva vṛndāni
muṣalena vyapothayat

He wielded His snake-like plough, smashing everything that came in His path. Then, without impediment, He slaughtered innumerable men, elephants, and horses with His great *muṣala*.

Text 32

gajena gajamās phālya
rathena rathayodhinam

hayena na ca hayārohaṁ
padātena padātinam

Although He fought on foot, He killed countless elephants, smashed all the chariots and killed the charioteers, slaughtered the horses and their soldiers, and massacred innumerable infantry.

Text 33

samara sa mahātejā
nṛpārka śatasaṁkule
vicaran vividhān mārgān
nidhāghe bhāskaro yathā

As the sun scorches everyone during summer, incomparably powerful Balarāma wandered within our ranks, commanded by thousands of powerful kings, demonstrating His superiority.

Text 34

rāmādan antaraṁ kṛṣṇaḥ
pragṛhyārka samaprabham
cakraṁ cakrabhṛtāṁ śreṣṭhaḥ
siṁhaḥ kṣudra mṛgaṁ yathā

Balarāma's younger brother, Kṛṣṇa, wielded His *cakra* as brilliant as the sun, scattering our warriors as a lion causes a herd of deer to panic and flee.

Texts 35-36

pravicālva mahāvīryaḥ
pādavegena taṁ girim
śatrusainye papātocvair
yaduvīraḥ pratāpavān

pranṛtyanniva śailendras
toyadhārābhi ṣecitaḥ
ghūrṇamāno viveśorvīṁ
vinirvāpya hutāśanam

Kṛṣṇa of the Yadu dynasty made the mountain tremble by the pressure of His feet as He jumped from the peak and landed within our midst. Indeed, by the force of His jump, that king of mountains appeared to dance while being bathed with the water of its streams. Indeed, the mountain sank within the ground, and the cascading water doused the fire.

Text 37

adīpya māna śikharad
āvaplutya janārdanaḥ
jaghāna vāhinīṁ rājaṁś
cakra vyagreṇa pāṇinā

O King, after jumping from the peak of the burning mountain, Kṛṣṇa began mercilessly slaughtering our soldiers with His Sudarśana *cakra.*

Text 38

vikṣipya vipulaṁ cakraṁ
gadāpātā danantaram
naranāgāśva vṛndāni
muṣalena vyacūrṇayat

Sometimes He would leave aside His Sudarśana *cakra* and pick up His club. As He continued to slaughter our soldiers, Balarāma smashed countless elephants, horses, and human beings with His *muṣala.*

Text 39

krodhānila samuddhṛta
cakralāṅgala vahninā
nirdagdhā mahatī senā
narendrārkābhi pālitā

By the blazing fire emanating from the wrath of Kṛṣṇa's Sudarśana *cakra* and the plough of Balarāma, our entire army was burnt to ashes.

Text 40

naranāgāśva kalilaṁ
pattidhvaja samākulam
rathānīkaṁ padātābhyaṁ
kṣaṇena vidalīkṛtam

Although the two brothers fought on foot without chariots, within a moment They annihilated thousands of elephants, horses, and well-equipped soldiers.

Texts 41-42

senāṁ prabhagnām ālokya
cakrānala bhayārditām
mahatā rathavṛndena
parivārya samantataḥ

tatrāhaṁ yuddhya mānastu
bhrātāsya balavān bale
sthito mamāgrataḥ śūro
gadāpāṇir halāyudhaḥ

When I saw my vast army retreating out of fear of the *cakra*, I approached the two brothers on my chariot, showering upon Them my arrows. Kṛṣṇa's powerful brother, Balarāma, picked up His plough and club and stood before me, accepting the challenge.

Text 43

dvādaśa akṣauhiṇīr hatvā
prabhinna iva kesarī
halaṁ saunandam utsṛjya
gadayā māmatāḍayat

Balarāma fought fiercely like an injured lion and destroyed twelve *akṣauhiṇīs* of soldiers within a very short time. Thereafter, leaving aside His *muṣala*, He picked up His club and began to strike me.

Text 44

vajrapāta nibhaṁ vegaṁ
pātayitvā mamopari
bhūyaḥ prahartu kāmo māṁ
vaiśākhenās thito mahīm

The blow of His club felt as powerful as a thunderbolt. After striking me with His club again and again, He employed another weapon called Vaiśākhi and challenged me.

Text 45

vaiśākhaṁ sthānam āsthāya
guhaḥ krauñcaṁ yathā purā
tathā māṁ dīrghanetrābhyām
īkṣate nirdahanniva

As in the distant past, Kārttikeya had shattered the Krauñca mountain, desiring to pierce my heart with His *vaiśākhi* weapon, Balarāma glared at me as if to burn me to ashes.

Text 46

tādṛgrūpaṁ samālokya
baladevaṁ raṇājire
jīvitārthī nṛloke'smin
kaḥ pumān sthātum arhati

After seeing Baladeva's incomparable form on the battlefield, what person who values his life would stand before Him?

Text 47

gṛhītvā sa gadāṁ bhīmāṁ
kāladaṇḍam ivodyatām
kālāṅ kuśena nirghūtāṁ
sthita evāgrato mama

Balarāma picked up His powerful club, and like death personified, stood before me. While twirling His club, He appeared to be inviting me to my funeral.

Texts 48-49

tato jalada gambhīra
svareṇā pūrayan nabhaḥ
vāguvācā śarīreṇa
svayaṁ lokapitāmahaḥ

prahartavyo na rājāyam
avadhyo'yaṁ tavānagha
kalpito'sya vadho'nyasmād
viramasva halāyudha

At that time, Brahmā, the universal grandfather, appeared unseen to others in the sky and spoke with a grave voice: O sinless one, do not strike this king, for he is not to be killed by You. He is destined to die at the hands of someone else. Therefore, O carrier of the plough, please desist.

Text 50

śrutvāṁ tena vākyena
cintāviṣṭo nivartitaḥ
sarvaprāṇa haraṁ ghoraṁ
brahmaṇā svayamīritam

After I heard this celestial voice from the sky, I morosely ceased fighting. The prediction of Brahmā was very unpalatable news.

Text 51

tenāhaṁ vaḥ pravakṣyāmi
nṛpāṇāṁ hitakābhyayā
śrutvā tvameva rājendra
kartum arhasi tad vacaḥ

Now, for the benefit of all the kings of the earth, I wish to request something of you, being confident that after hearing my appeal, you will act in a way that is conducive for our welfare.

Texts 52-53

tapasogreṇa mahatā
putrārthī toṣya śaṅkaram
prāptavān devadevaṁ tvām
avadhyaṁ māthurair janaiḥ

mahāmuniścāya sacūrṇamaśnan
unupasthito dvādaśca vārṣikaṁ vratam
surāsuraiḥ saṁstuta pādapaṅkajaḥ
sa labdha vānīpsita kāmasampadam

The great sage, Garga, who is glorified by both demigods and demons, underwent severe austerities for twelve years while observing a vow of celibacy and eating only iron ore. He performed these austerities, desiring to have a son. Becoming pleased with him, Śaṅkara fulfilled his desire to have a son as powerful as the king of heaven, Indra. You should know that, by the benediction of Lord Śiva, you cannot be killed by anyone who takes birth within the city of Mathurā.

Text 54

tapobalād gārgya muner mahātmano
varaprabhā vācchakalendu maulinaḥ
bhavantam āsādya janārdano himaṁ
vilīyate bhāskara raśminā yathā

You have been born as the embodiment of the power of the great sage Gargamuni's austerities, and the benediction of Lord Śiva, whose is decorated with the crescent moon. When Kṛṣṇa challenges you to a fight, He will be destroyed just as ice is melted by the rays of the sun.

Text 55

yatasva rājñāṁ vacana pracodito
vrajasva yātrāṁ vijayāya keśavam
praviśya rāṣṭraṁ mathurāṁ ca senayā
nihatya kṛṣṇaṁ prathayan svakaṁ yaśaḥ

With the support of all my allies, you should attack Kṛṣṇa at Mathurā. Surround the city and then launch your attack from all sides. By vanquishing Kṛṣṇa, your already glorious reputation will be greatly enhanced.

Text 56

māthuro vāsudevo'yaṁ
baladevaḥ sabāndhavaḥ
tau vijeṣyasi saṁgrāme
gatvā tāṁ mathurāṁ purīm

The two sons of Vasudeva, Kṛṣṇa and Balarāma, as well as Their friends and kinsmen, are residing at Mathurā. I am sure that when you attack Mathurā, you will easily defeat the two brothers in battle.

Text 57

śālva uvāca
ityevaṁ narapati bhāskara pranītaṁ
vākyaṁ te kathitam idaṁ hitaṁ nṛpāṇām
tatsarvaṁ saha sacivair vimṛśya buddhyā
yudyukaṁ kuru manujendra cātmaniṣṭham

Śālva said: O King, I have thus repeated the message of Jarāsandha, sent on behalf of all the kings that are his allies. Carefully consider the matter in consultation with your ministers and then do whatever you conclude to be in your best self-interest.

Thus ends the translation of the fifty-third chapter of the Viṣṇu Parva of Śri Harivaṁsa.

Chapter 54

Kālayavana's reply to Śālva

Text 1

vaiśampāyana uvāca
evaṁ kathayamānaṁ taṁ
śālvarājaṁ nṛpājñayā
uvāca paramaprīto
yavanādhi patirnṛpaḥ

Vaiśampāyana said: After hearing Śālva's recitation of Jarāsandha's message, Kālayavana spoke as follows.

Text 2

kālayavana uvāca
dhanyo'smyanu gṛhīto'smi
saphalaṁ jīvitaṁ mama
kṛṣṇa nigraha hetorya
niyukto bahubhir nṛpaiḥ

Kālayavana said: I consider myself to be very fortunate that all these prestigious kings have entrusted me with the responsibility of killing Kṛṣṇa. Indeed, I feel that today my life has become successful.

Texts 3-4

durjayastriṣu lokeṣu
surāsura gaṇairapi
tasya nigraha hetormā
avadhārya jayāśiṣam

prahṛṣṭai rājasiṁhaistair
avadhāryo jayo mama
teṣāṁ vācāmbu varṣeṇa
vijayo me bhaviṣyati

I have been asked to vanquish the person who cannot be conquered by the greatest demigods and demons. I am confident that with your nectarean blessings, my success is guaranteed.

Text 5

kariṣye vacanaṁ teṣāṁ
nṛpa sattama coditam
parājayo'pi rājendra
jayena sadṛśo mama

O foremost king, in accordance with the order of Jarāsandha, I will certainly fulfill the desire of these kings. Indeed, in this glorious mission, I will even consider defeat as victory.

Text 6

adyaiva tithi nakṣatraṁ
muhūrtaṁ karaṇaṁ śubham
yāsyāmi mathurāṁ rājan
vijetuṁ keśavaṁ raṇe

I consider today as the most auspicious day, this moment as the most auspicious moment, and the positions of the stars and planets to be most favorable, so I will leave for Mathurā to conquer Kṛṣṇa without delay.

Texts 7 & 8

vaiśampāyana uvāca
evamābhāṣya rājānaṁ
saubhasya patimūrjitam
satkṛtya ca yathānyāyaṁ
mahārha maṇbhuṣnaiḥ

brāhmaṇebhyo dadau vittaṁ
siddhādeśāya vai nṛpaḥ
purohitāya rājendra
pradadau bahuśo dhanam

Vaiśampāyana said: After speaking to Śālva, the master of the Saubha airplane, Kālayavana offered him some valuable jeweled ornaments. Thereafter, to insure victory over Kṛṣṇa, Kālayavana gave a huge quantity of wealth in charity to the *brāhmaṇas*.

Text 9

hutvāgniṁ vidhivad rājā
kṛta kautuka maṅgalaḥ
prasthānaṁ kṛtavān samyag
jetukāmo janārdanam

He then performed the traditional rituals that grant one auspiciousness while setting out to engage in battle, and also offered oblations into the sacrificial fire. After completing these, Kālayavana left his palace, harboring the desire to defeat Kṛṣṇa in battle.

Text 10

śālvo'pi bharataśreṣṭha
kṛtārtho hṛṣṭamānasaḥ
yavanendraṁ pariṣvajya
jagāma svapuraṁ nṛpaḥ

O descendent of Bharata, being very pleased by Kālayavana's hospitality, Śālva embraced him and departed for home.

Thus ends the translation of the fifty-fourth chapter of the Viṣṇu Parva of Śri Harivaṁsa.

Chapter 55

Lord Kṛṣṇa returns to Mathurā. The arrival of Garuḍa and his suggestion to establish Dvārakā

Text 1

janamejaya uvāca
vidarbhanagarād yāte
śakra tulya parākrame
kimarthaṁ garuḍo nītaḥ
kiṁ ca karma cakāra saḥ

Janamejaya said: When Lord Kṛṣṇa, who is as powerful Indra, returned to Mathurā from Vidarbha, why did He take Garuḍa? What did Garuḍa do there?

Text 2

na cāruroha bhagavān
vainateyaṁ mahābalam
etanme saṁśayaṁ brahman
brūhi tattvaṁ mahāmune

O great sage, Why didn't the almighty Lord Kṛṣṇa ride on the back of Garuḍa while returning to Mathurā? This is my doubt and so kindly tell me the truth of the matter.

Text 3

vaiśampāyana uvāca
śṛṇu rājan suparṇena
kṛtaṁ karmāti mānuṣam

vidarbhanagarīṁ gatvā
vainateyo mahādyutiḥ

Vaiśampāyana said: O King, whatever activities Garuḍa, the son of Vinatā, performed while at Vidarbha were beyond human capapbility.

Texts 4-6

asamprāpte ca nagarīṁ
mathurāṁ madhusūdane
manasā cintayā māsa
vainateyo mahādyutiḥ

yaduktaṁ devadevena
nṛpāṇām agrataḥ prabho
yāsyāmi mathurāṁ ramyāṁ
bhojarājena pālitām

iti tadvacana syānte
gamiṣyeti vicintayan
kṛtāñjali puṭaḥ śrī mān
praṇipatyā vravīdidam

When the slayer of the Madhu demon had announced to the assembled kings at Vidarbha that He would return to the beautiful city of Mathurā, which was ruled by the Bhoja king, Ugrasena, Garuḍa had volunteered to accompany Him. Now, as they were traveling, Garuḍa suddenly had a thought and so, with folded hands, he addressed the Lord as follows.

Text 7

garuḍa uvāca
deva yāsyāmi nagarīṁ

raivatasya kuśasthalīm
raivataṁ ca giriṁ ramyaṁ
nandana pratimaṁ vanam

Garuḍa said: My dear Lord, I would like to go to the city of Kuśathali, which is ruled by King Raivata. Nearby is a beautiful mountain named Raivata, where the gardens are as enchanting as the Nandana gardens of the demigods.

Text 8

rukmiṇodvā sitāṁ ramyāṁ
śailodadhi taṭāśrayām
vṛkṣagulma latākīrṇāṁ
puṣpareṇu vibhūṣitām

King Rukmī has taken shelter of that area between the mountain and the sea, which is filled with beautiful flowering trees and plants.

Text 9

gajendra bhujagā kīrṇām
ṛkṣavānara sevitām
varāha mahiṣākrāntāṁ
mṛgayūthair anekaśaḥ

Numerous elephants, serpents, gorillas, and monkeys reside in that province, as do herds of hogs, buffaloes, and deer.

Texts 10-13

tāṁ samantāt samālokya
vāsārthaṁ te kṣamāṁ kṣamā

yadi syād bhavato ramyā
praśastā nagarīti ca

kaṇṭadod dharaṇaṁ kṛtvā
āgamiṣye tavāntikam

vaiśampāyana uvāca
evaṁ vijñāpya deveśaṁ
praṇipatya janārdanam
jagama patagendro'pi
paścimābhi mukho balī
kṛṣṇo'pi yadubhi sārddhaṁ
viveśa mathurāṁ purīm

svairiṇya ugrasenaśca
nāgarāścaiva sarvaśaḥ
pratyudgamyār cayan kṛṣṇam
prahṛṣṭa janasaṅkulaṁ

I wish to go and see that place, to ascertain if it is suitable for Your pastimes. I have heard that it is a very beautiful place and if I find it so, I will destroy any disturbing elements before returning to You.

Vaiśampāyana said: After expressing his intentions in this way and offering obeisances to Lord Kṛṣṇa, Garuḍa, the kings of birds, departed through the sky towards the west. After some time, Lord Kṛṣṇa and His associates arrived at the outskirts of Mathurā. All of the inhabitants of Mathurā, headed by King Ugrasena and including singers and dancers, came out of the city to receive the Lord.

Text 14

janamejaya uvāca
śrutvābhiṣikaṁ rājendraṁ

bahubhir vasudhādhipaiḥ
kiṁ cakāra mahābāhur
ugraseno mahīpatiḥ

Janamejaya said: How did mighty-armed King Urgrasena react when he heard about how the kings had performed Kṛṣṇa's coronation at Vidarbha?

Texts 15-22

vaiśampāyana uvāca
śrutvābhisīktaṁ rājendraṁ
bahubhiḥ pārthivottamaiḥ
indreṇa kṛtasaṁdhānaṁ
dūtaṁ citrāṅgadaṁ kṛtam

ekaikaṁ nṛpater bhāgaṁ
śatasāhasra sammitam
rājendre tvarbudaṁ dattaṁ
mānaveṣu ca vai daśa

ye tatra samanuprāptā
na riktāste gṛhaṁ gatāḥ
śaṅkho yādava rūpeṇa
pradadau haricintitam

evaṁ nidhipatiḥ śrīmān
daivatair anumoditaḥ
iti śrutvātmika janāl
loka pravṛtti kānnarāt

cakāra mahatīṁ pūjāṁ
devatāya taneṣvapi
vasudevasya bhavane
toraṇo bhayapārśvataḥ

naṭānāṁ nṛtyageyāni
vādyāni ca samantataḥ
patākadhvaja mālāḍhyāṁ
kārayāmāsa vai nṛpaḥ

kaṁsarājasya ca sabhāṁ
vicitrāmbara suprabhām
patākā vividhākārā
dāpayāmāsa bhojarāṭ

toraṇaṁ gopuraṁ caiva
sudhāpaṅkānu lepanam
kārayāmāsa rājendro
rājendrasyā sanālayam

Vaiśampāyana said: The assembled kings had performed the *abhiṣeka* of Lord Kṛṣṇa, thus formally accepting Him as the king of all kings. Indra had sent his messenger, Citrāṅgada, to convey his intentions to the assembled kings in this regard. After that ceremony, each king was given one hundred thousand gold coins in charity. Indeed, some of the most prominent kings received ten million gold coins. Ordinary citizens were each given ten thousand gold coins. Whoever participated in that ceremony did not return home empty-handed. Śaṅkha, the master of the ocean, was present in the guise of a member of the Yadu dynasty and he supplied all the required wealth, having received the support of all the demigods.

When King Ugrasena heard all this news from his relatives, ordinary citizens, and spies, he arranged for a special worship of the Supreme Lord in the temple. The palace of Vasudeva was then lavishly decorated and musical performances were arranged all over Mathurā. King Ugrasena arranged to decorate the assembly hall of Kaṁsa, and indeed, by his order, the entire city was cleansed and decorated. Finally, he arranged a superior throne and palace for the king of kings, Lord Kṛṣṇa.

Text 23-25

naṭānāṁ nṛtyageyāni
vādyāni ca samantataḥ
patākā vanamālāḍhyāḥ
pūrṇakumbhāḥ samantataḥ

rājamārgeṣu rājendra
candanodaka secitam
vastrābharaṇakaṁ rājā
dāpayāmāsa bhūtale

dhūpaṁ pārśvobhaye caiva
candanāguru guggulaiḥ
guḍaṁ sarjarasaṁ caiva
dahyamānaṁ tatastataḥ

Dancers, singers, and musicians joyfully performed throughout the city. Water mixed with sandalwood paste was sprinkled over the roads, which were decorated with pitchers of water adorned with garlands of forest flowers. King Ugrasena had the entire courtyard of his palace covered with carpets. Heaps of flower garlands were seen here and there, and incense made from sandalwood, *aguru*, and *guggula* burned on both sides of the roads. Food for mass distribution was being prepared in many places.

Text 26

vṛddhastrījana saṅdhaiśca
gāyadbhiḥ stutimaṅgalam
arghaṁ kṛtvā pratīkṣante
sveṣu sthāneṣu yoṣitaḥ

The elderly ladies of Mathurā assembled and chanted prayers and auspicious hymns. The young ladies carried plates of auspicious articles to greet the Lord.

Texts 27-30

evaṁ kṛtvā purānandam
ugraseno narādhipaḥ
vasudeva gṛhaṁ gatvā
priyākhyānaṁ nivedya ca

rāmeṇa saha sammantrya
nirgato rathamantikam
tasmin nevāntare rājañ
śaṅkhadhvanira bhūnmahān

pāñcajanyasya ninadaṁ
śrutvā madhuravāsinaḥ
striyo vṛddhāśca bālāśca
sūtā māgadha vandinaḥ
viniryayur mahāsenā
rāmaṁ kṛtvāgrato nṛpa
arghyaṁ pādyaṁ puraskṛtya
ugrasenena dhīmatā

After making all arrangements for the ecstatic festival of Lord Kṛṣṇa's return to Mathurā, King Ugrasena went to Vasudeva's palace and informed him of how the kings of the world had performed Kṛṣṇa's *abhiṣeka*, and how the Lord would soon return home. King Ugrasena then talked with Balarāma for some time before going out of the city to greet Lord Kṛṣṇa.

O King, at that time, the blowing of conch shells was heard. When the residents of Mathurā—men, women, children, the elderly, singers, dancers, musicians, and chroniclers—heard the tumultuous sound of Lord Kṛṣṇa's Pāñcajanya conch shell, they took *pādya*, *arghya* and other articles for worship and went out of the city, led by Balarāma and King Ugrasena.

Text 31

dṛṣṭipanthānam āsādya
ugraseno mahīpatiḥ
avatīrya rathācchubhrāt
pādamārgeṇa cāgrataḥ

As soon as King Ugrasena saw Kṛṣṇa in the distance, he hurriedly alighted from his brilliant chariot and proceeded toward the Lord on foot.

Texts 32-34

dṛṣṭvā'sīnaṁ rathe ramye
divyaratna vibhūṣitam
aṅgeṣvā bharaṇaṁ caiva
divyaratna prabhāyutam
vanamālo rasaṁ divyaṁ
tapantamiva bhāskaram
cāmaraṁ vyajanaṁ chatraṁ
khagendra dhvajamucchritam

rājala kṣaṇa sampūrṇam
āsannārkam ivojjvalam
śriyābhi bhūtaṁ deveśaṁ
durnirīkṣya taraṁ harim

King Ugrasena saw Lord Kṛṣṇa seated upon a beautiful chariot. He was decorated with jeweled ornaments, making Him appear even more effulgent. Upon His chest was a garland of forest flowers. Servants with *cāmaras* stood on both sides of the

Lord and a gorgeous umbrella was held over His head. The flag of His chariot bore the emblem of Garuḍa. Being the embodiment of all qualities befitting royalty, the Lord shone so brightly, it was difficult to gaze upon Him.

Text 35

dṛṣṭvā sa rājā rājendra
harṣa gadgadayā girā
babhāṣe puṇḍarīkākṣaṁ
rāmaṁ balaniṣūdanam

While gazing upon the extraordinary beauty of Kṛṣṇa, King Urgasena spoke to lotus-eyed Balarāma, the slayer of His enemies, in a voice that was choked with love.

Text 36

rathena na mayā gantuṁ
yukta pūrveti cintya vai
avatīrṇo mahābhāga gaccha
tvaṁ syandanena ca

O supremely fortunate one, I had left my chariot, feeling that it would be more befitting for me to approach Your elder brother on foot. I would be most pleased if You would accept my chariot as Your own.

Texts 37-42

viṣṇunā chadmarūpeṇa
gatvemāṁ mathurāṁ purīm
anuprakāśita ātmānaṁ
devendratvaṁ nṛpārṇave

tamahaṁ stotum icchāmi
sarvabhāvena keśavam
pratyuvāca mahātejā
rājānāṁ kṛṣṇapūrvajaḥ

na yuktaṁ nṛpate stotuṁ
vrajantaṁ devasattamam
vinā stotreṇa saṁtuṣṭas
tava rājañ janārdanaḥ

tuṣṭasya stutinā kiṁ te
darśanena tava stutiḥ
rājendratvam anuprāpya
āgatastava veśmani

na tvayā stutavān rājan
divyaiḥ stotrair amānuṣaiḥ
evamābruva māṇautau
samprāptau keśavāntikam

arghyodyata bhujaṁ dṛṣṭvā
sthāpayitvā rathottamam
uvāca vadatāṁ śreṣṭha
ugrasenaṁ narādhipam

Lord Viṣṇu appeared at Mathurā, assuming a human-like form. At Vidarbha, however, He appeared before the assembled kings and revealed Himself as the supreme controller and indestructible Lord. Now, upon His return, I wish to worship Him with great reverence.

Kṛṣṇa's elder brother, Balarāma, said: My dear King Ugrasena, ruler of men, it is not proper for you to offer prayers to Lord Kṛṣṇa. Kṛṣṇa is pleased to accept you as His family member, and so your affection for Him is not on the platform of awe and reverence. Rest assured that Kṛṣṇa will be very pleased simply to see you. Now He is recognized as the emperor of the world and thus glorified by everyone. Your relationship as His elder should not be disturbed.

While talking in this manner, Balarāma and King Ugarsena approached Lord Kṛṣṇa. When Lord Kṛṣṇa saw King Ugrasena standing with *arghya* in his hand, He halted His chariot and spoke as follows.

Text 43

yanmayā cābhiṣiktastvaṁ
mathureśo bhavatviti
nayuktaman yathā kartuṁ
mathurādhi pate svayam

O King of Mathurā, I had not installed you upon the royal throne for this purpose! Don't degrade your royal lineage by acting in this manner, which does not befit you.

Text 44

arghyam ācamanīyaṁ ca
pādyaṁ cāsmai niveditam
na dātur mahase rājan
eṣa me manasaḥ priyaḥ

At the time of your installation, I had worshiped you with offerings of *pādya*, *arghya* and *ācamanīya*. Therefore, you should not offer these articles back to Me. This is My desire.

Text 45

tavābhiprāyaṁ vijñāya
vravībhi nṛpate vacaḥ

tvameva mathuro rājā
nānyathā kartum arhasi

O ruler of men, I am fully aware of your intention. You alone are the king of Mathurā and you will continue to be so. You should not reverse the position that I awarded you.

Text 46

sthānabhāgaṁ ca nṛpate
dāsyāmi tava dakṣiṇam
yathā nṛpāṇāṁ sarveṣāṁ
tathā te sthāpito'grataḥ

I will regularly give you a share of whatever wealth I procure. I have given much wealth to all the kings, and have also brought your share.

Text 47

śatasāhastriko bhāgo
vastrā bharaṇa varjitaḥ
āruhasva rathaṁ śubhraṁ
cāmīkara vibhūṣitam

Besides gifts of cloth and ornaments, I will give you one hundred thousand gold coins. You should now ascend this white chariot decorated with gold.

Texts 48-53

cāmaraṁ vyajanaṁ chatraṁ
dhvajaṁ ca manujeśvara

divyābharaṇa saṁyuktaṁ
mukuṭaṁ bhāskaraprabham

dhārayasva mahābhāga
pālayasva purīmimām
putrapautraiḥ pramudito
mathurāṁ paripālaya

jitvāri gaṇasaṅghāṁśca
bhojavaṁśaṁ vivarddhaya
devadevādya anantāya
śauriṇe vajrapāṇinā

preṣitaṁ devarājena
divyābharaṇam ambaram
māthurāṇāṁ ca sarveṣāṁ
bhāgā dīnārakā daśa

sūta māgadha bandīnām
ekaikasya sahasrakam
vṛddha strijana saṅghānāṁ
ganikānām śatam śatam

nṛpeṇa saha tiṣṭhanti
vikadru pramukhāśca ye
daśa sāhasriko bhāgas
teṣāṁ dhātrā prakalpitaḥ

O most fortunate king, these *cāmaras*, umbrellas, flags, and celestial ornaments are for you. This crown, which is as brilliant as the sun, is for your use. Along with your sons and grandsons, continue ruling the inhabitants of the city of Mahturā. Increase the glories of the Bhoja dynasty by defeating their enemies. Indra, the wielder of the thunderbolt, has sent celestial garments and ornaments for Balarāma, the master of the demigods and original cause of creation, who appeared in the dynasty of Surasena and is non-different from Ananta Śeṣa. All the leading citizens of Mathurā should be given ten thousand gold coins, including the singers, dancers, musicians, and orators. Please give each of the elderly ladies who chanted auspicious hymns one hundred gold coins. Give each of the principal members of the Yadu dynasty, such as Vikadru, ten thousand gold coins. These gifts have been ordained by Indra.

Text 54

vaiśampāyana uvāca
evaṁ sampūjya rājānaṁ
māthurāṇāṁ camū mukhe
kṛtvā sumahadānandāṁ
mathurāṁ madhusūdanaḥ

Vaiśampāyana said: In this way, Lord Madhusūdana submerged King Ugrasena and all the other inhabitants of Mathurā in an ocean of bliss before entering the city.

Text 55

divyābharaṇa mālyaiśca
divyāmvara vilepanaiḥ
dīpyamānāḥ samantācca
devā iva triviṣṭape

As the demigods happily reside in the heavenly planets, Lord Kṛṣṇa and the people of Mathurā, who decorated themselves with celestial ornaments, flower garlands, and sandalwood paste, continued to live in peace and harmony.

Texts 56-57

bherīpaṭaha nādena
śaṅka dundubhi niḥsvanaiḥ
vṛṁhitena ca nāgānāṁ
hayānāṁ heṣitena ca

siṁhanādena śūrāṇāṁ
rathanemi svanena ca
tumulaḥ sumahānāsīn
meghanāda ivāmbare

The tumultuous sounds of the drums, conch shells, horns, elephants, and horses, as well as the roaring of warriors and the rumbling of chariot wheels seemed like the rumbling of clouds in the sky during the monsoon.

Text 58

bandhibhiḥ stūyamānaṁ ca
namaścakrur api prajāḥ
dattvā dānaman antaṁ ca
na yayau vismayaṁ hariḥ

The orators glorified Lord Kṛṣṇa while all the inhabitants of Mathurā offered their obeisances. In spite of giving such a huge amount of wealth in charity, Lord Hari never became proud like a conditioned soul.

Text 59

svabhāvonnata bhāvatvād
dṛṣṭapūrvāt tato'dhikam
anaṁkāra bhāvācca
vismayaṁ na jagāma ha

By nature Lord Kṛṣṇa was very kind and magnanimous. He had previously given even vaster amounts of charity and yet pride never manifested within His mind. That is the nature of the Absolute Truth, the Supreme Personality of Godhead.

Text 60

dīpyamānaṁ svavapuṣā
āyāntaṁ bhāskara prabham
dṛṣṭvā mathura vāsinyo
namaścakruḥ pade pade

As Lord Kṛṣṇa, whose form illuminated all directions, entered Mathurā, the ladies followed, offering their respects at every step.

Text 61

eṣa nārāyaṇaḥ śrī mān
kṣirārṇava niketanaḥ
nāgaparyaṅkam utsṛjya
prāptp'yaṁ mathurāṁ purīm

While walking, the ladies spoke to one another: He is the same Lord Nārāyaṇa who resides on the ocean of milk. He left His bed of Śeṣa and came to Mathurā.

Text 62

baddhvā baliṁ mahāvīryaṁ
durjayaṁ tridaśair api
śakrāya pradadau rājyaṁ
trailokyaṁ vajrapāṇaye

Long ago, He arrested the powerful King Bali, who was

unconquerable even by the demigods, and returned the kingdom of the three worlds to Indra, the wielder of the thunderbolt.

Texts 63-64

hatvā daityagaṇān sarvān
kaṁsaṁ ca balināṁ varam
bhojarājāya mathurāṁ
dattvā keśini ṣūdanaḥ

nābhiṣiktaḥ svayaṁ rājye
na cāsīno nṛpāsane
rājendratvaṁ ca samprāpya
mathurāmā viśat tataḥ

He killed Keśi and many other demons in Vraja. He awarded the kingdom of Mathurā to the Bhoja king, Ugrasena, after killing Kaṁsa. Although He was expected to sit upon the throne after killing Kaṁsa, He preferred to install His maternal grandfather. Now He has returned to Mathurā after being recognized as the emperor of the world.

Text 65

evamanyonya saṁjalpaṁ
śrutvā pura nivāsināṁ
bandi māgadha sūtānām
idam ūcur gaṇādhipāḥ

As the ladies were conversing among themselves in this manner, they were joined by the singers, musicians, and orators, whose only pleasure was in glorifying Lord Kṛṣṇa. They spoke as follows.

Text 66

kiṁ vā śakyāmahe vaktuṁ
guṇānāṁ te guṇodadhe
mānuṣe ṇaika jihvena
prabhāvotsāha sambhavān

O ocean of compassion, how can we human beings who have only one tongue properly describe Your transcendental qualities and influence?

Text 67

sa tatra bhogī nāgendraḥ
kadācid deva buddhimān
dvisāhasreṇa jihvena
vāsukiḥ kathayiṣyati

My dear Lord, we think that the king of the serpents, Vāsuki, who resides in Pātālaloka, would be better qualified to describe Your glories with his two thousand tongues.

Text 68

kiṁ tvadbhutam idaṁ loke
mānavendreṣu bhūtale
na bhūtaṁ na bhaviṣyaṁ ca
śakrādāsanam agatam

Has anyone heard that it the past a throne was dispatched from the heavenly planets for the use of a king on earth? I doubt that such an astonishing thing will not be repeated in the future.

Text 69

sabhāva taraṇaṁ caiva
kalaśair āgataṁ svayam
na śrutaṁ na ca dṛṣṭaṁ vā
tena manyāmahe'd bhūtam

Has an assembly hall of the demigods descended to the earth at any other time? Did celestial pitchers appear in the sky and perform an *abhiseka*, as was done for Lord Keśava? Such are the wonderful pastimes of the Lord!

Texts 70-71

dhanyā devī mahābhāgā
devakī yoṣitāṁ varā
bhavantaṁ tridaśa śreṣṭhaṁ
dhṛtvā garbheṇa keśavam

kṛṣṇaṁ padma palāśākṣaṁ
śrī puñja mamarārcitam
netrābhyāṁ snehapūrṇābhyāṁ
vīkṣate mukhāpaṅkajam

Devakī-devī is certainly the foremost of women because she carried Lord Keśava within her womb. Now, with glances of love, she observes the lotus-like dark-complexioned face of the Supreme Lord, who is worshiped by the demigods.

Texts 72-89

iti saṁjalpa mānānāṁ
śṛṇvantau pṛthagīritam
ugrasenaṁ puraskṛtya
bhrātarau rāmakeśavau

prākāradvāri samprāptyā
varcayāmāsa vai tadā
arghyam ācamanaṁ dattvā
pādyaṁ pādyeti cābravīt

ugrasenas tato dhīmān
keśavasya rathāgrataḥ
praṇamya śirasā kṛṣṇaṁ
gajamāruhya vīryavān

dhanavat toyadhāreṇa
vavarṣa kanakāmbubhiḥ
dhanaughair varṣamāṇastu
samprāptaḥ pitṛveśmani

mathurādhi patiḥ śrīmān
uvāca madhusūdanam
rājendratvam anuprāpya
yuktaṁ me nṛpaveśmani

sthāpituṁ devarājena
dattaṁ siṁhāsanaṁ prabho
neṣyāmi mathureśasya
sabhāṁ bhuja balārjitām

prasādayiṣye bhagavan
na kopaṁ kartum arhasi
devakī vasudevaśca
rohiṇī ca viśāmpate

na kiṁcit karaṇe śaktā
harṣaklama vimohitā
kaṁsamātā tato rājan
arcayāmāsa keśavam

nānādigdeśa jānītaṁ
kaṁsenopārjitaṁ dhanam
deśakālaṁ samālokya
pādayugme nyavedayat
ugrasenaṁ samāhūya
uvāca śrlakṣṇayā girā

śrī kṛṣṇa uvāca
na cāhaṁ mathurā kāṅkṣī
na mayā vittakāṅkṣayā

ghātitas tava putro'yaṁ
kālena nidhanaṁ gataḥ
yajasva vividhān yajñān
dadasva vipulaṁ dhanam

jayasva ripupsainyāni
mama bāhubalāśrayāt
tyajasva manasastāpaṁ
kaṁsanāśod bhavaṁ bhayam

nayasva vittanicayaṁ
mayā dattaṁ punastava
iti prāśvāsya rājānaṁ
kṛṣṇastu halinā saha

praviveśa tataḥ śrīmān
mātā pitro rathāntikam
ānanda paripūrṇābhyāṁ
hṛdayābhyāṁ mahābalau

pitṛmātrostu pādān vai
namaścakra turānatau
tasmin muhūrte nagarī
mathurā tu babhūva sā

svargalokaṁ parityajya
avatīrṇa vāmarāvatī
vasudevasya bhavanaṁ
samīkṣya puravāsinaḥ

manasā cintayā māsur
devalokaṁ na bhūtalam
visṛjya mathureśaṁ tu
mahiṣī sahitaṁ tadā

bhavanaṁ vasudevasya
praviśya balakeśavau
nyasta śastrābubhau vīrau
svagṛhe svairacāriṇau

As the singers, dancers, and orators were speaking in this way, the two brothers, Kṛṣṇa and Balarāma, led by King Ugrasena, arrived at the outer gate of the city. Intelligent King Ugrasena stood in front of Kṛṣṇa's chariot and said: Bring *pādya* and *arghya*.

Thereafter, the king personally worshiped Kṛṣṇa with this paraphernalia and then offered obeisances. After worshiping the Lord, the king mounted an elephant and began sprinkling scented water on the road, like a cloud showering rain. Being moistened by that water, Lord Kṛṣṇa gradually came to the palace of His father.

There, King Ugrasena the king of Mathurā said to Kṛṣṇa, the killer of the Madhu demon: My dear Lord, You have been installed as the emperor of the earth. It seems most appropriate if You bring the throne given by Indra here and rule the kingdom. My dear Lord, You are the actual king of Mathurā because it was attained by Your exhibition of strength. I wish to take You into the royal assembly so please comply with my desire. Devakī, Vasudeva, and Rohiṇi are so overwhelmed by affection that they have not been able to greet You properly.

Then Kaṁsa's mother, Padmāvati, worshiped Lord Keśava and without considering proper time and place, offered at His lotus feet all the wealth that her son had attained by conquering numerous kings.

Lord Kṛṣṇa then spoke to King Ugrasena very sweetly: O King, I do not want to be the master of the kingdom of Mathurā. I did not kill your son with a desire to enjoy wealth or prestige. He met his death by the arrangement of providence. My dear King, you should perform sacrifices, give charity, and conquer your enemies under the shelter of My supreme prowess. Give up your anxiety and accept this vast amount of wealth.

After pacifying King Ugrasena and Queen Padmāvati and bidding them farewell, Lord Kṛṣṇa and His elder brother, Balarāma, went to Their father's palace. There, the two mighty-armed heroes offered Their obeisances at the feet of their father and mother. At that time, the people of Mathurā appeared so ecstatic that it seemed as if Svarga had descended upon the earth. To the citizens of Mathurā, Vasudeva's palace looked like an abode of the demigods.

Text 90

tataḥ kṛtāhnikau bhūtvā
sukhāsīnau kathāntare
etasmin neva kāle tu
mahotpāto babhūva ha

After the two brothers had performed Their daily duties and were seated together comfortably, it appeared that a great calamity had suddenly occurred.

Texts 91-108

babhramuśca ghanākāśe
celuśca bhuvi parvatāḥ

samudāḥ kṣubhitāḥ sarve
vibhrānto bhogināṁ varaḥ

kampitā yādavāḥ sarve
nyubjāśca patitā bhuvi
tau tān nipatitān dṛṣṭvā
rāmakṛṣṇau tu niścalau

mahatā pakṣavātena
vijñātau patagottamam
dadarśa samanuprāptaṁ
divyasrag anulepanam

praṇamya śirasā tābhyāṁ
saumyarūpī kṛtāsanaḥ
taṁ dṛṣṭvā samanuprāptaṁ
sacivaṁ sāmparāyikam

dhṛtimantaṁ garutmantam
uvāca balisūdanaḥ
svāgataṁ khecara śreṣṭha
surasenāri mardana

vinatā hṛdayānanda
svāgataṁ keśavapriya
tamuvāca tataḥ kṛṣṇaḥ
sthitaṁ deham ivāparam

tulyasām arthyayā vācā
āsīnaṁ vinatātmajam

śrī kṛṣṇa uvāca
yāsyāmaḥ patagaśreṣṭha
bhojasyāntaḥ puraṁ mahat

tatra gatvā sukhāsīnā
mantrayāmo manogatam

vaiśampāyana uvāca
praviṣṭau tau mahāvīryau
baladeva janārdanau

vainateya tṛtīyau ca
guhyaṁ mantram athābruvan
avadhyo'sau kṛto'smākaṁ
sumahacca riporbalam

vṛtaḥ sainyena mahatā
mahadbhiśca narādhipaiḥ
bahulāni ca sainyāni
hantaṁ varṣa satairapi

na śakṣyāmaḥ kṣayaṁ kartuṁ
jarāsaṅdhasya vāhinīm
ato'rthaṁ vainateya tvāṁ
vravīmi mathurāṁ purīm
vasatorā vayoḥ śreyo
na bhaved iti me matiḥ

garuḍa uvāca
devadevaṁ namaskṛtya
gato'haṁ bhavato'ntikāt
vāsārtham īkṣituṁ bhūmiṁ
tava deva kuśasthalīm
gatvāhaṁ khe samāsthāya
samantād avalokya tām

dṛṣṭvāhaṁ vivudha śreṣṭha
purīṁ lakṣaṇa pūjitām

sāgarānūpa vipulāṁ
prāgudakya plavaśītalām

sarvatodadhi madhyasthānam
abhedyāṁ tridaśairapi
sarvaratnā karavatīṁ
sarvakāma phaladrumām

sarvatur kusumākīrṇāṁ
sarvataḥ sumanoharām
sarvāśramādhi vāsāṁ ca
sarvakāma guṇairyutām

naranārī samākīrṇaṁ
nityāmoda vivarddhinīm
prākāra parikhopetāṁ
gopurāṭ ṭāla mālinīm

vicitra catvara pathāṁ
vipula dvāra toraṇam
yantrargala vicitrāḍhyāṁ
hemaprākāra śobhitām

Clouds filled the sky, the earth began to shake, the seas became agitated, and even Śeṣa, the foremost of serpents, became confused. The members of the Yadu dynasty trembled vigorously and then fell to the ground unconscious. Only Kṛṣṇa and Balarāma remained undisturbed, for They understood by the movements of the air that Garuḍa, the king of birds, had arrived.

Thereafter, Garuḍa appeared before the two Lords. He was decorated with beautiful flower garlands and smeared with sandalwood paste. He bent his head to offer obeisances and then cheerfully sat on an *āsana*. When Lord Kṛṣṇa saw His carrier, Garuḍa, before Him, He spoke as follows: O foremost of birds, destroyer of the enemies of the demigods, you are most welcome. O giver of pleasure to Vinatā, let Us go to King Ugrasena's palace, where We can discuss Our future course of action.

Vaiśampāyana said: Kṛṣṇa, Balarāma, and Garuḍa entered Ugrasena's palace and began their consultation. Kṛṣṇa was the first to speak: O son of Vinatā, both Jarāsandha and Kālayavana are not to be killed by Me. Both are exceedingly powerful and surrounded by subordinate kings, and they possess vast armies. Indeed, Jarāsandha's army is so extensive that We would not be able to exterminate all his soldiers in one hundred years. For this reason, I think that it is best for Us not to remain at Mathurā. That is My conviction.

Garuḍa responded by saying: My dear Lord, You are the master of all living beings. With Your permission I had gone to Kuśasthali, hoping to find a suitable residence for You. Indeed, I carefully studied the entire area from the sky and after doing so, I concluded that a very wonderful city could be established there. Kuśasthali is strategically very good because it is situated in the sea and thus surrounded by water, which also cools the atmosphere. If You were to make Your capital there, even the demigods would be unable to attack. Construct a beautiful city with gold and jewels and fill it with wish-fulfilling trees and gardens of flowers that bloom in all seasons. Let this city be inhabited by the members of all four *āśramas*. Boundary walls, residential buildings, roads, and gates should be constructed so that everywhere the eye turns, the view is very pleasing.

Text 109

naranāgāśva kalilāṁ
rathasainya samākulām
nānādigdeśajā kīrṇāṁ
divyapuṣpa phaladrumām

The city should be well-protected by the four divisions of our army—infantry, cavalry, chariot warriors, and soldiers riding on elephants. Let it be populated with people from all lands. Celestial trees that supply delicious fruit and fragrant flowers will increase its beauty.

Text 110

patākādhvaja mālāḍhyāṁ
mahābhavana śālinīm
bhīṣaṇīṁ ripusaṅghānāṁ
mitrāṇāṁ harṣavardhanīm

The city should be decorated with colorful flags and banners, for that will greatly enhance its beauty, as will the spacious residential quarters. Indeed, this wonderful city should create fear in the minds of our enemies and joy in the minds of our friends.

Texts 111-12

manujendrādhi vāsebhyo
viśiṣṭo nagarottamām
raivataṁ ca giriśreṣṭhaṁ
kuru deva surālayam

nandana pratimaṁ divyaṁ
puradvārasya bhṛṣaṇam
kārayasvādhi vāsaṁ ca
tatra gatvā surottama

My dear Lord, this city should provide a residence suitable for the king of kings. Nearby Raivataka Mountain is a playground of the demigods, and the forests there rival the Nandana forest of Indra. I suggest that You go and reside there.

Texts 113-127

kumārīṇāṁ pracāraśca
suramāṇyo bhaviṣyati
nāmnā dvāravatī jñeyā
triṣu lokeṣu viśrutā

bhaviṣyati pure ramyā
śakrasyevā marāvatī
yadi syāt saṁvṛtāṁ bhūmiṁ
pradāsyati mahodadhiḥ

yatheṣṭaṁ vividhaṁ karma
viśvakarmā kariṣyati
maṇimuktā pravālabhir
vajra vaidūrya saprabhaiḥ

divyair abhiprāya yutair
divyaratnai strilokajaiḥ
divyastambha śatākīrṇan
svarge deva sabhopamān

jāmbunada mayāñchrubhrān
sarvaratna viibhūṣitān
divyadhvaja patākāḍhyān
devagandharva pālitān

candrasūrya pratīkāśān
prāsādān kāraya prabho

vaiśampāyana uvāca
evaṁ kṛtvā tu saṁkalpaṁ
vainatey'tha keśavam
praṇamya śirasā tābhyāṁ
niṣasāda kṛtāsanaḥ

kṛṣṇo'pi rāmasahito
vicintya hita mīritam

prakāśa kartu kāmau tau
visṛjya vinatātmajam
satkṛtya vidhivad rājan
mahārhavara bhūṣaṇaiḥ

modete sukhinau tatra
suraloke yathāmarau
tasya tad vacanaṁ śrutvā
bhojarājo mahāyaśāḥ

kṛṣṇaṁ snehena vistrabhdhaṁ
vabhāṣe vacanāmṛtam
kṛṣṇa kṛṣṇa mahābāho
yadūnāṁ nandivarddhana

śrūyatāṁ vacanaṁ tvādya
vakṣyāmi ripusūdana
tvayā vihīnāḥ sarve sma
na śaktāḥ sukhamāsitum
pure'smin viṣayānte vā
patihīnā iva striyaḥ
tvatsanāthā vayaṁ tāta
tvadvāhu balamāśritāḥ

vibhīmo na narendrāṇāṁ
sendrāṇāmapi mānada
vijayāya yaduśreṣṭha
yatra yatra gamiṣyasi

tatra tvaṁ sahito'smābhir
gacchethā yādavarṣabha

tasya rājño vacaḥ śrutvā
sasmitaṁ devakīsutaḥ

yatheṣṭaṁ bhavatāmadya
tathā kartāsmya saṁāyam

This city will be known as Dvāravatī, or Dvārakā, and it will become renowned throughout the three worlds, equal to the city of Indra in the heavenly planets, and even young girls will be able to wander about freely without fear. If the deity of the ocean gives a portion of its domain to us, then such a city can be established.

My dear Lord, by Your order, Viśvakarmā can come and manifest this city according to Your desire, displaying the full extent of his artistic skill. He can construct beautiful buildings decorated with diamonds, pearls, jewels, coral, and emeralds—whatever valuable jewels are available within the three worlds—so that it resembles the assembly halls of the demigods. The buildings should be supported by thousands of pillars and covered with gold. White marble palaces should be decorated with colorful flags so that they appear as effulgent as the sun.

Vaiśampāyana said: After presenting his proposal to Lord Kṛṣṇa, Vinatā's son, Garuḍa, offered his obeisances to both Kṛṣṇa and Baralāra and sat down. Kṛṣṇa and Balarāma carefully considered Garuḍa's proposal and then expressed Their approval. Kṛṣṇa satisfied Vinatā's son, Garuḍa, by giving him some of His ornaments, and then bade him farewell.

Thereafter, Kṛṣṇa and Balarāma continued to happily reside at Mathurā like two demigods. When the king of the Bhojas, King Ugrasena, heard about Garuḍa's proposal, he spoke to Lord Kṛṣṇa with great affection: O mighty-armed Lord, who enhances the happiness of the Yadu dynasty, as a woman without a husband cannot live happily, so without You, all of us Yādavas cannot bear to live in Your absence. Under the shelter of Your protection, we do not care for even the demigods, headed by

Indra. Wherever you go to attain victory over your enemies, kindly take us with You.

After hearing these words of King Ugrasena, Lord Kṛṣṇa, the son of Devakī, smiled and said: O King, rest assured that I will do whatever you desire.

Thus ends the translation of the fifty-fifth chapter of the Viṣṇu Parva of Śri Harivaṁsa.

Chapter 56

Kālayavana and Jarāsandha attack Mathurā. Lord Kṛṣṇa and the Yādavas depart from Mathurā and establish the city of Dvārakā

Text 1

vaiśampāyana uvāca
kasyacit tvatha kālasya
sabhyāṁstān yadusaṁsadi
babhāṣe puṇḍarīkākṣo
hetu madvākyam uttamam

Vaiśampāyana said: Thereafter, on a fine day, lotus-eyed Lord Kṛṣṇa spoke to everyone seated within the royal assembly.

Text 2

yādavānām yaṁ bhūmir
mathurā rāṣṭramālinī
vayaṁ caiveha sambhūtā
vraje ca parivarddhitāḥ

This transcendental abode of Mathurā is the abode of the Yādavas. We were born here and then grew up at Vraja.

Text 3

tadidānīṁ gataṁ duḥkhaṁ
śatravaśca parājitāḥ
nṛpeṣū janitaṁ vairaṁ
jarāsandhena vigrahaḥ

At present we live here peaceful because many of Our enemies have been defeated. However, We have created enmity with other powerful kings who do not accept Our authority, especially Jarāsandha.

Text 4

vāhanāni ca naḥ santi
pādātaṁ cāpyanantakam
ratnāni ca vicitrāṇi
mitrāṇi ca bahūni ca

We have ample chariots and countless warriors. Our treasury is full of wealth and jewels, and we have many strong friends and allies.

Text 5

iyaṁ ca māthurī bhūmir
alpā gamyā parasya tu
vṛddhiścaiva parāsmākaṁ
balato mitra tastathāa

However, Mathurā is a small city and not very well fortified so that our enemies can easily penetrate our defenses. Although we may increase the strength of our army and win more allies, this weakness will remain.

Text 6

kumāra kaṭyo yāścemāḥ
padātīnāṁ gaṇāśca ye
eṣāmapīha vasatāṁ
sammardam upalakṣaye

With ten million young soldiers not yet married, and countless infantry at our disposal, the small city of Mathurā appears congested.

Text 7

atra no rocate mahyaṁ
nivāso yadupuṅgavāḥ
purīṁ niveśayiṣyāmi
mama tat kṣantum arhatha

For this reason, O foremost of Yādavas, I do not wish to reside here anymore and am planning to establish a new city. I hope you will forgive this audacity of Mine.

Text 8

etad yadanurūpaṁ vo
mamābhi prāyajaṁ vacaḥ
bhavāya bhavatāṁ kāle
yaduktaṁ yadusaṁsadi

I have thus revealed to you My intention, and you should know that it is for your benefit. Kindly let Me know if you approve of My proposal or not.

Text 9

tamūcuryā davāḥ sarve
hṛṣṭena manasā tadā
sādhyatāṁ yadabhipretaṁ
janasyāsya bhavāya vai

In response, all of the Yādavas joyfully spoke in one voice:

O master, You should do whatever you feel is right for the welfare and prosperity of the members of the Yadu dynasty.

Text 10

tataḥ sammantryāmāsur
vṛṣṇayo mantram uttamam
avadhyo'saukṛto'smākaṁ
sumahacca riporbalam

Thereafter, all the members of the Vṛṣṇi dynasty consulted among themselves as follows: Jarāsandha and Kālayavana cannot to be killed by us, for that is the arrangement of providence. The strength of our enemies is formidable.

Text 11

kṛtaḥ sainya kṣayaścāpi
mahāniha narādhipaiḥ
bahulāni ca sainyāni
hantuṁ varṣa śatairapi
na śakṣyāmo hyatasteṣām
apayāne'bhavanmatiḥ

Although our allies have vanquished many of our enemies in battle, there are countless more waiting to attack us, and we could not eliminate them even by fighting for one hundred years. Therefore, the plan to reside elsewhere in a more secure place is praiseworthy.

Text 12

tasmiṁś caivāntare rājā
sakāla yavanastadā

sainyena tadvidhenaiva
mathurām abhyupāgamat

Meanwhile, both Kālayavana and Jarāsandha, along with their huge armies, attacked the city of Mathurā.

Text 13

tato jarāsandhabalaṁ
durnivāryam abhūt tadā
te kālayavanaṁ caiva
śrutvedaṁ pratipedire

First Jarāsandha launched such a sudden and forceful attack that it took the Yādavas by surprise. Then, when the Yādavas learned of Kālayavana's arrival, they lost all hope of defending themselves.

Text 14

keśavaḥ punarevāha
yādavān satyasaṁgaraḥ
adyaiva divasaḥ puṇyo
niryāmaḥ svabalānugāḥ

Lord Kṛṣṇa then told the Yādavas: Today is the auspicious day when we should leave Mathurā, taking our army with us.

Text 15

tato niścakramuḥ sarve
yādavāḥ kṛṣṇaśāsanāt
odhā iva samudrasya
balaugha pratināditāḥ

As advised by Lord Kṛṣṇa, all the Yādavas quickly left Mathurā, creating quite a commotion throughout the city.

Texts 16-17

saṁgṛhya te kalatrāṇi
vasudeva purogamāḥ
susannaddhairga jairmattai
rathair aśvaiśca daṁśitaiḥ

āhatya dundubhīn sarve
svajana jñāti bāndhavāḥ
niryayur yādavāḥ sarve
mathurām apahāya vai

The Yādavas, headed by Vāsudeva, took their wives and departed from Mathurā after placing their belongings on the backs of intoxicated elephants, horses, and chariots. Along with their relatives, they sounded drums, announcing their departure from Mathurā.

Texts 18-19

syandanaiḥ kāñcanāpīḍair
mattaiśca varavāraṇaiḥ
sūtaiḥ plutaiśca turagaiḥ
kaśāpārṣṇi praṇoditaiḥ

svāni svāni balāgrāṇi
śobhayantaḥ prakarṣiṇaḥ
pratyaṅmukhā yuyurhṛṣṭā
vṛṣṇayo bharatarṣabha

O descendent of Bharata, in a cheerful mood, the

members of the Vṛṣṇi dynasty proceeded towards the west on chariots decorated with gold, the foremost of elephants, and excellent horses that moved by the order of their masters. They were surrounded by their powerful army and so it was a very beautiful sight.

Text 20

tato mukhya tamāḥ sarve
yādavā raṇakovidāḥ
anīkāgrāṇi karṣanto
vāsudeva purogamāḥ

They were followed by Lord Kṛṣṇa and other principal Yādavas, all of who were very expert warriors.

Texts 21-22

te sma nānā latācitraṁ
nārikela vanāyutam
kīrṇaṁ nāgabalaiḥ kāntaṁ
ketakī khaṇḍa maṇḍitam

tāla punnāga bakula
drākṣāvana ghanaṁ kacit
anūpaṁ sindhurājasya
prapetur yadupuṅgavāḥ

In due course of time, the great heroes of the Yadu dynasty arrived at a place partially flooded by the ocean. It was very verdant land and thus pleasing to see. The jasmine flower was especially seen in profusion, and there were numerous palm, *punnāga*, and *bakula* trees, as well as grape vines.

Text 23

te tatra ramaṇīyeṣu
viṣayeṣu sukhāpriyāḥ
mumudur yādavāḥ sarve
devāḥ svargatā iva

The Yādavas took great pleasure in that enchanting place and stopped to entertain themselves in that very pleasing atmosphere, like demigods in the heavenly planets.

Text 24

puravāstu vicitvan
sa kṛṣṇastu paravīrahā
dadarśa vipulaṁ deśaṁ
sāgareṇopa śobhitam

Lord Kṛṣṇa, the vanquisher of His foes, surveyed the land, trying to ascertain where He should establish His wonderful city and while doing so, His gaze fell upon the sea.

Text 25

vāhanānāṁ hitaṁ caiva
sitakā tāmra mṛttikam
pura lakṣaṇa sampannaṁ
kṛtāspadam iva śriyā

The shore of the ocean at that place was filled with copper-colored sand, and the area provided by the ocean seemed ideal for constructing a city, even as a residence for the goddess of fortune.

Text 26

sāgarānila saṁvītaṁ
sāgarāmbu niṣevitam
viṣayaṁ sindhurājasya
śobhitaṁ puralakṣaṇaiḥ

This place was served by breezes cooled by the water of the sea and it appeared to be very suitable for constructing a grand city.

Text 27

tatra raivatako nāma
parvato nātidūrataḥ
mandarodāra śikharaḥ
sarvato'bhi virājate

Near the shore was a well-known hill named Raivataka, which was a delight for the eyes from any angle of vision. Its high peak reminded one of Mount Mandara.

Text 28

tatrai kalavya saṁvāso
droṇenādhyu ṣitaściram
prabhūta purūṣopetaḥ
sarvaratna samākulaḥ

Droṇācārya's disciple Ekalavya had resided at that place and many people came there because it was known to be a source of many valuable jewels.

Text 29

vihāra bhūmis tatraiva
tasya rājñaḥ sunirmitā
nāmnā dvāravatī nāma
svāyatāṣṭā padopamā

Beside that hill was the place of King Revata's pleasure pastimes, which was square like a chess board and included the city of Dvāravatī.

Text 30

keśavena matistatra
puryarthe viniveśitā
niveśaṁ tatra sainyānāṁ
rocayanti sma yādavāḥ

Lord Kṛṣṇa decided to established His city at this place, and all of the Yādavas agreed that it was suitable for them and their army.

Text 31

te rakta sūryadivase
tatra yādava puṅgavāḥ
senā pālāṁśca saṁcakruḥ
skandhāvāra niveśanam

At that time, the sun was about to set. The leading Yādavas appointed guards and hurriedly set up their camp.

Text 32

dhruvāya tatra nyavasat
keśavaḥ saha yādavaiḥ
deśo pura niveśāya sa
yadupravaro vibhuḥ

Lord Kṛṣṇa, the foremost member of the Yadu dynasty, was satisfied that this was the best place to establish a city for Himself and the other Yādavas.

Text 33

tasyāstu vidhivan nāma
vāstūni ca gadāgrajaḥ
nirmame puruṣaśreṣṭho
manaso yādavottamaḥ

Within His mind, Lord Kṛṣṇa, the Supreme Personality of Godhead and the elder brother of Gada, contemplated the entire design of the city with its various residential quarters.

Text 34

evaṁ dvāravatīṁ caiva
purīṁ prāpya sabāndhavāḥ
sukhino nyavasan rājan
svarge devagaṇā iva

In this way, Lord Kṛṣṇa, along with the other members of the Yadu dynasty, began to reside in the city of Dvārakā, just as the demigods reside in heaven.

Text 35

kṛṣṇo'pi kālayavanaṁ
jñātvā keśi niṣūdanaḥ
jarāsandha bhayāccaiva
purīṁ dvāravatīṁ yayau

Realizing that Kālayavana was about to attack Mathurā with the support of Jarāsandha, Kṛṣṇa departed and went to Dvārakā.

Thus ends the translation of fifty-sixth chapter of the Viṣṇu Parva of Śri Harivaṁsa.

Chapter 57

Kālayavana killed by King Mucukunda.

Text 1

janamejaya uvāca
bhagavañ chrotum icchāmi
vistareṇa mahātmanaḥ
caritaṁ vāsudevasya
yaduśreṣṭhasya dhīmataḥ

Janamejaya said: O powerful sage, my desire to hear about the pastimes of the Supreme Lord, Kṛṣṇa, the son of Vasudeva and supremely intelligent member of the Yadu dynasty, increases at every moment.

Texts 2-4

kimarthaṁ ca parityajya
mathurāṁ madhusūdanaḥ
madhyadeśasya kakudaṁ
dhāma lakṣmyāśca kevalam
śṛṅgaṁ pṛthivyāḥ svālakṣyaṁ
prabhūta dhana dhānyavat
āryāḍhya jala bhūyiṣṭham
adhiṣṭhāna varottamam

ayuddhenaiva dāśārhas
tyaktavān dvijasattama
sa kālayavanaścāpi
kṛṣṇe kiṁ pratyapadyata

Why did Madhusūdana leave Mathurā, the transcendental abode of the Lord and His consort, the goddess of fortune, Lakṣmī. Indeed, Mathurā is the most sanctified place on earth, it is the most enchanting of all places of pilgrimage, and it is blessed with great prosperity. It has always been an abode for saintly persons and it is situated by the side of a most sacred river. Certainly, it is the foremost place of residence on this earth. O foremost of those who are twice-born, why did Lord Kṛṣṇa relinquish Mathurā without a fight? After finding that the Lord had fled, what did Kālayavana do?

Text 5

dvārakā ca samāsādya
vāridurgāṁ janārdanaḥ
kiṁ cakāra mahābāhur
mahāyogī mahātapāḥ

What did Lord Janārdana, the master of mystic powers, do after going to Dvāraka, which was surrounded by the water of the ocean?

Text 6

kiṁvīryaḥ kālayavanaḥ
kena jātaśca vīryavān
yamasahyaṁ samālakṣya
vyapa yāto janārdanaḥ

How powerful was Kālayavana? Who were his parents? Considering him to be unbearably powerful, Lord Kṛṣṇa left Mathurā.

Text 7

vaiśampāyana uvāca
vṛṣṇīnām andhakānāṁ ca
gurur gārgo mahāmanāḥ
brahmacārī purā bhūtvā
na sma dārān sa vindati

Vaiśampāyana said: My dear King, long ago, the exalted sage Gargamuṇi, the family priest of the Vṛṣṇi and Andhaka dynasties, observed celibacy while undergoing severe austerities. At that time, he remained completely aloof from women.

Text 8

tathā hi vartamānaṁ tam
ūrdhvaretasam avyayam
śyālo'bhiśastavān gārgyama
upamāniti rājani

The great sage Gargamuṇi controlled his mind and senses, so that they never became agitated. However, his brother-in-law accused him in an assembly of learned men that he was unfit to beget a child.

Text 9

so'bhiśas tastadā rājan
nagare tvajitaṁ jaye
alipsaṁstu striyaṁ caiva
tapastepe sudāruṇam

Although the great sage conquered the unconquerable Supersoul of all living entities, he was wrongly criticized. As a result, he recommenced his penance, performing it with even greater severity and determination.

Text 10

tato dvādaśa varṣāṇi
so'yaścūrṇam abhakṣayat
ārādhayan mahādevam
acintyaṁ śūlapāṇinam

Gargamuṇi worshiped Lord Śiva, who carries a trident and whose form is inconceivable. He continued his austerities for twelve years, sustaining his life by eating iron ore and nothing more.

Text 11

rudrastasmai varaṁ prādāt
samarthaṁ yudhi nigrahe
vṛṣṇinām andhakānāṁ ca
sarvatejo mayaṁ sutam

Being pleased by the sage's austerities, Mahādeva appeared before him and awarded him the benediction that in the future he would have a powerful son who would be capable of defeating the great heroes of the Vṛṣṇi and Andhaka dynasties.

Text 12

tataḥ śuśrāva taṁ rājā
yavanādhi patirvaram
putra prasavajaṁ devād
aputraḥ putrakāmitā

A Yavana king happened to hear about this benediction

of Mahādeva. By the arrangement of providence, the Yavana had no son and desperately wanted one.

Text 13

sa nṛpastamu pānāyya
sāntvayitvā dvijottamam
taṁ ghoṣamadhye yavano
gopastrīṣu samāsṛjat

The Yavana king brought Gargamuṇi to his palace and gave him facility to freely mingle with the cowherd women in the pastures.

Text 14

gopālī tapsarās tatra
gopastrī veṣadhāriṇī
dhārayāmāsa gārgyasya
garbhaṁ durdharam acyutam

There was an Apsarā named Gopālī residing in that cow pasture, having assumed the guise of a cowherd girl. It was she who bore the incomparable son of Gargamuṇi.

Text 15

mānuṣyāṁ gārgyabhāryāyāṁ
niyogācchūla pāṇinaḥ
sa kālayavano nāma
jajñe śuro mahābalaḥ

Thus, by the influence of Mahādeva's benediction,

Gargamuṇi begot a powerful and heroic son named Kālayavana from the womb of the Apsarā who had assumed a human form.

Text 16

aputrasyātha rājñastu
vavṛdhe'ntaḥ pure śiśuḥ
tasminn uparate rājan
sa kālayavano nṛpaḥ

O King, thereafter the child happily grew up in the palace of his foster father. After the death of his foster father, Kālayavana ascended the throne and continued to rule the kingdom of Yavanas.

Text 17

yuddhābhi kāmo nṛpatiḥ
paryapṛcchad dvijottamān
vṛṣṇyandhaka kulaṁ tasya
nāradena niveditam

Having a strong desire to engage in warfare, King Kālayavana inquired from the *brāhmaṇas*, asking them to name the greatest warriors on earth. The great sage Nārada Muni then informed him about the Vṛṣṇi and Andhaka dynasties.

Text 18

jñātvā tu varadānaṁ tan
nāradān madhusūdanaḥ
upapraikṣata tejasvī
varddhantaṁ yavaneṣu tam

Although the all-powerful Lord Madhusūdana knew that

Kālayavana had received information from the great sage Nārada, He paid no heed to the Yavana king.

Text 19

samṛddho hi yadā rājā
yavanānāṁ mahābalaḥ
tata evaṁ nṛpā mlecchāḥ
saṁśrityānuya yustadā

As Kālayavana became more and more prosperous and influential, many other kings, especially the rulers of the *mlecchas*, took shelter of him, becoming his followers.

Text 20

śakāstu ṣārā daradāḥ
pāradāḥ śṛṅgalāḥ khasāḥ
pahlavāḥ śataśaścānye
mlecchā haima vatāstathā

Indeed, many thousands of *mleccha* clans, such as the Śakas, Thusārs, Daradas, Pāradas, Śriṅgalas, Khasas, and Phallavas, who resided in the Himālayas, joined him.

Text 21

sa tai parivṛto rājā
dasyubhiḥ śalabhiriva
nānāveṣā yudhaibhīmmair
mathurāmabhya vartata

All of these *mlecchas* were plunderers who dressed as dacoits and carried weapons. Being accompanied by these ferocious *mlecchas*, King Kālayavana attacked the city of Mathurā.

Texts 22-23

gajavāji kharoṣṭrāṇām
ayutairar budairapi
pṛthivīṁ kampayāmāsa
sainyena mahatā vṛtaḥ

reṇunā sūryamārgaṁ tu
samavacchādya pārthivaḥ
mūtreṇa śakṛtā caiva
sainyena sasṛje nadīm

Kālayavana had many hundreds of thousands of warriors mounted upon elephants, horses, donkeys, and camels. Being surrounded by his vast army, he began to create havoc so that even the earth began to tremble and the sun became covered by the dust stirred up by the feet of the soldiers. Incredibly, a river was created by the stool and urine evacuated by the soldiers and their animals.

Text 24

aśvoṣṭra śakṛtāṁ rāśor
niṣrūteti janādhipa
tato'śva śakṛdityevaṁ
nāma nadyā badhūva ha

O ruler of men, that river was filled with huge mounds of camel dung and horse dung and because of this, it was called Aśvaśvakṛt.

Text 25

tatsainyaṁ mahadāyād vai
śrutvā vṛṣṇyandhak āgraṇīḥ
vasudevaḥ samānāyya
jñātī nidam uvāca ha

When Vasudeva, the king of the Vṛṣṇi and Andhaka dynasties, heard of Kālayavan's attack with his vast army, he immediately summoned his associates and spoke as follows.

Text 26

idaṁ samutthitaṁ ghoraṁ
vṛṣṇyandhaka bhayaṁ mahat
avadhyaścāpi naḥ śatrur
varadānāt pinākinaḥ

We now find ourselves in a very dangerous position. Indeed, a calamity has befallen the Vṛṣṇi and the Andhaka dynasties because our greatest enemy, Kālayavana, who cannot be killed by us due to the benediction of Mahādeva, the wielder of the trident, has attacked our city.

Text 27

sāmādayo'bhyupāyāśca
vihitāstasya sarvaśaḥ
matto madabalābhyāṁ
tu yuddhameva cikīrṣati

Although we may try to subdue our enemy by various means, rest assured that we will not succeed. He is intoxicated with pride due to his incomparable strength and is determined to conquer us.

Text 28

etāvāniha vāsaśca
kathito nāradena me
etāvati ca vaktavyaṁ
sāmaiva paramaṁ matam

The great sage Nārada had advised us to reside here until such an occurrence as this. It is said that the best way to deal with a very proud and powerful enemy is to behave with him in a very pleasant and humble manner.

Texts 29-30

jarāsandhaśca no rājā
nityameva na mṛṣyate
tathānye pṛthivī pālā
vṛṣṇicakra pratāpitāḥ

kecit kaṁsa vadhāccāpi
viraktās tadgatā nṛpāḥ
samāśritya jarāsandham
asmānicchanti vādhitum

Jarāsandha is very envious of us and will never forgive us. Many kings that we had previously defeated, and others that were allied with Kaṁsa, are ready to assist Jarāsandha, hoping to gain revenge.

Texts 31-33

bahavo jñātayaś caiva
yadūnāṁ nihatā nṛpaiḥ
varddhituṁ naiva śakṣyāma
pure'smin niti keśavaḥ

apayāne matiṁ kṛtvā
dūtaṁ tasmai sasarjaha
tataḥ kumbhe mahāsarpaṁ
bhinnāñjana cayopamam

ghoram āśīviṣaṁ kṛṣṇaṁ
kṛṣṇam prākṣepayat tadā
tatastaṁ mudrayitvā tu
svena dūtena hārayat

These sinful kings have already killed many of our relatives. If we remain at Mathurā, we will continuously face the wrath of our enemies. Considering this, Kṛṣṇa also decided that we should establish ourselves somewhere else. Hoping to avoid this inconvenience, the Lord had sent an envoy to Kālayavana. He had placed a black poisonous snake inside a pitcher. After carefully closing the lid, he sent it as a gift with His envoy to Kālayavana.

Texts 34-36

nidarśanārthaṁ govindo
bhīṣayāmāsa taṁ nṛpaṁ
sa dūtaḥ kālayavane
darśayāmāsa taṁ ghaṭam
kālasarpopamaḥ kṛṣṇa
ityuktvā bharatavarṣabha
tatkālayavano buddhvā
trāsanaṁ yādavaiḥ kṛtam

pipīlikānāṁ caṇḍānāṁ
pūrayāmāsa taṁ ghaṭam
sa sarpo bahubhis tīkṣṇaiḥ
sarva tastaiḥ pipīlikaiḥ

bhakṣyamāṇaḥ kilāṅgeṣu
bhasmībhūto'bhavat tadā

Lord Govinda wanted to frighten Kālayavana by sending him a poisonous snake. O descendent of Bharata, the messenger handed the pitcher to Kālayavana, saying that Lord Kṛṣṇa is as formidable as a black snake. Kālayavana felt insulted by the Yādavas and in a fit of anger he gathered thousands of ants and put them in the pitcher. These carnivorous ants covered the snake and bit it until it died.

Text 37

taṁ mudrayitvā tu ghaṭaṁ
tathaiva yavanādhipaḥ
preṣayāmāsa kṛṣṇāya
bhāhulyam upavarṇayan

Kālayavana then tightly closed the pitcher and sent it back to Lord Kṛṣṇa, demonstrating that he was not at all one to be intimidated.

Text 38

vāsudevastu taṁ dṛṣtvā
yoga vihata ātmanaḥ
utsṛjya mathurāmāśu
dvārakām abhijagmivān

When Lord Kṛṣṇa understood that His attempt to frighten Kālayavana had failed, He immediately left Mathurā and went to Dvārakā.

Text 39

vairasyāntaṁ vidhitsaṁstu
vāsudevo mahāyaśāḥ
niveśya dvārakāṁ rājan
vṛṣṇīnāś cāsya caiva ha

Desiring to cause the destruction of the envious Kālayavana, Lord Vāsudeva established the city of Dvārakā and then brought all the members of the Vṛṣṇi dynasty there, giving them all assurances. Thereafter, the Lord returned to Mathurā.

Text 40

padātiḥ puruṣa vyaghro
bāhu praharanas tadā
ājagāma mahāvīryo
mathurāṁ madhusūdanaḥ

Lord Madhusūdana, whose intentions cannot be thwarted, traveled to Mathurā on foot and with no weapons other than his two mighty arms.

Text 41

taṁ dṛṣṭvā niryayau dṛṣṭaḥ
sa kālayavano ruṣā
prekṣāpūrvaṁ ca kṛṣṇo'pi
niścakarṣa mahābalaḥ

When Kālayavana saw that Kṛṣṇa had come to Mathurā, he immediately came out of the palace that he had occupied, feeling both elation and anger. However, after revealing His presence to Kālayavana, Kṛṣṇa quickly fled.

Text 42

athānvagacchad govindaṁ
jighṛkṣūr yavaneśvaraḥ
na caina maśakad rājā
grahītuṁ yogadharmiṇam

Kālayavana, the ruler of the Yavanas, chased Lord Govinda, desiring to arrest him. However, as much as he tried, he could not catch Kṛṣṇa, the master of all mystic powers.

Text 43

māndhātustu suto rājā
mucukundo mahāyaśāḥ
purā devāsure yuddhe
kṛtakarmā mahābalaḥ

Long ago, when the demigods and demons fought a great battle, Māndhātā's son, the illustrious Mucukunda, fought very bravely on behalf of the demigods.

Text 44

vareṇa cchandito devair
nidrāmeva gṛhītavān
śrāntasya tasya vāgevaṁ
tadā prādur abhūt kila

Being very pleased with Mucukunda, the demigods asked him to accept a benediction. Mucukunda then requested that he might enjoy an undisturbed sleep for as long as he would desire. He had become exhausted from fighting and before sleeping, he spoke as follows.

Text 45

prasuptaṁ bodhayed yo māṁ
taṁ daheyam ahaṁ surāḥ
cakṣuṣā krodhadīptena
evamāha punaḥ punaḥ

My dear rulers of the planets, I request that if while sleeping someone disturbs me, then my angry glance should burn the intruder to ashes.

Text 46

evamastivati taṁ śakra
uvāca tridaśaiḥ saha
sa surair abhya anujñāto
hyadrirājam upāgamat

Upon hearing this, the demigods heartily agreed, saying, "So be it." Thereafter, as instructed by the demigods, Mucukunda approached the king of the mountains.

Text 47

sa parvata guhāṁ kāṁcit
praviśya śramakarśitaḥ
suṣvāpa kālametaṁ vai
yāvat kṛṣṇasya darśanam

Being exceedingly fatigued from fighting, King Mucukunda entered a mountain cave and slept for a very long time, until he fortunately received the *darśana* of Lord Kṛṣṇa.

Text 48

tatsarvaṁ vāsudevāya
nāradena niveditam
varadānaṁ ca devebhyas
tejastasya ca bhūpateḥ

The great sage Nārada had approached Lord Kṛṣṇa, the son of Vasudeva, and narrated to Him everything about Mucukunda's benediction received from the demigods, and the power of his fiery glance.

Text 49

kṛṣṇo'nu gamyamānaśca
tena mlecchena śatruṇā
tāṁ guhāṁ mucukundasya
praviveśa vinītavat

Therefore, as Lord Kṛṣṇa was being chased by the king of the *mlecchas*, Kālayavana, He entered the cave where Mucukunda was sleeping.

Text 50

śiraḥsthāne tu rājarṣer
mucukundasya keśavaḥ
saṁdarśana pathaṁ tyaktvā
tasthau buddhimatāṁ varaḥ

Lord Kṛṣṇa, the foremost of intelligent personalities, carefully avoided disturbing Mucukunda. He simply stood in a corner of that dark cave.

Text 51

anupraviśya yavano
dadarśa pṛthivīpatim
sa taṁ suptaṁ kṛtāntābham
āsasāda sudurmatiḥ

Feverishly chasing Lord Kṛṣṇa, Kālayavana entered the cave and saw the sleeping Mucukunda. Thinking him to be Kṛṣṇa, wicked-minded Kālayavana stood in front of Mucukunda, who for him was just like death personified.

Text 52

vāsudevaṁ tu taṁ matvā
ghaṭṭayāmāsa pārthivam
pādenātma vināśāya
śalabhaḥ pāvakaṁ yathā

Just as a fly enters the fire for its own destruction, Kālayavana kicked Mucukunda in the chest, thinking him to be Kṛṣṇa.

Text 53

mucukundastu rājarṣiḥ
pādasparśa prabodhitaḥ
nidrācchedena cukrodha
pādasparśena tena ca

As soon as he was kicked, Mucukunda woke up with a start and upon seeing the Yavana king before him, he became furious.

Text 54

saṁsmṛtya sa varaṁ śakrād
avaikṣata tamagrataḥ
sa dṛṣṭamātraḥ krodhena
samprajajvāla sarvaśaḥ

King Mucukunda remembered the benediction received from Indra as gazed upon Kālayavana standing in front of him. Indeed, as he angrily gazed upon Kālayavana, the Yavana burst into flames.

Text 55

dadāha pāvakastaṁ tu
śuṣkaṁ vṛkṣam ivāśaniḥ
kṣaṇena kālayavanaṁ
netratejo vinirgataḥ

Just as a thunderbolt burns dry wood to ashes, the blazing fire emanating from Mucukunda's eyes, which were red with rage, burned Kālayavana to ashes within a moment.

Text 56

taṁ vāsudevaḥ śrī mantam
ccirasuptaṁ narādhipam
kṛtakāryo'bravīd dhimān
vacanam uttamam

In this way the supremely intelligent Lord Kṛṣṇa accomplished His purpose. Thereafter, He spoke as follows to the powerful King Mucukunda, who had woken up after a very long sleep.

Text 57

rājaṁścira prasupto'si
kathito nāradena me
kṛtaṁ me sumahatkāryaṁ
svasti te'stu vrajāmyaham

Nārada Muni had told me everything about you and so I decided to employ your services in accomplishing My mission. As I depart I wish that you may achieve auspiciousness.

Text 58

vāsudevam upālakṣya
rājā hṛsvaṁ pramāṇataḥ
pariṣkṛtaṁ yugaṁ mene
kālena mahatā tadā

When King Mucukunda saw the son of Vasudeva's short stature, he could understand that a long time had passed and that now it was Kali-yuga.

Text 59

uvāca rājā govindaṁ
ko bhavān kimihāgataḥ
kaśca kālaḥ prasuptasya
yadi jānāsi kathyatām

King Mucukunda inquired: Who are you? Why have you come here? How long have I been sleeping? Kindly tell me.

Text 60

śrī kṛṣṇa uvāca
somavaṁśod bhavo rājā
yayātir nāma nāhuṣaḥ
tasya putro yadurjyeṣṭhaś
catvāro'nye yavīyasaḥ

Śrī Kṛṣṇa said: O King, long ago lived a king named Yayāti, the son of Nāhuṣa of the Candra dynasty. He had five sons and the eldest one was named Yadu.

Text 61

yaduvaṁśāt samutpannaṁ
vasudevātmajaṁ vibho
vāsudevaṁ vijānīhi
nṛpate māmihāgatam

I am the son of Vasudeva in the Yadu dynasty. For this reason I am also known as Vāsudeva, O ruler of men.

Text 62

tretāyuge prasupto'si
vidito me'si nāradāt
idaṁ kaliyugaṁ viddhi
kimanyat karavāṇi te

I was told by Nārada that you have been sleeping since Tretā-yuga. Now is the conjunction of Dvāpara and Kali *yugas*. What else can I do for you?

Text 63

mama śatrus tvayā dagdho
devadatta varo nṛpa
avadhyo yo mayā saṁkhye
bhaved varṣa śatairapi

You served Me by killing My enemy, who had received a benediction from the demigods that he would not be killed by Me, even if I were to fight with him for one hundred years.

Text 64

vaiśampāyana uvāca
ityuktaḥ sat tu kṛṣṇena
nirjagāma guhāmukhāt
anvīya mānaḥ kṛṣṇena
kṛtakāryeṇa dhīmatā

Vaiśampāyana said: When Lord Kṛṣṇa finished speaking, King Mucukunda came out of the cave, and Kṛṣṇa followed him.

Text 65

tato dadarśa pṛthivīm
āvṛtāṁ hṛsvakair naraiḥ
svalpotsāhair alpabalair
alpavīrya parākramaiḥ
pareṇādhiṣṭhitaṁ caiva
rājyaṁ kevalam ātmanaḥ

King Mucukunda saw that the people on earth were very short in stature. Their enthusiasm, strength, and influence had decreased remarkably. Only his kingdom was still intact, although it was ruled by someone else.

Text 66

prītyā visṛjya govindaṁ
praviveśa mahad vanam
himavantam agād rājā
tapase dhṛtamānasaḥ

King Mucukunda bade farewell to Lord Kṛṣṇa with great affection. He was determined to perform austerities, and for that purpose he departed the Himālayas.

Text 67

tataḥ sa tapa āsthāya
vinirmucya kalevaram
āruroha divaṁ rājā
karmabhiḥ svairjitāśubhaiḥ

In a forest of the Himālayas, he practiced severe austerities before giving up his material body. In this way, he ultimately attained the heavenly planets.

Text 68

vāsudevo'pi dharmātmā
upāyena mahāmanāḥ
ghātayitvā't manaḥ śatruṁ
tatsainyaṁ pratyapadyata

Now that Kālayavana was gone, the Supreme Personality of Godhead, Lord Vāsudeva, returned to Mathurā and easily dispersed the enemy soldiers.

Text 69

prabhūta ratha hastyaśva
varma śastrāyudha dhvajam
ādāyopa yayau dhīmān
sa sainyaṁ nihateśvaram

After the death of Kālayavana, Kṛṣṇa took his innumerable chariots, elephants, horses, and weapons, and whatever else was of value.

Text 70

nivedayāmāsa tato narādhipe
tadugrasene pratipūrṇa mānasaḥ
janārdano dvāravatīṁ ca tāṁ pure
maśobhayat tena dhanena bhūriṇā

In this way, Lord Kṛṣṇa felt great satisfaction upon achieving victory over His enemies. Much of the spoils of war were given to King Ugrasena, and with the great wealth He enhanced the beauty of Dvārakā.

Thus ends the translation of the fifty-seventh chapter of the Viṣṇu Parva of Śri Harivaṁsa

Chapter 58

By Lord Kṛṣṇa's order, Viśvakarmā constructs Dvārakā

Text 1

vaiśampāyana uvāca
tataḥ prabhāte vimale
bhāskare udite tadā
kṛtajāpyo hṛṣīkeśo
vanānte niṣasādaha

Vaiśampāyana said: Thereafter, on a sunny Saturday morning, after getting up from His bed, Lord Kṛṣṇa sat within a garden and performed His morning religious duties of chanting and hearing the scriptures.

Text 2

paricakṛama taṁ deśaṁ
durgasthāna diḍṛkṣayā
upatasthuḥ kulaprāgyā
yādavā yadunandanam

After finishing His morning duties, Lord Kṛṣṇa wandered about, accompanied by elderly members of the Yadu dynasty, ascertaining an ideal location for constructing His palace.

Text 3

rohiṇyām ahani śreṣṭhe
svasti vācya dvijottamān

puṇyāha ghoṣair vipulair
durgasyā rabdhavān kriyām

After choosing the best location for His palace, the Lord had qualified *brāhmaṇas* perform the required rituals invoking auspiciousness on a Saturday during the period of Rohiṇī *nakṣatra*. Later in the day, the construction commenced.

Text 4

tataḥ paṅkaja patrākṣo
yādavān keśisūdanaḥ
provāca vadatāṁ śreṣhto
devān vṛtra ripuryathā

Just as Indra, the enemy of Vṛtrāsura, makes announcements to the assembled demigods, lotus-eyed Lord Kṛṣṇa, the killer of the Keśi demon and foremost of eloquent speakers, announced as follows.

Text 5

kalpiteyaṁ mayā bhūmiḥ
paśyadhvaṁ devasadmavat
nāma cāsyāḥ kṛtaṁ puryāḥ
khyātiṁ yadupayāsyati

My dear Yādavas, just see how, by My inconceivable potency, I have transformed this land so that it appears like an abode of the demigods. I have decided upon a name for our new place of residence, which will become famous throughout the three worlds.

Text 6

iyaṁ dvāravatī nāma
pṛthivyāṁ nirmitā mayā
bhaviṣyati pure ramyā
śakrasyeva amarāvatī

This city, created by Me, will be known in this world as Dvāravatī, or Dvārakā, and will rival the abode of Indra, Amarāvatī.

Text 7

tānyevāsyāḥ kārayiṣye
cinhānyāya tanāni ca
catvarān rājamārgāṁśca
samyagantaḥ purāṇi ca

I will arrange for opulent residences, temples, palaces, and avenues so that it exactly resembles Indra's city, Amarāvatī.

Text 8

devā ivātra modantu
bhavanto vigatajvarāḥ
bādhamānā ripūnugrān
ugrasena purogamāḥ

As the demigods enjoy celestial happiness at Amarāvatī, under the leadership of King Ugrasena, I wish for all of you to reside here very happily, creating envy in the minds of our enemies.

Text 9

gṛhyantāṁ veśma vāstūni
kalpyantāṁ trika catvarāḥ
mīyantāṁ rājamārgāśca
prāsādasya ca yā gatiḥ

The paraphernalia for performing the ceremony for laying the foundation should be collected. All the roads and intersections should systematically demarked and there should be a grand highway leading to My place.

Text 10

preṣyantāṁ śilpimukhyā vai
niyuktā veśmakarmasu
niyujyantāṁ ca deśeṣu
preṣyakarma karājanāḥ

We should summon the foremost artisans, who are masters of the art of constructing buildings. We should also set up temporary camps near the construction site for the laborers.

Text 11

evamukte tu yadavo
g'rhasaṁgraha tatparāḥ
yathāniveśaṁ saṁhṛṣṭās
cakrur vāstu parigraham

Upon receiving Lord Kṛṣṇa's instructions, all the Yādavas jubilantly began collecting the required materials for the construction. The paraphernalia for the laying of the foundation was separately gathered by qualified persons.

Text 12

sūtrahastās tato mānaṁ
cakruryādava sattamāḥ
puṇye'hani mahārāja
dvijātīn abhipūjya ca

Thereafter, on an auspicious day, the Yādavas first worshiped the qualified *brāhmaṇas* and then began demarking the boundaries of the buildings and roads with string.

Text 13

vāstudaivata karmāṇi
vidhinā kārayanti ca
stha patīnatha govindos
tatrovāca mahāmatiḥ

They very respectfully worshiped the presiding deity of that place, carefully observing all the prescribed rules and regulations. Lord Kṛṣṇa then called for all the laborers and spoke to them as follows.

Text 14

asmadarthe suvihitaṁ
kriyatāmatra mandiram
vivikta catvara pathaṁ
suniviṣṭeṣṭa daivatam

First you should construct beautiful temples for the worship of the demigods and thereafter make the roads so that they appear very attractive, especially the intersections.

Texts 15-16

te tatheti mahābāhum
uktvā sthapatayas tadā
durgakarmāṇi saṁskārān
upakalpya yathāvidhi

yathānyāyaṁ nirmimire
durgāṇyāyata nāni ca
sthānāni nida dhuścātra
brahmādīnāṁ yathākramam

After receiving the orders of mighty-armed Lord Kṛṣṇa, the laborers immediately began the preliminary work of construction, such as clearing and leveling the land. Thereafter, following the procedures laid down in the scriptures, they built numerous palaces and temples for the worship of the demigods, beginning with Brahmā.

Text 17

apamāgneḥ sureśasya
dṛṣa dolūkha lasya ca
cāturdaivāni catvāri
dvārāṇi nidadhuśca te

They constructed four marvelous gates dedicated to the *lokapālas*, Varuṇa, Agni, Indra, and Vayu.

Texts 18-21

śuddhākṣa maindraṁ bhallāṭaṁ
puṣpadantaṁ tathaiva ca
teṣu veśmasu yukteṣu
yādaveṣu mahātmasu

puryāḥ kṣipraṁ niveśārthaṁ
cintayāmāsa mādhavaḥ
tasya daivotthitā buddhir
vimalā kṣiprakāriṇī

puryāḥ priyakarī sā vai
yadūnāma bhivarddhinī
śilpimukhyastu devānāṁ
prajāpati sutaḥ prabhuḥ

viśvakarmā svamatyā vai
purīṁ saṁsthāpayiṣyati
manasā samanudhyāya
tasyā gamana kāraṇāt
tridaśābhi mukhaḥ kṛṣṇo
vivikte samapadyata

These sculptors prepared deities of many demigods, including Śuddhākṣa, Aindra, Bhallāṭa, and Puṣpadanṭa, which were then installed at various places throughout the city. As the Yādavas enthusiastically engaged in the construction of the buildings, Lord Kṛṣṇa, the husband of Lakṣmī, began to think about how the city could be completed very quickly. Lord Kṛṣṇa, who always considered the welfare and prosperity of the Yādavas, thought: Prajāpati's son, Viśvakarmā, the architect of the demigods, is the most expert person in this field. I am sure he would be very happy to employ his skills in constructing this wonderful city.

After making up His mind in this way, Lord Kṛṣṇa went to a solitary place and invoked Viśvakarmā from the world of the celestials.

Text 22

tasminneva tataḥ kāle
śilpācāryo mahāmatiḥ
viśvakarmā suraśreṣṭhaḥ
kṛṣṇasya pramukhe sthitaḥ

As soon as he was thought of, the greatly intelligent and expert architect of the demigods appeared before Lord Kṛṣṇa.

Text 23

viśvakarmovāca
śakreṇa preṣitaḥ kṣipraṁ
tava viṣṇo dhṛtavrata
kiṅkaraḥ samanu prāptaḥ
śādhimāṁ kiṁ karomi te

Viśvakarmā said: My dear Lord Viṣṇu, Indra ordered me to immediately come here. I am Your obedient servant and am prepared to execute whatever You may desire. Please instruct me—what can I do for You?

Text 24

yathāsau devadevo me
saṅkaraśca yathāvyayaḥ
tathā tvaṁ devo mānyo me
viśeṣo nāsti vaḥ prabho

My dear Lord, I consider You to be on the level of Brahmā, the lord of the demigods, and Saṅkara, the eternal master of material nature. My understanding is that there is no real difference between You three.

Text 25

trailokya jñāpikāṁ vācam
utsṛjyasva mahābhuja
eṣo'smi paridṛṣṭārthaṁ
kiṁ karomi praśādhi mām

O mighty-armed one, You are the master of everyone within the three worlds. Please consider me to be Your eternal servant. I am an accomplished architect that now stands before You. Please order me—what service can I perform?

Text 26

śrutvā vinītaṁ vacanaṁ
keśavo viśvakarmaṇaḥ
pratyuvāca yaduśreṣṭhaḥ
kaṁsarir atulaṁ vacaḥ

After hearing the humble speech of Viśvakarmā, Lord Kṛṣṇa, the foremost member of the Yadu dynasty and killer of Kaṁsa, replied as follows.

Text 27

śutārtho devaguhyasya
bhavān yatra vayaṁ sthitāḥ
avaśyaṁtviha kartavyaṁ
sadanaṁ me surottama

Long ago, you were present during an emergency meeting of the demigods and so you are aware of how they prayed for My incarnation to remove the burden of the earth. Now, I would like you to construct a suitable palace for Me.

Text 28

tadiyaṁ pūḥ prakāśārthaṁ
niveśyā mayi suvrata
matprabhāvānu rūpaiśca
gṛhaiśceyaṁ samantataḥ

Kindly display the full extent of your architectural skill for My sake. Indeed, I entrust you with the responsibility of constructing this entire city, full of palatial buildings that match My personal influence and opulence.

Text 29

uttamā ca pṛthivyāṁ vai
yathā svarge' amarāvatī
tatheyaṁ hi tvayā kāryā
śakto hyasi mahāmate

As Amarāvatī is the best of all cities in the heavenly planets, this city should be the foremost city on earth. I am confident that you are capable of fulfilling My desire.

Text 30

mama sthānam idaṁ kāryaṁ
yathā vai tridive tathā
martyāḥ paśyantu me lakṣmīṁ
puryā yadukulasya ca

This city should be made to resemble My transcendental abode of Vaikuṇṭha so that the people of this world can fully appreciate My opulence and influence, and that of My associates, the members of the Yadu dynasty.

Text 31

evamuktas tataḥ prāha
viśvakarmā matīśvaraḥ
kṛṣṇam akliṣṭa karmāṇaṁ
devāmitra vināśanam

After being instructed by Lord Kṛṣṇa, Viśvakarmā, the son of Prajāpati and performer of wonderful architectural feats, replied to the vanquisher of the enemies of the demigods.

Text 32

sarvametat kariṣyāmi
yat tvayābhihitaṁ prabho
pure tviyaṁ janasyāsya
na paryāptā bhaviṣyati

O Lord, I will certainly execute whatever You have ordered. However, I must inform you that, in my opinion, this land is not sufficient for the vast number of people assembled here.

Texts 33-34

bhaviṣyati ca vistīrṇā
vṛddhir asyāstu śobhanā
catvāraḥ sāgarā hyasyāṁ
viccariṣyanti rūpiṇaḥ

yadīcchet sāgaraḥ kiñcid
utsraṣṭumapi toyarāṭ
tataḥ svāyata lakṣaṇyā
puri syāt puruṣottama

O Supreme Lord, if You so desire, I can extend the area of this land while retaining its beauty. You should petition the presiding deity of the ocean, asking him to provide some more land so that this city can be constructed with all pleasing characteristics.

Text 35

evamuktas tataḥ kṛṣṇaḥ
prāgeva kṛtaniścayaḥ
sāgaraṁ saritāṁ nātham
uvāca vadatāṁ varaḥ

After hearing Viśvakarmā's suggestion, Lord Kṛṣṇa, the foremost of eloquent speakers, made up His mind to acquire more land from the ocean-god. With this in mind, He addressed Sāgara, the lord of the ocean, as follows.

Text 36

samudra daśa ca dve ca
yojanāni jalāśaye
pratisaṁhṛya tāmātmā
yadyasti mayi mānyatā

O Sāgara, if you have respect for Me then fulfill My wish by providing Me with an additional twelve *yojanas* of land by withdrawing your water from it.

Text 37

avakāśo tvayā date
purīṁ māmakaṁ balam
paryāpta viṣayā ramyā
samagraṁ visahiṣyati

If you allow Me to utilize this land, I can extend My city so that it will be large enough to accommodate the burden of My vast army.

Text 38

tataḥ kṛṣṇasya vacanaṁ
śrutvā nadanadīpatiḥ
sa mārutena yogena
utsasarja jalāśayam

As soon as the presiding deity of the rivers and seas heard the request of Lord Kṛṣṇa, he immediately called for the assistance of the wind-god and withdrew the water from the required area of land.

Text 39

viśvakarmā tataḥ pṛta
puryāḥ saṁlakṣya vāstu tat
govinde caiva sammānaṁ
kṛtavān sāgaras tadā

Viśvakarmā was very pleased to see the extended area he would have to work with. Thus, as was befitting his position, the presiding deity of the ocean rendered service to Lord Kṛṣṇa.

Text 40

viśvakarmā tataḥ kṛṣṇam
uvāca yadunandanam
adya prabhṛti govinda
sarve samadhirohata

Viśvakarmā then addressed Lord Kṛṣṇa, the descendent of Yadu: O Govinda, You will be able to reside in this city beginning from this very day.

Texts 41-42

manasā nirmitā ceyaṁ
mayā puḥ pravarā vibho
acireṇaiva kālena
gṛhasambādha mālinī

bhaviṣyati pure ramya
sudvārā prāgyatoraṇā
cayāṭṭālaka keyūrā
pṛthivyāṁ kakudopamā

My dear Lord, I have already conceived of the city within my mind. In a short while, all of the palaces and other residential quarters will manifest themselves, making the entire city very attractive. The doors will increase the beauty of all the buildings due to their exquisite artistry. Everywhere, courtyards, halls, pillars, and residential buildings will decorate the city so that it appears like the crown of the earth.

Text 43

antaḥpuraṁ ca kṛṣṇasya
paricaryākṣayaṁ mahat
cakāra tasyāṁ puryā vai
deśe tridaśa pūjite

Viśvakarmā then constructed an especially magnificent palace for Lord Kṛṣṇa in the heart of the city, which was envied by even the demigods.

Text 44

tataḥ sā nirmitā kāntā
puri dvārāvatī tadā
mānasena prayatnena
vaiṣṇavī viśvakarmaṇā

Viśvakarmā conceived of the entire city of Dvārakā within his mind, and then manifested it as the transcendental abode of Lord Viṣṇu.

Text 45

vidhāna vihitadvārā
prākāra varaśobhitā
parikhācaya saṁguptā
sāṭṭa prākāra toraṇā

The city gates were built according to injunctions of the literature dealing with architecture. Throughout the city were many raised platforms, high walls, massive gates, and pillars that greatly enhanced its beauty.

Text 46

kāntanārī naragaṇā
vaṇigbhi rupaśobhitā
nānāpaṇya gaṇāīrṇā
khecarīva ca gāṁ gatā

The city became filled with gloriously handsome men and beautiful women. Countless merchants opened shops that provided the necessities of life. Indeed, it appeared as if a celestial city had miraculously manifested on the earth.

Text 47

prapāvāpī prasannodā
udyānair upaśobhitā
samantataḥ saṁvṛtāṅgī
vanitevāya tekṣaṇā

The ponds, lakes, and wells within the city were filled with crystal-clear water. The reservoirs of water and the flower gardens and orchards enhanced the beauty of the city. It appeared as if the city were like a charming girl with wide eyes who modestly covered herself.

Text 48

samṛddha catvaravatī
veṁottama dhanācitā
rathyā koṭi sahasrāḍhyā
śubhrarāja pathottarā

The avenues within the city were majestic and the multi-storied palaces seemed to touch the clouds. There were many thousands of roads and small lanes winding here and there.

Text 49

bhūṣayantī samudraṁ sā
svargamindra purī yathā
pṛthivyāṁ sarva ratnānām
ekā nicayaśālinī

As the abode of Indra increases the beauty of the heavenly planets, this city enhanced the beauty of the sea. It appeared to be a storehouse of all kinds of precious jewels available on earth.

Text 50

surāṇām api sukṣetrā
sāmantak ṣobha kāriṇī
aprakāśaṁ tadākāsaṁ
prāsādair upakurvatī

The city of Dvārakā became a place of pilgrimage even for the demigods. Indeed, it created envy and agitation within the minds of neighboring kings. With its massive palaces, the city seemed to cover the sky.

Text 51

pṛthivyāṁ pṛthurāṣṭrāyāṁ
janaugha pratināditā
odyaiśca vārirājasya
śiśirī kṛtamārutā

The city of Dvārakā bustled with the activity of countless men and women. The cool breezes coming from the sea and the gentle sound of the waves created a soothing atmosphere that greatly pleased the inhabitants.

Text 52

anūpopa vanaiḥ kāntaiḥ
kāntyā janamanoharā
satārakā dyauriva sā
dvārakā pratyarājata

The enchanting city of Dvārakā, which was surrounded on all sides by the sea, as well as very lovely forests and gardens, captivated the minds all living entities. With its innumerable inhabitants, it appeared like the sky filled with stars and planets.

Texts 53-55

prākāreṇārka varṇena
śāta kaumbhena saṁvṛtā
hiraṇya prativarṇaiśca
gṛhair gambhīra niḥsvnaiḥ

śubhramegha pratīkāśair
dvāraiḥ saudhaiśca śobhitā
kacit kvacid udagrāgrair
upāvṛta mahāpathā

tāmāvaasat purīṁ kṛṣṇaḥ
sarve yādavanandanāḥ
abhepreta janākīrṇāṁ
somaḥ khamiva bhāsayan

The raised platforms and boundary walls were made of gold, as were many of the residential quarters. The doors of the palaces were as white as clouds in autumn. The pillars were beautifully made so that they enchanted the mind. The buildings were so tall that their shadows fell a great distance on the roads. Lord Kṛṣṇa and the other members of the Yadu dynasty began to reside at Dvārakā very happily. Just as the moon illuminates all directions with its pleasing rays, the city was filled with godly person who were very pleasing to everyone.

Text 56

viśvakarmā ca tāṁ kṛtvā
purīṁ śakrapurīmiva

jagāma tridivaṁ devo
govindenābhi pūjitaḥ

After completing the construction of Dvārakā, which appeared like Indra's abode, Viśvakarmā returned to the heavenly planets after being duly gratified by Lord Kṛṣṇa.

Text 57

bhūyaśca buddhir abhavat
kṛṣṇaśca viditātmanaḥ
janānimān dhanau ghaiśca
tarpayeya mahaṁ yadi

Thereafter, Lord Kṛṣṇa thought: If I can please all the inhabitants of Dvārakā with gifts of abundant wealth—that would be very nice.

Text 58

savai śravaṇa saṁspṛṣṭām
nidhīnām uttamaṁ nidhim
śaṅkhamāhya yatopendro
niśi sve bhavane prabhuḥ

Lord Kṛṣṇa, who had previously appeared as Upendra, then summoned Śaṅkha, an associate of Kuvera, the treasurer of the demigods, calling him at night to His residence.

Text 59

sa śaṅkhaḥ keśavāhvānaṁ
jñātvā hi nidhirāṭ svayam
ājagāma samīpaṁ vai
tasya dvāravatī pateḥ

Understanding that Lord Kṛṣṇa had summoned him, that master of wealth, Śaṅkha, quickly went to meet Him at Dvārakā.

Text 60

sa śaṅkhaḥ prāñjalir bhūtvā
vinayāda vaniṁ gataḥ
kṛṣṇaṁ vijñāpayāmāsa
yathāvai śravaṇaṁ tathā

After coming before t he Lord, Śaṅkha folded his hand and then offered obeisances by falling flat onto the ground, just as he would have done in the presence of Kuvera. Then he began to speak as follows.

Text 61

bhagavān kiṁ mayā kāryaṁ
surāṇāṁ vittarakṣiṇā
niyojaya mahābāho yat
kāryaṁ yadunandana

My dear Lord, I am the protector of the demigods' wealth. O mighty-armed descendent of Yadu, what can I do for You? Kindly order me according to Your desire.

Text 62

tamuvāca hṛṣīkeśaḥ śaṅkhaṁ
guhyakam uttamam
janāḥ kṛśaghanā ye'smiṁs
tān dhanenābhipūraya

Lord Kṛṣṇa replied to the best of Guhyakas: My dear Śaṅkha, I want you to give sufficient wealth to those in this city who are feeling difficulty in properly maintaining themselves and their families.

Text 63

necchāmyana śitaṁ draṣṭuṁ
kṛśaṁ malinam eva ca
dehīti caiva yācantaṁ
nagaryāṁ nirdhanaṁ naram

I do not want to see anyone suffering from poverty in this city. No one should have to fast due to lack of food. I do not want to see anyone weak from hunger, or begging from others just to survive.

Texts 64-66

vaiśampāyana uvāca
gṛhītvā śāsanaṁ mūrdhnā
nidhirāṭ keśavasya ha
nidhīnājñā payāmāsa
dvāravatyāṁ gṛhe gṛhe

dhanau ghairabhi varṣadhvaṁ
cakruḥ sarvaṁ tathā ca te
nādhano vidyate tatra
kṣīṇa bhāgyo'pi vā naraḥ

kṛśo vā malino vāpi
dvāravatyāṁ kathaṁcana
dvāravatyāṁ puri purā
keśavasya mahātmanaḥ

Vaiśampāyana said: Śaṅkha happily accepted Lord Kṛṣṇa's order and ordered his subordinates: Go to each and every house in Dvārakā and distribute sufficient wealth to the inhabitants. The order of Śaṅkha was faithfully carried out so that not a single resident of Dvārakā, the abode Lord Keśava, was without sufficient wealth.

Text 67

cakāra vāyor āhvānaṁ
bhūyaśca puruṣottamaḥ
tatrastha eva bhagavān
yādavānāṁ priyaṁkaraḥ

Soon thereafter, the Supreme Personality of Godhead, Lord Kṛṣṇa, who always acted for the welfare of the Yādavas, summoned the predominating deity of air, Vāyu, to Dvārakā.

Text 68

prāṇayonistu bhūtānām
upatasthe gadādharam
ekamasīnam ekānte
devaguhya dharaṁ prabhum

Immediately, Vāyu, who sustains the lives of all living entities, appeared before Lord Kṛṣṇa as He was sitting alone in a solitary place at Dvārakā.

Text 69

kiṁ mayā deva kartavyaṁ
sarvagenāśu gāminā
yathaiva dūto devānāṁ
tathaivāsmi tavānagha

Vāyu said: My dear Lord, I can travel anywhere throughout the universe with incredible speed. Kindly tell me—what service can I perform for Your satisfaction? Just as I am the servant of the king so heaven, I am naturally Your eternal servant.

Text 70

tamuvāca tataḥ kṛṣṇo
rahasyaṁ puruṣo hariḥ
mārutaṁ jagataḥ prāṇaṁ
rūpiṇaṁ samupasthitam

Thus the wind-god, the life of the universe, appeared to render service to Lord Kṛṣṇa. When the Supersoul of all living entities and destroyer of all sins saw him, He spoke very mysteriously as follows.

Text 71

gaccha māruta deveśam
anumānya sahāmaraiḥ
sabhāṁ sudharmām ādāya
devebhyastva mihānaya

O Māruta, quickly go to Indra, the king of the demigods, offer My respects to him, and then with their permission, bring the Sudharmā assembly hall here.

Text 72

yādavā dhārmikā hyete
vikrāntāśca sahasraśaḥ
tasyāṁ viśeyurete vai
na tu yā kṛtrimā bhavet

The many thousands of members of the Yadu dynasty need a suitable assembly hall that is indestructible and worthy of their prestigious position.

Text 73

yā hyskṣayā sabhā ramyā
kāmagā kāmarūpiṇī
sā yadūn dhārayet sarvān
yathaiva tridaśāṁs tathā

I want the Sudharmā assembly hall, which is indestructible, very beautiful, capable of going anywhere at will, and capable of assuming any form according to the desire of the members of the assembly. It will be able to accommodate all the members of the Yadu dynasty, just as it does all the assembled demigods.

Text 74

saṁgṛhya vacanaṁ tasya
kṛṣṇasyākliṣṭa karmaṇaḥ
vāyurātmopama gatir
jagāma tridivālayam

By the order of Lord Kṛṣṇa, who can effortlessly perform even extraordinary activities, Vāyu departed for the heavenly planets.

Text 75

so'numānya surān sarvān
kṛṣṇavākyaṁ nivedya ca
sabhāṁ sudharmām ādāya
punarāyān mahītalam

After approaching the demigods, headed by Indra, he offered his respects and then informed them of Lord Kṛṣṇa's desire. Thereafter, with their permission, he brought the Sudharmā assembly hall to earth.

Text 76

sudharmāya sudharmo tāṁ
kṛṣṇāyākliṣṭa kāriṇe
devo devasabhāṁ dattvā
vāyurantara dhīyata

After presenting the Sudharmā assembly hall to Lord Kṛṣṇa, Vāyu, who is capable of performing very wonderful activities, mysteriously disappeared from Dvārakā.

Text 77

dvāravatyāstu sā madhye
keśavena niveśitā
sudharmā yadumukhyānāṁ
devānāṁ tridive yathā

Lord Kṛṣṇa placed the Sudharmā assembly hall in the middle of the city of Dvārakā. Just as it had served as the assembly hall of the demigods in heaven, it became the assembly hall of the Yādavas on earth.

Text 78

evaṁ divyaiśca bhogaiśca
jalajaiścāvyayau hariḥ
dravyair alaṁkaroti sma
purīṁ svāṁ pramadāmiva

In this way, Lord Hari collected many celestial objects of enjoyment, as well as a great quantity of jewels from the ocean, and beautified His abode of Dvārakā, just as a man decorates his young wife.

Text 79

maryādāścaiva saṁcakre
śreṇīśca prakṛtatīs tathā
balādhyakṣāṁśca yuktāṁśca
prakṛtīśāṁs tathaiva ca

He prescribed religious principles that were to be followed by everyone in the city. He instructed the merchants, his subjects in general, the commanders-in-chief of his army, and the administrators of the government to follow the principles that He prescribed.

Text 80

ugrasenaṁ narapatiṁ
kāśyaṁ cāpi purohitam
senāpatim anādhṛṣṭiṁ
vikadruṁ mantripuṅgavam

He installed Ugrasena as the king of Dvārakā, and He appointed the learned scholar of Kāśī, Sāndipani Muṇi, the royal priest. He made Anādhṛṣṭi the commander-in-chief of the army and Vikadru the prime minister.

Text 81

yādavānāṁ kulakārān
sthavirān daśa tatra vai

matimān sthāpayāmāsa
sarvakāryeṣvan antarān

Lord Kṛṣṇa appointed ten elderly and experienced Yādavas—Uddhava, Vasudeva, Kaṅka, Vipṛthu, Śvaphalka, Citraka, Gada, Satyaka, Balabhadra and Pṛthu—as advisors to help the king in important matters of governance.

Text 82

ratheṣvati ratho yenta
dārukaḥ keśavasya vai
yodha mukhyaśca yodhānāṁ
pravaraḥ sātyakiḥ kṛtaḥ

Dāruka became Lord Kṛṣṇa's chariot driver and Sātyaki was made the leader of all the warriors.

Text 83

vidhānam eva kṛtvātha
kṛṣṇaḥ puryām aninditaḥ
mumude yadubhiḥ sārddhaṁ
lokasraṣṭāḥ mahītale

In this way, Lord Kṛṣṇa, whose glories are spotless, arranged the city of Dvārakā in a scientific manner so that He could reside there happily in the company of the Yādavas.

Text 84

revatasyātha kanyāṁ ca
revatiṁ śīla sammatām
prāptavān baladevastu
kṛṣṇasyānu mate tadā

At that time, with the permission of Lord Kṛṣṇa, His elder brother Balarāma married King Raivata's chaste and well-behaved daughter, Revatī.

Thus ends the translation of the fifty-eighth chapter of the Viṣṇu Parva of Śri Harivaṁsa.

Chapter 59

Rukmiṇi's marriage to Śiśupāla arranged. Kṛṣṇa kidnaps Rukmiṇi, followed by fierce fighting

Text 1

vaiśampāyana uvāca
etasmin neva kāle tu
jarāsandhaḥ pratāpavān
nṛpānudyo jayāmāsa
cedirāja priyepsayā

Vaiśampāyana said: At that time, the powerful King Jarāsandha regrouped his forces for the pleasure of the king of Cedi.

Text 2

sutāyā bhīṣmaka syātha
rukmiṇyā rukmabhūṣaṇaḥ
śiśupālasya nṛpater
vivāho bhavitā kila

He sent messengers to all his allies saying that King Bhīṣmaka's daughter, Rukmiṇī, who would be decorated very lavishly with gold ornaments, would soon marry Śiśupāla.

Text 3

dantavaktrasya tanayaṁ
suvaktram amitaujasam
sahasrākṣa samaṁ yuddhe
māyāśata viśāradam

King Jarāsandha then summoned the greatly powerful Suvakra, the son of Dantavakra, who was expert at creating illusions, employing them to bewilder his enemies. It was said that he was as powerful as thousand-eyed Indra.

Text 4

pauṇḍrasya vāsudevasya
tathā putraṁ mahābalam
sudevaṁ vīrya sampannaṁ
pṛthagakṣauhi ṇīpatim

Jarāsandha also summoned Pauṇḍraka Vāsudeva's greatly powerful son, Sudeva, the commander-in-chief of one *akṣauhini* of soldiers.

Texts 5-7

ekalavyasya putraṁ ca
vīryavantaṁ mahābalam
putraṁ ca pāṇḍyarājasya
kaliṅgādhi patiṁ tathā

kṛtāpriyaṁ ca kṛṣṇena
veṇudāriṁ narādhipam
aṅśūmantaṁ tathā krāthaṁ
śruta dharmāṇam eva ca

nivṛtta śatruṁ kaliṅgaṁ
gāndhārādhi patiṁ tathā
prasahya ca mahāvīryaṁ
kauśamvyadhi pameva ca

He also summoned Ekalavya's greatly influential son,

the son of the king of Pāndya, the king of Kaliṅgadeśa who was defeated by Lord Kṛṣṇa, King Venudāri, Kratha's sons Aṁśumān and Śrutadharmā, the king of Gāndhāra, and the king of Kauśāmbi.

Text 8

bhagadatto mahāsenaḥ
śalaḥ śālvo mahābalaḥ
bhūriśravā mahāsenaḥ
kuntivīryaśca vīryavān
svayaṁ varārthaṁ samprāptā
bhojarāja niveśane

Also invited to Śiśupāla's marriage were King Bhagadatta and with his vast army, King Śala, the powerful Sālva, King Bhuriśrava and his huge army, and the greatly powerful Kuntivīrya. They all arrived at the palace of King Bhīṣmaka.

Text 9

janamejaya uvāca
kasmin deśe nṛpo jajñe
rukmī vedavidāṁ varaḥ
kasyānvavāye dyutimān
sambhūto dvijasattama

Janamejaya said: O best of those who are twice-born, in which country and in which family did King Rukmī, who was a greatly learned scholar of the Vedas, take birth?

Text 10

vaiśampāyana uvāca
rājarṣer yādavasyāsīd

vidarbho nāma vai sutaḥ
vindhyasya dakṣiṇe pārśve
vidarbhāyāṁ nyaveśayat

Vaiśampāyana said: O King, there was a king named Yādava who had a son named Vidarbha who resided in the kingdom of Vidarbha, located south of Vindhya mountains.

Text 11

kratha kaiśika mukhyāstu
putrāstasya mahābalāḥ
babhūvur vīrya sampannāḥ
pṛthag vaṁśakarā nṛpāḥ

This King Vidarbha had many powerful sons, including Kratha, Kauśika, who were all very influential. They founded their own separate dynasties.

Text 12

tasyānvavāye bhīmasya
jajñire vṛṣṇayo nṛpāḥ
krathasya tvaṁśumān vaṁśe
bhīṣmakaḥ kaiśikasya tu

The kings of the Vṛṣṇi dynasty, such as Bhīma, originally belonged to the dynasty of the saintly King Yādava. Aṅśumān was born in the family of King Kratha and King Bhīṣmaka was born in the family of Kauśika.

Text 13

hiraṇya rometyāhuryaṁ
dākṣiṇātyeśvaraṁ nṛpāḥ

agastya guptām āśāṁa
kuṇḍinastho'nvaśān nṛpaḥ

King Bhīṣmaka was also called Hiraṇyaromā and Dakṣiṇātyeśvara. He resided in the city of Kuṇḍina, and ruled South India under the able guidance of Agastya Muṇi.

Texts 14-15

rukmī tasyābhavat putro
rukmiṇī ca viśāmpate
rukmī cāstrāṇi divyāni
drumāt prāpa mahābalaḥ

jāmadagnyāt tathā rāmād
brāhmam astram avāptavān
prāsparddhata sa kṛṣṇena
nityam adbhuta karmaṇā

O ruler of men, King Bhīṣmaka had a son named Rukmī and a daughter named Rukmīṇi. The greatly powerful Rukmī received celestial weapons from Druma, the king of the Kiṁpuruṣas. He also acquired the *brahmāstra* from Jamadagni's son, Paraśurāma. Rukmī was always very envious of Kṛṣṇa and took every opportunity to insult Him.

Text 16

rukmiṇī tvabhavad rājan
rūpeṇā sadṛśī bhuvi
cakame vāsudevastāṁ
śravādeva mahādyutiḥ

O King, it is impossible to properly describe the beauty of Princess Rukmiṇī. She was incomparable. When the supremely powerful son of Vasudeva, Lord Kṛṣṇa, heard about her qualities, His heart became attracted to her.

Text 17

sa tayā cābhilaṣitaḥ
śravādeva janārdanaḥ
tejo vīrya balopetaḥ
sa me bhartā bhavediti

In the same way, Rukmīṇi became attracted to Lord Kṛṣṇa simply by hearing about His transcendental qualities, and thus she desired Him as her husband.

Texts 18-19

tāṁ dadau na ca kṛṣṇāya
dveṣād rukmī mahābalaḥ
kaṁsasya vadhasaṅtāpāt
kṛṣṇāyām amita tejase

yācamānāya kaṁsasya
dveṣyo'yam iti cintayan
caidyasyārthe sunīthasya
jarāsaṅdhastu bhūmipaḥ
varayāmāsa tāṁ rājā
bhīṣmakaṁ bhīma vikramam

The greatly powerful Rukmī steadily maintained his hatred for Kṛṣṇa and for that reason, he adamantly opposed the marriage of his sister to Him. He became even more antagonistic toward Kṛṣṇa after hearing the news of Kaṁsa's death. Thus, even though his father tried to persuade him to sanction his sister's marriage to Kṛṣṇa, he would not budge. For the pleasure of

King Śiśupāla, the son of the Cedi King, Sunītha, Jarāsandha, the emperor of the earth, asked King Bhīṣmaka to give his daughter in marriage to him.

Text 20

cedirājasya tu vasor
āsīt putro vṛhadrathaḥ
magadheṣu purā yena
nirmito'sau girivrajaḥ

The Cedi king, Uparicara Vasu, had a son named Bṛhadratha who long ago established a city called Girivraja within the kingdom of Magadha.

Text 21

tasyānvavāye jajñe'sau
jarāsandho mahābalaḥ
vasoreva tadā vaṁśe
damaghoṣo'pi cedirāṭ

Jarāsandha was born in the dynasty of Uparicara Vasu, as was Damaghoṣa. Later on, Damaghoṣa became the King of Cedi.

Text 22

damaghoṣasya putrāstu
pañca bhīma parākramāḥ
bhaginyāṁ vasudevasya
śrutaśravasi jajñire

Damaghoṣa had five very powerful sons, who were born from the womb of his wife, Śrutaśravā, the sister of Vasudeva.

Text 23

śiśupālo daśagrīvo
raibhyo'tho padiśo bali
sarvāstra kuśalā vīrā
vīryavanto mahābalāḥ

The names of these five sons were Śiśupāla, Daśagrīva, Raimya, Upadiśa, and Bali. All of them were expert in the use of weapons and very powerful warriors.

Text 24

jñāteḥ samāna vaṁśasya
sunīthaḥ pradadau sutam
jarāsandhastu sutavad
dadarśainaṁ jugopa ca

Jarāsandha was a relative of Damaghoṣa, having been born in the same family. That is why Damaghoṣa gave his son, Śiśupāla, for him to raise. Jarāsandha treated Śiśupāla like his own son and gave him all protection.

Text 25

jarāsandhaṁ puraskṛtya
vṛṣṇiśatruṁ mahābalam
kṛtānyāgāṁsi caidyena
vṛṣṇīnāṁ cāpriyaisiṇā

Hoping to diminish the reputation of the Vṛṣṇi dynasty, the Cedi king committed many atrocities against them while keeping Jarāsandha, who was also their enemy, in front.

Text 26

jāmātā tvabhavat tasya
kaṁsas tasmin hate yudhi
kṛṣṇārthaṁ vairam abhavaj
jarāsandhasya vṛṣṇibhiḥ

King Kaṁsa was the brother-in-law of Jarāsandha. After Kaṁsa was killed by Lord Kṛṣṇa, Jarāsandha became envious of the entire Vṛṣṇi dynasty.

Text 27

bhīṣmakaṁ varayāmāsa
sunīthārthe ca rukmiṇīm
tāṁ dadau bhauṣmakaścāpi
śiśupālāya vīryavān

Jarāsandha requested King Bhīṣmaka to hand over his daughter Rukmiṇī to Sunītha's son Śiśupāla. The powerful King Bhīṣmaka agreed to this proposal.

Text 28

tataścaidyam upādāya
jarāsandho narādhipaḥ
yayau vidarbhān sahito
dantavaktreṇa yāyinā

Following this development, Jarāsandha along with his assistant, Dantavakra, took Śiśupāla and went to the kingdom of Vidarbha.

Text 29

anujñātaśca pauṇḍreṇa
vāsudevena dhīmatā
aṅgavaṅga kaliṅgānām
īśvaraḥ sa mahābalaḥ

The wise King Pauṇḍraka Vāsudeva also approved of Jarāsandha's maneuvers. Mighty-armed Jarāsandha was the king of Aṅgadeśa, Baṅgadeśa, and Kaliṅgadeśa.

Text 30

mānayiṣyaṁśca tān rukmī
pratyud gamya narādhipān
parayā pūjayo petāṁs
tān ināya purīṁ prati

When the three powerful kings arrived at Vidarbha, Rukmī came to welcome them. He greeted them very respectfully and after exchanging some words with them, he brought them to his palace.

Text 31

pitṛṣvasuḥ priyārthaṁ ca
rāmakṛṣṇā vubhāvapi
prayayur vṛṣṇayaś cānye
rathais tatra balānvitāḥ

The two brothers, Kṛṣṇa and Balarāma, also went to Vidarbha for the pleasure of their aunt. Along with Them came many powerful heroes of the Vṛṣṇi dynasty, riding upon their chariots.

Text 32

kratha kauśika bhartā tān
pratigṛhya yathāvidhi
pūjayāmāsa pūjārhān
bahiścaiva nyaveśayat

Kratha and Kauśika greeted Kṛṣṇa and Balarāma, worshiped Them in accordance with scriptural injunctions, and then arranged their residence outside his palace.

Texts 33-34

śvobhāvini vivāhe ca
rukmiṇī niryayau bahiḥ
caturyujā rathenaindre
devatāyatane śubhe

indrāṇīm arcayiṣyantī
kṛta kautuka maṅgalā
dīpyamānena vapuṣā
balena mahatā vṛtā

The day before her *svayamvara*, Princess Rukmiṇī performed the required rituals, appearing very bright-faced. According to her family tradition, she went to the temple of goddess Durgā to seek her blessings. For this purpose, she mounted a chariot drawn by four horses and went to the temple during the period of Jeṣṭhā *nakṣatra*, surrounded by a huge army.

Text 35

tāṁ dadarśa tadā kṛṣṇo
lakṣmīṁ sākṣādiva sthitām

rūpeṇāgrayeṇa sampannāṁ
devatāyatana antike

As this procession was wending its way to the temple of Goddess Durgā, Kṛṣṇa's gaze suddenly fell upon the most enchanting Princess Rukmiṇī, who appeared non-different from Lakṣmī, the goddess of fortune.

Text 36

vahneriva śikhāṁ dīptāṁ
māyāṁ bhūmitatāmiva
pṛthivīmiva gambhīrām
utthitāṁ pṛthivītalāt

Rukmiṇī appeared like a flame of blazing fire, the energy of the Supreme Lord, or the personified earth whose nature is very grave.

Text 37

marīcimiva somasya
saumyāṁ strīvigrahāṁ bhuvi
śrīmi vāgryāṁ vinā padmaṁ
bhaviṣyāṁ śrī sahāyinīm
kṛṣṇena manasā dṛṣṭāṁ
durnirīkṣyāṁ surairapi

She appeared as if the moon rays had taken the form of a beautiful girl and appeared on the earth. She looked just like Lakṣmī without a lotus flower in her hand, or else a companion of Lakṣmī. Lord Kṛṣṇa gazed upon Rukmiṇī, whose *darśana* is rarely achieved even by the demigods.

Text 38

śyāmāvadātā sā hyāsīt
pṛthucārvāyata ekṣaṇā
tāmraiṣṭha nayanāpāṅgī
pīnoruja ghanastanī

Rukmiṇī was sixteen years old at that time. Her complexion was like the color of gold. Her eyes were broad and beautiful. The color of her lips and the corners of her eyes were that of copper. Her thighs, hips, and breasts were rounded and fleshy.

Text 39

vṛhatī cāru sarvāṅgī
tanvī śaśisitānanā tāmra
tuṅga nakhī subhrir
nīlakuñcita murdhajā

She was tall and thin. Her entire body had a most charming appearance. Her face was very beautiful and fair like the full moon. Her nails were raised and reddish. Her eyebrows were very attractive and she had black curly hair.

Text 40

atyarthaṁ rūpataḥ kāntā
pina śroṇi payodharā
tīkṣṇa śuklaiḥ samairdantaiḥ
prabhāsadbhir alaṁkṛtā

In fact, Princess Rukmiṇī was extraordinarily beautiful. Her hips and waist beautifully formed. Her lovely teeth were spotlessly white, equal in size, and shiny.

Text 41

ananyā pramadā loke
rūpeṇa yaśasā śriyā
rukmiṇī rūpiṇī devī
pāṇḍurakṣauma vāsinī

As far as Her beauty, fame, and nature are concerned, Rukmiṇī had no rival anywhere within the world. In one word, she was matchless. She wore a bright silk *sāri*. Princess Rukmiṇī appeared like a celestial goddess.

Text 42

tāṁ dṛṣṭvā vavṛdhe kāmaḥ
kṛṣṇasya priyadarśanām
haviṣevā nalasyārcir
manastasyāṁ samādadhat

As the flames of a fire increase by pouring ghee, while gazing at the most enchanting Princess Rukmiṇī, Lord Kṛṣṇa's desire to have her increased. He fixed His mind on her and gave His heart to her.

Text 43

rāmeṇa saha niścitya
keśavastu mahābalaḥ
tatpramāthe'karod buddhiṁ
vṛṣṇibhiḥ praṇidhāya ca

Thereafter, Lord Kṛṣṇa consulted Balarāma and other members of the Vṛṣṇi dynasty about what should be done and finally, with everyone's consent, He decided to kidnap Rukmiṇī.

Text 44

kṛte tu devatākārye
niṣkāmantīṁ surālayāt
unmathya sahasā kṛṣṇaḥ
svaṁnināya rathottamam

Meanwhile, Princess Rukmiṇī completed her worship of Goddess Durgā and slowly came out of the temple. At that time, Lord Kṛṣṇa suddenly came and picked her up, placing her on His chariot, and hastily departed.

Text 45

vṛkṣam utpāṭya rāmo'pi
jaghānā patataḥ parān
samanahyanta dāśārhās
tadājñaptāśca sarvaśaḥ

All the assembled kings were taken by surprise but after regaining their composure, they prepared to attack Lord Kṛṣṇa. At that time, Balarāma uprooted a gigantic tree and began killing all the inimical kings and soldiers. Following the order of Balarāma, all the Yādavas joined the fray.

Text 46

te rathair vividhākāraiḥ
samucchrita mahādhvajaiḥ
vājibhir vāraṇaiścaiva
parivavrur halāyudham

The members of the Yadu dynasty were all very powerful warriors. They came on their chariots decorated with flags, and on horses and elephants and surrounded Lord Balarāma.

Text 47

ādāya rukmiṇīṁ kṛṣṇo
jagāmāśu purīṁ prati
rāme bhāraṁ tamāsajya
yuyudhāne ca vīryavān

Lord Kṛṣṇa entrusted the responsibility of fighting to His elder brother, Balarāma, and Sātyaki, so that He could leave Vidarbha and go to Dvārakā with Rukmiṇī.

Texts 48-51

akrūre vipṛthau caiva
gade ca kṛtavarmaṇi
cakradeve sudeve ca
sāraṇe ca mahābale

nivṛtta śātrau vikrānte
bhaṅgakāre vidūrthe
ugrasenāt maje kaṅke
śatadyumne ca keśavaḥ

rājādhi deve mṛdure
prasene citrake tathā
atidānte vṛhaddurge
śvaphalke satyake pṛthau

vṛṣṇyandhakeṣu cānyeṣu
mukhyeṣu madhusūdanaḥ
gurumāsajya taṁ bhāraṁ
yayau dvāravatīṁ prati

Besides Balarāma and Sātyaki, Lord Kṛṣṇa entrusted

the fighting to Akrūra, Vipṛthu, Gada, Kṛtavarmā, Cakradeva, Sudeva, the powerful Sāraṇā, Nivṛtta-śātru, the powerful Bhaṅgakāra, Vidūrtha, Ugrasena's son Kaṅka, Śatadyumna, Rājādhideva, Mṛdura, Prasena, Citraka, Atidāna, Vṛhad-durga, Śvaphalka, Satyaka, and Pṛthu, as well as many other principal warriors from the Vṛṣṇi and Anḍhaka dynasties. After doing so, Lord Kṛṣṇa left for Dvārakā.

Text 52

dantavaktro jarāsandhaḥ
śiśupālaśca vīryavān
saṁnaddhā niryayuḥ kruddhā
jighānsanto janārdanam

Meanwhile, Dantavakra, Jarāsandha, and Śiśupāla put on their armor, picked up their weapons, and departed in an angry mood with a desire to kill Lord Kṛṣṇa.

Text 53

aṅgavaṅga kaliṅgaiśca
sārddhaṁ pauṇḍaraśca
vīryavān niryau cedirājastu
bhrātṛbhiḥ sa mahārathaiḥ

The powerful king of Cedi, Śiśupāla, was ably supported by the kings and warriors of Aṅga, Baṅga, Kaliṅga, and Puṇḍra-deśa. With great enthusiasm, they marched towards the battlefield.

Text 54

tān pratyagṛhṇan saṁrabdhā
vṛṣṇivīrā mahārathāḥ

saṁkarṣaṇaṁ puraskṛtya
vāsavaṁ maruto yathā

To counteract the forward march of the enemies, all the warriors of the Vṛṣṇi dynasty kept Balarāma in front, just as the demigods keep Indra in front of them while engaged in battle.

Text 55

āpantaṁ hi vegena
jarāsandhaṁ mahābalam
ṣāḍbhir vivyādha nārācair
yuyudhāno mahāmṛdhe

In that great battle, Sātyaki released six powerful arrows at Jarāsandha as he advanced toward him, causing injury.

Text 56

akrūro dantavaktraṁ tu
vivyādha navabhiḥ śaraiḥ
taṁ pratya vidhyat kāruṣo
vāṇair daśabhirā śugaiḥ

Akrūra wounded Dantavakra with nine arrows. In retaliation, Dandavakra, the king of Karuṣa, released ten powerful arrows.

Text 57

vipṛthuḥ śuśupālaṁ tu
śarair vivyādha saptabhiḥ
aṣṭabhiḥ pratya viddhyat taṁ
śiśupālaḥ pratāpavān

Vipṛthu discharged seven arrows at Śiśupāla, injuring him. Powerful Śiśupāla retaliated by severely injuring Vipṛthu with seven arrows.

Text 58

gaveṣaṇastu caidyaṁ tu
ṣaḍbhir vivyādha mārgaṇaiḥ
atidāntas tathāṣṭābhir
bṛhad durgaśca pañcabhiḥ

Thereafter, Gaveṣana with six arrows, Atidānta with eight arrows, and Bṛhaddurga with five arrows seriously injured the king of Cedi, Śiśupāla.

Text 59

prati vivyādha tāṁścaidyaḥ
pañcabhiḥ pañcabhiḥ śaraiḥ
jaghānāśvāṁśca caturaś
caturbhir vipṛthoḥ śaraiḥ

Śiśupāla retaliated by sending five arrows toward each of them. He then killed the four horses of Vipṛthu with four powerful arrows.

Texts 60-61

bṛhad durgasya bhallena
śiraściccheda cārihā
gaveṣaṇasya sūtaṁ tu
prāhiṇod yamasādanam

hatāśvaṁ tu rathaṁ tyaktvā
vipṛthustu mahābalaḥ

āruroha rathaṁ śīghraṁ
bṛhad durgasya vīryavān

Śiśupāla, the slayer of his enemies, cut off Bṛhad-durga's head with a trident and also sent the charioteer of Gaveṣaṇa to the abode of Yamarāja. Vipṛthu dismounted his disabled chariot and mounted Bṛhad-durga's chariot.

Text 62

vipṛthoḥ sārathiścāpi
gaveṣaṇarathaṁ drutam
āruhya javanā naśvān
niyantum upacakrame

In this situation, Viprthu's chariot driver quickly went and sat on Gaveṣaṇa's chariot, taking up the reins and bringing the horses under control.

Text 63

te kruddhāḥ śaravarṣeṇa
sunīthaṁ samavākiram
nṛtyantaṁ rathamārgeṣu
cāpahastāḥ kalāpinaḥ

Becoming enraged, Gaveṣaṇa quickly picked up his bow and proceeded to shower his arrows on Śiśupāla, who appeared to be dancing on the battlefield.

Text 64

cakradevo dantavaktraṁ
vibhedor asi patriṇā

ṣaḍrathaṁ pañcabhiścaiva
vivyādha yudhi mārgaṇaiḥ

Cakradeva then pierced Dantavakra's chest with a sharp arrow. He then released five more arrows that injured Ṣaḍratha.

Text 65

tābhyāṁ sa viddho daśabhir
vāṇair marmātigaiḥ śitaiḥ
tato balī cakradevaṁ
bibheda daśabhiḥ śaraiḥ

In retaliation, both Dandavakra and Ṣaḍratha released a shower of arrows, wounding Cakradeva severely. Śiśupāla's brother Balī then released ten arrows at Cakradeva.

Text 66

pañcabhiścāpi vivyādha
so'pi dūrād vidūratham
vidūratho'piṁ taṁ ṣaḍbhir
vivyādhājau śitaiḥ śaraiḥ

Balī also injured Vidūratha with five sharp arrows. In retaliation, Vidhūratha injured Balī with six very powerful arrows.

Texts 67-69

triśatā pratyavidhyat taṁ
balī bāṇair mahābalam
kṛtavarmā vibhedājau
rājaputraṁ tribhiḥ śaraiḥ

nyahanat sārathiṁ cāsya
dhvajaṁ ciccheda socchritam
prativivyādha taṁ kruddhaḥ
pauṇḍraḥ ṣaḍbhiḥ śilīmukhaiḥ

dhanuśccheda cāpyasya
bhallena kṛtavarmaṇaḥ
nivṛtta śatruḥ kāliṅgaṁ
vibheda niśitaiḥ śaraiḥ
tomareṇāṁ sadeśe taṁ
nirvibheda kaliṅgarāṭ

Balī then discharged thirty arrows at Vidhuratha. Meanwhile, Kṛtavarmā caused grave injury to Pauṇḍraka Vāsudeva's son. He also killed Pauṇḍraka's charioteer and cut down his flag. This made Pauṇḍraka mad with rage and he retaliated by releasing six arrows at Kṛtavarmā and cut his bow into pieces with a trident. At that time, Nivṛtaśatru pierced the king of Kaliṅga's body with many sharp arrows. In retaliation, the king of Kaliṅga picked up a club and struck Nivṛtaśatru, breaking his shoulder.

Text 70

gajenāsādya kaṅkastu
gajamaṅgasya vīryavān
tomareṇa vibhedāṅgaṁ
vibhedāṅgaśca taṁ śaraiḥ

The powerful Kaṅka induced his elephant to attack the elephant upon which rode the king of Aṅgadeśa. He then injured him by striking him with his club. In turn, Aṅgarāja shot many arrows at Kaṅka, wounding him.

Text 71

citrakaśca śvaphalkaśca
satyakaśca mahārathaḥ
kaliṅgasya tathānīkaṁ
nārācair vibhiduḥ śataiḥ

Meanwhile, Citraka, Śvaphalka, and the great charioteer Satyaka, each released one hundred arrows, piercing the bodies of the soldiers supporting the king of Kaliṅga.

Text 72

taṁ nisṛṣṭa drumeṇājau
baṅgarājasya kuñjaram
jaghāna rāmaḥ saṁkruddho
vaṅgarājaṁ ca sayuge

Thereafter, in a fit of rage, Lord Balarāma picked up a tree devoid of leaves and first killed the elephant of the king of Baṅga and then sent him to the abode of Yamarāja.

Text 73

taṁ hatvā rathamāruhya
dhanurādāya vīryavān
saṅkarṣaṇo jaghānograir
nārācaiḥ kaiśikān bahūn

After killing the king of Baṅga, Lord Saṅkarṣaṇa picked up His bow and arrows and mounted a chariot. He then killed many soldiers belonging to Kauśika with His formidable arrows.

Text 74

ṣaḍbhir nihatya kāruṣān
maheṣvāsān sa vīryavān
śataṁ jaghāna saṁkruddho
māgadhānāṁ mahābale

Lord Balarāma appeared to be exceedingly angry. He released six arrows that killed the foremost warriors of Kāruṣadeśa. He then sent many distinguished heroes of the vast army of the king of Magadha to the abode of Yamarāja.

Text 75

nihatya tān mahāvāhur
jarāsandhaṁ tato'bhyayāt
tamāpatantam vivyādha
nārācair māgadhastribhiḥ

After destroying many of His sinful enemies in this way, mighty-armed Balarāma attacked Jarāsandha. To check His advance, the king of Magadha injured Him with three sharp arrows.

Text 76

taṁ vibhedāṣṭabhiḥ kruddho
nārācair musalāyudhaḥ
ciccheda cāsya bhallena
dhvajaṁ hema pariṣkṛtam

Lord Baladeva, the carrier of the *muṣala*, released eight arrows that pierced Jarāsandha's body, and cut down his gold plated flag with a trident.

Text 77

tad yuddham abhavad ghoraṁ
teṣāṁ devā suropamam
sṛjatāṁ śaravarṣāṇi
nighnatāmita retaram

In this fierce battle, showers of arrows were seen all over the battlefield. Indeed, it resembled a battle between the demigods and demons in times long past.

Text 78

gajairgajā hi saṁkruddhāḥ
saṁnipetuḥ sahasraśaḥ
rathai rathāśca saṁrabdhāḥ
sādinaścāpi sādibhiḥ

With great anger, thousands of elephants charged other elephants, thousands of chariots collided with other chariots, and thousands of cavalry collided with the opposing cavalry.

Text 79

padātayaḥ padātīṁśca
śakticarmāsi pāṇayaḥ
chindantaś cottamāṅgāni
viceruryudhi te pṛthak

The infantry soldiers fought with their counterparts by hurling missiles and wielding swords and shields. They charged each other wildly, severing one another's heads.

Text 80

asīnaṁ pātyamānānāṁ
kavaceṣu mahāsvanaḥ
śarāṇāṁ patatāṁ śabdaḥ
pakṣiṇāmiva śuśruve

The battlefield was permeated with frightful sounds of swords, smashed armor, arrows, colliding shields, and so on. The combined sound appeared like the sound of chirping birds.

Text 81

bherīśaṅkha mṛdaṅgānāṁ
veṇūnāṁ ca mṛdhe dhvanim
jugūha ghoṣaḥ śastrāṇāṁ
jyāghoṣaśca mahātmanām

Also heard on that battlefield was a commotion created by soldiers bragging and challenging one another, as well as the sounds of drums of various sizes, *mṛdaṅgas*, and flutes. The combined sound filled the entire sky.

Thus ends the translation of the fifty-ninth chapter of the Viṣṇu Parva of Śri Harivaṁsa.

Chapter 60

After defeating Rukmī, Kṛṣṇa returns to Dvārakā with Rukmīṇi

Text 1

vaiśampāyana uvāca
kṛṣṇena hriya māṇāṁ tāṁ
rukmī śrutvā tu rukmiṇīm
pratijñām akarot kruddhaḥ
samakṣaṁ bhīṣmakasya ha

Vaiśampāyana said: When Rukmī heard that Kṛṣṇa had kidnapped Rukmiṇī and was running away, he came before his father, Bhīṣmaka, and made this promise.

Text 2

rukmyuvāca
ahatvā yudhi govindam
anānīya ca rukmiṇīm
kuṇḍinaṁ na pravekṣyāmi
satyametad vravimyaham

Rukmī said: I will not return to Kuṇḍiṇapura unless I kill Kṛṣṇa in battle and bring back my sister, Rukmiṇī. This is my promise.

Text 3

āsthāya sa rathaṁ vīraḥ
samudagrāyudha dhajam

javena prayayau kruddho
balena mahatā vṛtaḥ

After making this oath, valiant Rukmī, who was filled with rage, equipped himself with powerful weapons, mounted a chariot that was decorated with a beautiful flag, and chased Kṛṣṇa, taking with him a vast army.

Texts 4-5

tamanvayur nṛpāścaiva
dakṣiṇā pathavartinaḥ
krārtho'śumāñ śrutarvā ca
veṇudāriśca vīryavān

bhīṣmakasya sutāścānye
rathena rathināṁ varāḥ
kratha kaiśika mukhyāśa
sarva eva mahārathāḥ

Many powerful kings from South India, Kratha's son Aṅśumān, Śrūtarvā, and the powerful Veṇudārī followed Rukmī. The other sons of Bhīṣmaka also followed him, riding upon chariots. The other great warriors from Kratha and Kauśīka's kingdom also assisted Rukmī in that fight.

Text 6

te gatvā dūram adhvānaṁ
saritaṁ narmadāmanu
govindaṁ dadṛśūḥ kruddhāḥ
sahaiva priyayā sthitam

After traveling a great distance, all these kings saw Lord

Kṛṣṇa sitting with Rukmiṇī on a chariot by the side of the River Narmadā, and immediately they became filled with rage.

Text 7

avasthāpya ca tatsainyaṁ
rukmī madabalān vitaḥ
cikīrṣūrdvai rathaṁ yuddhaṁ
abhyayān madhusūdanam

Rukmī was very proud of his strength. He ordered all the kings to refrain from proceeding further and then went alone to fight with Lord Kṛṣṇa.

Text 8

sa vivyādha catuḥṣaṣṭyā
govindaṁ niśitaiḥ śaraiḥ
taṁ pratyavidhyat saptatyā
bāṇairyudhi janārdanaḥ

Rukmī initiated the battle by releasing sixty-four arrows that pierced Lord Kṛṣṇa. Lord Kṛṣṇa then retaliated by releasing seventy arrows at Rukmī.

Text 9

ata mānasya ciccheda
dhvajaṁ cāsya mahābalaḥ
jahāra ca śiraḥ kāyāt
sārathes tasya vīryavān

Next, Lord Kṛṣṇa cut down Rukmī's flag and pierced his chariot driver with an arrow in the heart.

Text 10

taṁ kṛccha gatamājñāya
parivabrur janārdanam
dākṣiṇātyā jighāṁsanto
rājānaḥ sarva evahi

When the other kings saw that Rukmī was in great danger, they immediately rushed at Kṛṣṇa and surrounded Him, determined to kill Him.

Text 11

tamaṁśumān mahābāhur
vivyādha daśabhiḥ śaraiḥ
śrutarvā pañcabhiḥ kruddho
veṇudāriśca saptabhiḥ

Mighty-armed Aṅśumān released ten arrows, Śutarvā discharged five arrows, and Veṇudārī angrily shot seven arrows at Lord Kṛṣṇa, injuring Him.

Text 12

tatoṁ'śumantaṁ govindo
vibhedorasi vīryavān
niṣasāda rathopasthe
vyathitaḥ sa narādhipaḥ

To counter their attack, Lord Govinda pierced Aṅśumān's chest with a sharp arrow. Being injured by Lord Kṛṣṇa, Aṅśumān stopped fighting and sat down in the back of his chariot.

Text 13

śrutarvaṇo jaghānāśvāṁś
caturbhiś caturaḥ śaraiḥ
veṇudārer dhvajaṁ chittvā
bhujaṁ vivyādha dakṣiṇam

Kṛṣṇa then killed the four horses of Sutarvā with four arrows and cut down Veṇudārī's flag while piercing both sides of his body.

Text 14

tathaiva ca śrutar vāṇaṁ
śarair vivyādha pañcabhiḥ
śiśriye sa dhvajaṁ śānto
nyaṣīdacca vyathānvitaḥ

Kṛṣṇa then wounded Sutarvā with five sharp arrows, causing him severe pain so that he had to support himself by leaning on his flagpole.

Text 15

muñcantaḥ śaravarṣāṇi
vāsudevaṁ tato'bhyuḥ
kratha kaiśika mukhyāśca
sarva eva mahārathāḥ

Thereafter, all the principal warriors from Kratha and Kauśika's kingdom showered countless arrows upon Lord Kṛṣṇa, hoping to subdue Him.

Text 16

bāṇair bāṇāṁśca ciccheda
teṣāṁ yudhi janārdanaḥ
jaghāna caiṣāṁ saṁrabdhaḥ
patamānāṁśca tāñcharān

Lord Kṛṣṇa very swiftly countered all these kings, cutting their arrows to pieces and angrily destroying the other weapons released against Him.

Text 17

punaranyāṁś catuḥṣāṣṭyā
jaghāna niśitaiḥ śaraiḥ
kruddhānā patato vīrān
adrivat sa mahābalaḥ

Remaining immovable like a mountain, Kṛṣṇa employed sixty-four sharp arrows to kill the enemy warriors that were attacking Him.

Text 18

vidrutaṁ svabalaṁ dṛṣṭvā
rukmī krodha vaśaṁgataḥ
pañcabhir niśitair bāṇair
vivyādhorasi keśavam

When Rukmī saw how his soldiers and their leaders were fleeing the battlefield out of fear of Lord Kṛṣṇa, he became mad with rage and released five arrows that pierced His chest.

Text 19

sārathiṁ cāsya vivyādha
sāyaykair niśitai ṣtribhiḥ
ājaghāna śareṇāsya
dhvajaṁ ca nataparvaṇā

Rukmī also injured Kṛṣṇa's chariot driver with three arrows, and with a crescent-shaped arrow, cut off His flag.

Text 20

keśavastva ritaṁ dṛṣṭvā
kruddho vivyādha mārgaṇaiḥ
dhanuściccheda cāpyasya
yatamānasya rukmiṇaḥ

Kṛṣṇa became highly enraged while watching Rukmī release arrows at an incredible rate, injuring everyone who came before him. He retaliated by wounding Rukmī and breaking his bow.

Text 21

athānyad dhanurādāya
rukmī kṛṣṇa jighāṁsayā
prāduścakāra cānyāni
divyānyastrāṇi vīryavān

Being without any weapon in his hands, powerful Rukmī picked up another bow that he found lying on the ground, desiring to kill Kṛṣṇa without delay. Finally, when he saw that his arrows were futile, Rukmī began to invoke celestial weapons.

Text 22

astrair astrāṇi saṁvārya
tasya kṛṣṇo mahābalaḥ
punaściccheda taccāpaṁ
ratheṣāṁ ca tribhiḥ śaraiḥ

Mighty-armed Lord Kṛṣṇa perfectly counteracted all Rukmī's celestial weapons with His own. Thereafter, Kṛṣṇa released three arrows that again broke Rukmī's bow, as well as the axle of his chariot.

Text 23

sa cchinna dhanvā virathaḥ
khaḍgam ādāya carma ca
utpapāta rathād vīro
gurutmāniva vīryavān

When Rukmī saw that his bow was broken and his chariot disabled, he picked up a sword and shield and jumped to the ground, like Garuḍa swooping from the sky.

Text 24

tasyābhi patataḥ khaḍgaṁ
cchiccheda yudhi keśavaḥ
nārācaiśca tribhiḥ kruddho
vidhedainam athorasi

Then, when Rukmī charged at Kṛṣṇa, sword in hand, the Lord broke his sword to pieces and in a fit of anger pierced his heart with three sharp arrows.

Text 25

sa papāta mahābāhur
vasudhāmanu nādayan
visaṁjño murcchito rājā
vrajeṇeva mahāsuraḥ

Being unable to tolerate the pain, mighty-armed Rukmī fell to the ground unconscious, creating a loud sound, as if a giant demon has been felled by the thunderbolt of Indra.

Text 26

tāṁśca rājñaḥ sarvān
punar vivyādha mādhavaḥ
rukmiṇaṁ patitaṁ dṛṣṭvā
vyadravanta narādhipāḥ

As Lord Mādhava continued to pierce the other kings with His arrows, seeing how their leader, Rukmī, was lying upon the ground injured, they began fleeing from the battlefield.

Text 27

viceṣṭamānaṁ taṁ bhūmau
bhrātaraṁ vīkṣya rukmiṇī
pādayornya patad viṣṇor
bhrāturjīvita kāṅkṣiṇī

When Rukmiṇī saw her brother in that pitiful condition, she clasped the lotus feet of Lord Kṛṣṇa, desiring his welfare.

Text 28

tāmutthāpya pariṣvajya
sāntvayāmāsa keśavaḥ
abhayaṁ rukmiṇe dattvā
prayayau svapurīṁ tataḥ

Being very merciful, Lord Kṛṣṇa picked up Rukmiṇī and embraced her. After pacifying her and giving assurances to Rukmī, He proceeded toward Dvārakā.

Text 29

vṛṣṇayo'pi jarāsandhaṁ
bhaṅktvā tāṁścaiva pārthivān
prayayur dvārakāṁ dṛṣṭāḥ
puruskṛtya halāyudham

Meanwhile, the other members of the Vṛṣṇi dynasty chased the retreating kings, including Jarāsandha, shouting jubilantly. Thereafter, they returned to Dvārakā, keeping Lord Balarāma in front.

Text 30

prayāte puṇḍarīkākṣe
śrutarbābhyetya saṁgare
rukmaṇa rathamāropya
prayayau svāṁ purīṁ prati

After lotus-eyed Lord Kṛṣṇa departed, King Sutarvā returned to the battlefield, slowly picked up the unconscious and injured Rukmī, placed him on his chariot, and set out for Kuṇḍinapura.

Text 31

anānīya svasāṛaṁ tu
rukmī māna madānvitaḥ
hīnapratijño naicchat sa
praveṣṭuṁ kuṇḍinaṁ puram

When Rukmī, who was always very proud, remembered his vow to never return home without his sister, he refused to enter Kuṇḍinapura.

Text 32

vidarbheṣu nivāsārthaṁ
nirmame'nyat puraṁ mahat
tad bhoja kaṭamityeva
babhūva bhuvi viśrutam

Thereafter, Rukmī established a new city for his residence, which came to be known as Bhojakaṭa, within the kingdom of Vidarbha.

Text 33

tatraujasā mahātejā
dakṣiṇāṁ diśamanvagāt
bhīṣmakaḥ kuṇḍine caiva
rājovāsa mahābhujaḥ

The greatly powerful Rukmī resided in that city and continued to rule a large portion of South India, while his father, mighty-armed King Bhīṣmaka, remained at Kuṇḍinapura.

Text 34

dvārakāṁ cāpi samprāpte
rāme vṛṣṇi balānvite
rukmiṇyāḥ keśavaḥ pāṇiṁ
jagāha vidhivat prabhuḥ

After Lord Balarāma returned to Dvārakā with the army of the Vṛṣṇi dynasty, Lord Kṛṣṇa married Rukmiṇī according to the injunctions of the revealed scriptures.

Text 35

tataḥ saha tayā reme
priyayā prīyamāṇayā
sītayeva purā rāmaḥ
paulomyeva puraṁdaraḥ

Just as long ago Lord Rāmacandra enjoyed life with Sītā, or as Indra, the king of the demigods, enjoys life with Śacī, the daughter of the sage Puloma, Lord Kṛṣṇa continued to happily reside with His dear wife, Rukmiṇī.

Text 36

sā hi tasyā bhavajjyeṣṭhā
patnī kṛṣṇasya bhāminī
pativratā guṇopetā
rūpa śīla guṇānvitā

Rukmiṇī was Kṛṣṇa's first and seniormost wife. She was very beautiful, chaste, humble, well-behaved, and decorated with all good qualities.

Texts 37-39

tasyāṁ utpādayāmāsa
putrān daśa mahārathān
cārudeṣṇaṁ sudeṣṇaṁ ca
pradyumnaṁ ca mahābalam

suṣeṇaṁ cāruguptaṁ ca
cārubāhuṁ ca vīryavān
cāruvindaṁ sucāruṁ ca
bhadracāruṁ tathaiva ca

cāruṁ ca balināṁ śreṣṭhaṁ
sutāṁ cārumatīṁ tathā
dharmārtha kuśalāste tu
kṛtāsrā yuddha durmadāḥ

Thereafter, Lord Kṛṣṇa begot ten powerful sons in the womb of His wife, Rukmiṇi—Cārudeṣṇa, Sudeṣṇa, the powerful Pradyumṇa, Suṣeṇa, Cārugupta, Cārubāhu, Cāruvinda, Sucāru, Bhadracāru and the best of heroic personalities Cāru. In addition, Lord Kṛṣṇa begot a daughter named Cārumatī. All of His sons were pious, expert in the art of releasing weapons, and powerful warriors.

Texts 40-44

mahiṣīraṣṭa kalyāṇīs
tato'nyā madhusūdanaḥ
upayeme mahābāhur
guṇopetāḥ kulodbhavāḥ

kālindīṁ mitravindāṁ ca
satyāṁ nāgnajitīṁ api

sutāṁ jāmbavataś cāpi
rohiṇīṁ kāmarūpiṇīm

madrarāja sutāṁ cāpi
suśīlāṁ śubhalocanām
sātrājitīṁ satyabhāmāṁ
lakṣmaṇāṁ cāruhāsinīm

śaivyasya ca sutāṁ tanvīṁ
rūpeṇāpsaraso pamām
strī sahasrāṇi cānyāni
ṣoḍaśātula vikramaḥ

upayeme hṛṣīkeśaḥ
sarvā bheje sa tāḥ samam
parārdhya vastrābharaṇāḥ
kāmaiḥ sarvaiḥ sukhocitāḥ
jajñire tāsu putrāśca
tasya vīrāḥ sahasraśaḥ

After some time, mighty-armed Lord Madhusūdana married eight other beautiful women that had been born in aristocratic families, and who were all very pious and reservoirs of transcendental qualities. These queens were 1. Surya's daughter Kālindī, 2. Mitravindā, the daughter of Rājādhidevī, Kṛṣṇa's aunt from Avantī, 3. Satyā, the daughter of Nagnajit, the king of Ayodhyā, 4. Jāmbavatī, the daughter of Jāmbavān, 5. Rohiṇī, who was also known as Bhadrā and could assume any form at will. She was also known as Kaikeyī because she was the daughter of the king of Kaikeya, and she was the daughter of Kṛṣṇa's aunt, Śrūtakīrtī, 6. Lakṣmaṇā, the very gentle and beautiful-eyed daughter of the king of Madra, 7. Satyabhāmā, the daughter of Satrājit, and 8. Gāndhārī, the daughter of King Śaivya. She was as beautiful as an Apsarā.

Thereafter, Lord Kṛṣṇa married sixteen thousand more women. Indeed, the unlimitedly powerful Lord Kṛṣṇa expanded Himself into sixteen thousand forms and married all these queens, who were gorgeously dressed and decorated with ornaments. All of them became fully satisfied, experiencing great transcendental happiness in the association of the Lord. Lord Kṛṣṇa begot thousands of powerful sons within the wombs of these queens.

Text 45

śāstrārtha kuśalāḥ sarve
balavanto mahārathāḥ
yajvānaḥ puṇyakarmāṇo
mahābhāgā mahābalāḥ

All of Kṛṣṇa's sons were well-versed in the scriptures. They were very powerful warriors, performers of numerous sacrifices, and very fortunate. They were all very pious by nature and had immense strength .

Thus ends the translation of the sixtieth chapter of the Viṣṇu Parva of Śri Harivaṁsa.

Chapter 61

The marriage of Pradyumna and Śubhāṅgī, the daughter of Rukmī. The marriage of Aniruddha and Rukmī's grand-daughter, Rukmavatī. Lord Balarāma kills Rukmī after gambling with dice

Text 1

vaiśampāyana uvāca
tataḥ kāle vyatīte tu
rukmī mahati vīryavān
duhituḥ kārayāmāsa
svayaṁvaram ariṁdam

Vaiśampāyana said: After a long time had passed, the powerful King Rukmī, the vanquisher of his enemies, arranged for the *svayamvara* of his daughter.

Text 2

tatrāhūtā hi rājāno
rājaputrāśca rukmiṇāḥ
samājagmur mahāvīryā
nānādigbhyaḥ śriyānvitāḥ

After receiving Rukmī's invitation, many powerful and influential kings and princes began to arrive at Bhojakata from far-off lands.

Text 3

tatrājagāma pradyumnaḥ
kumārair aparair vṛtaḥ

sāhitaṁ cakame kanyā
sa ca tāṁ śubhalocanām

Many princes of the Yadu dynasty, headed by Pradyumna, also arrived. Rukmī's daughter chose Pradyumna within her heart and Pradyumna also desired to marry the beautiful-eyed princess.

Text 4

śubhāṅgī nāma vaidarbhī
kānti dyuti samanvitā
pṛthivyām abhavat khyātā
rukmiṇas tanayā tadā

The princess of Vidarbha was named Śubhāṅgī. She was beautiful and very intelligent. Indeed, the daughter of Rukmī was known throughout the world for her exquisite beauty.

Text 5

upaviṣṭeṣu sarveṣu
pārthiveṣu mahātmasu
vaidarbhīm varayāmāsa
pradyumnam arisūdanam

As all the invited kings and princes were seated, Princess Śubhāṅgī slowly entered the arena of the *svayamvara* and selected Pradyumna as her husband.

Text 6

sa hi sarvāstra kuśalaḥ
siṁha saṁhanano yuvā

rūpeṇā pratimo loke
keśavasyāt majo'bhavat

Pradyumna was as strong as a lion, he was in the prime of his youth, and he was very a very expert wielder of weapons. In terms of beauty, the son of Lord Kṛṣṇa had no comparison within the world.

Text 7

varyorūpa gūṇopetā
rājaputrī ca sābhavat
narāyaṇīvendrasenā
jātakāmā ca taṁ prati

The princess was very young, extremely beautiful, and possessed all good qualities. As Nārāyaṇī Indrasenā was devoted to her husband, the great sage Mṛdula, Śubhāṅgī loved Pradyumna.

Text 8

vṛtte svayaṁvare jagmū
rājānaḥ svapurāṇi te
upādāya ca vaidarbhīṁ
pradyumno dvārakāṁ yayau

At the completion of the *svayamvara* all the assembled kings and princes departed for their respective kingdoms while Pradyumna took his newly-wedded wife and returned to Dvārakā.

Text 9

reme saha tayā vīro
damanyantyā nalo yathā
sa tasyāṁ janayāmāsa
devagarbhopamaṁ sutam

Thereafter, Pradyumna enjoyed life with his wife just as King Nala had happily passes his days with Damayantī. In due course of time, he begot a son within the womb of Śubhāṅgī who was as powerful as a demigod.

Text 10

aniruddham iti khyātaṁ
karmaṇā pratimaṁ bhuvi
dhanurvede ca vede ca
nītiśāstre ca pāragam

His name was Aniruddha and he became known as an unrivaled hero who performed extraordinary feats. He was very well-versed in the Vedas and scriptures dealing with morality, and he was unmatched with the bow.

Text 11

abhavat sa yadā rājan
aniruddho vayo'nvitaḥ
tadāsya rukmiṇaḥ pautrīṁ
rukmiṇī rukmasaṇibhā
patnyarthe varayāmāsa
nāmnā rukmavatīti sa

O King, when Aniruddha reached the prime of his youth, Rukmiṇī asked Rukmī to give his grand-daughter, named Rukmavatī, whose complexion was golden, to him in marriage.

Texts 12-13

aniruddha guṇairdātuṁ
kṛtabuddhir nṛpastataḥ
prītyāhi rukmiṇoyasya
rukmiṇyāścāpyupa grahāt

visparddhannapi kṛṣṇena
vairaṁ tyajya mahāyaśāḥ
dadāmītya vravīd rājā
prītimāñ janamejaya

My dear Janamejaya, King Rukmī was attracted by the transcendental qualities of Aniruddha and so he already desired that his grand-daughter marry him. Therefore, in spite of his enmity towards Lord Kṛṣṇa, upon seeing Rukmiṇī's eagerness, Rukmī happily agreed to the proposal, declaring: Yes, I will give my grand-daughter to Aniruddha!

Text 14

keśavaḥ saha rukmiṇyā
putraiḥ saṁkarṣaṇena ca
anyaiśca vṛṣṇibhiḥ sārddhaṁ
vidarbhān sabalo yayau

Lord Kṛṣṇa and Rukmiṇī then traveled to Vidarbha, along with many of His sons, headed by Pradyumna, His brother Balarāma, and the army of the Vṛṣṇi dynasty.

Text 15

saṁyuktā jñātayaścaiva
ruimiṇaḥ suhṛdaśca ye
āhūtā rukmiṇā te'pi
tatrājagmur narādhipāḥ

Rukmī invited many kings, relatives, and well-wishers to the marriage, so that it was celebrated with great pomp and happiness.

Text 16

śubhe tithau mahārāja
nakṣatre cābhi pūjite
vivāhaḥ so'niruddhasya
babhūva paramotsavaḥ

O King, on an auspicious day, at an auspicious moment, under the influence of an auspicious star, the marriage of Prince Aniruddha was performed.

Text 17

pāṇau gṛhīte vaidarbhyās
tvaniruddhena tatra vai
vaidarbha yādavānāṁ ca
babhūva paramotsavaḥ

As Aniruddha accepted the hand of the Vidarbha princess, Rukmavatī, all the members of the Yadu dynasty and residents of Vidarbha jubilantly witnessed the occasion.

Texts 18-22

remire vṛṣṇyastatra
pūjyamānā yathāmarāḥ
athāśma kānāmadhipo
veṇudārir udāradhīḥ

akṣaḥ śrutarvā cāṇuraḥ
krāthaścaivāṁśu mānapi

jayatsenaḥ kaliṅgānām
adhipaśca mahābalaḥ

pāṇḍyaśca nṛpatiḥ śrīmān
ṛṣīkādhi patistathā
ete sammantrya rājāno
dākṣiṇātyā maharddhayaḥ

abhigamyā bruvan sarve
rukmiṇaṁ rahasi prabhum
bhavāna kṣeṣu kuśalo
vayaṁ cāpi riraṁsavaḥ

priyadyūtaśca rāmo'sā
vakṣeṣva nipuṇo'pi ca
te bhavantaṁ puraskṛtya
jetumicchāma taṁ vayam
ityukto rocayāmāsa rukmī
dyūtaṁ mahārathaḥ

The Yādavas were very pleased by the hospitality of the people of Vidarbha. One day some kings from South India—the noble Veṇudārī the king of Aśmaka, Akṣa, Śutarvā, Cāṇura, Kratha's son Aṅśumān, Jayatsena the king Kaliṅga, Pāṇḍya, and Ṛṣika—approached Rukmī in a solitary place and said: You are a very cunning player with dice and we are also very eager to play. On the other hand, although very fond of the game, Balarāma is a poor player. We would like you to compete with Balarāma at the dice board and defeat Him.

Rukmī liked this idea and so immediately agreed to challenge Balarāma to play with dice.

Text 23

te śubhāṁ kāñcanas tambhāṁ
kusumair bhūṣitājirām
sabhāmāvi viśur hṛṣṭāḥ
siktāṁ candana vāriṇā

At the appointed time, all the kings cheerfully entered the gaming room, whose golden pillars were decorated with flower garlands. Water mixed with sandalwood paste had been sprinkled over the floor.

Text 24

tāṁ praviśya tataḥ sarve
śubhra sraganu lepanāḥ
sauvarṇeṣvā saneṣvāsām
cakrire vijigīṣavaḥ

The kings were also decorated with beautiful flower garlands and sandalwood paste and after entering the hall, they sat down on golden thrones. They all had one thing in common—the desire that Lord Balarāma meet with defeat.

Text 25

āhūto baladevastu
kitavair akṣakovidaiḥ
bāḍhamitya bravīd dhṛṣṭaḥ
saha dīvyāma paṇyatām

Lord Balarāma was then invited by the gamblers to play dice. He happily agreed, saying: Let the play begin. You may all place your bets.

Text 26

nikṛtyā vijigīṣanto
dākṣiṇātyā narādhipāḥ
maṇimuktāḥ suvarṇaṁ ca
tatrāninyuḥ sahasraśaḥ

With a desire to win by cheating, the kings from South India had brought thousands of gold coins, diamonds, and pearls.

Text 27

tataḥ prāvartata dyūtaṁ
teṣāṁ rati vināśanam
kalahasyās padaṁ ghoraṁ
durmatīnāṁ kṣayāvaham

At the agreed time, the game started. Gambling with dice is known to destroy the mutual love and understanding of those who play by creating enmity and quarrel. This is not only true of pious souls but evil-minded people as well.

Text 28

niṣkāṇāṁ ca sahasrāṇi
suvarṇasya daśāditaḥ
rukmiṇā saha sampāte
baladevo glahaṁ dadau

To start, Lord Baladeva played with Rukmī with ten thousand gold coin as the wager.

Text 29

taṁ jigāya tato rukmī
yatamānaṁ mahābalam
tāvadevā paraṁ bhūyo
baladevaṁ jigāya saḥ

Although Lord Baladeva tried His best to win, Rukmī easily defeated Him. Rukmī also won the next game with the same wager.

Text 30

asakṛjjīya mānastu
rukmiṇā keśavāgrajaḥ
suvarṇa koṭīrjagrāha
glahaṁ tasya mahātmanaḥ

Being defeated again and again at dice, Kṛṣṇa's elder brother Balarāma thought for awhile and then placed ten million gold coins as his wager.

Text 31

jitamityeva hṛṣṭo'tha
tamāhṛvaṭir abhāṣata
śṛlādhyamānaśca cikṣepa
prahasan muṣalāyuḍhaṁ

By nature Rukmī was a very crooked person. Being very happy to see so much wealth, after the roll of the dice he exclaimed: I have won all this as well.

All the kings present began to glorify Rukmī, who then ridiculed Balarāma, the holder of the *muṣala*, as follows.

Text 32

avidyo durbalaḥ śrīmān
hiraṇyam amitaṁ mayā
ajeyo baladevo'yam
akṣadyūte parājitaḥ

This Balarāma is uneducated and weak. He pretended to be unconquerable, but today He has been comprehensibly defeated by me. I have won all His gold coins.

Text 33

kaliṅga rājas tacchrutvā
prajahāsa bhṛśaṁ tadā
dantān saṁdarśayan hṛṣṭas
tatrā kruddhayad halāyudhaḥ

Upon hearing Rukmī speak in this way, the happiness of the king of Kaliṅga knew no bounds as he laughed loudly while purposely displaying his teeth. This made Balarāma furious.

Texts 34-35

rukmiṇastad vacaḥ śrutvā
parājaya nimittajam
nigṛhya māṇastīkṣṇābhir
vāgbhir bhīṣmaka sūnunā

roṣam āhārayāmāsa
jitaroṣo'pi dharmavit
saṁkruddho dharṣaṇāṁ prāpya
rauhiṇeyo mahābalaḥ

Rukmī's insulting words were intolerable for Rohiṇī's son, Balarāma, and so He became highly enraged. Of course, as the Personality of Godhead, He was the foremost knower of religious principles and could very well control His anger. Still, for the purpose of nourishing His pastimes, He appeared to be filled with uncontrollable rage.

Texts 36-37

dhairyānmanaḥ saṁnidhāya
tato vacanam abravīt
daśakoṭi sahasrāṇi
glahaṁ eko mamāparaḥ

enaṁ sampari gṛhīṣva
pātayākṣān narādhipa
kṛṣṇakṣāṁllohita akṣāṁśca
deśz'smis tvadhipāṁsule

Still, desiring to continue the gain, Lord Baladeva remained patient, carefully controlling His mind and anger. He then said: O king of Vidarbha, let us roll the dice one final time with a wager of ten million gold coins. Roll the black and red dice and see if you can win. Your kingdom is well-known for being firmly fixed in the mode of passion.

In this way, Rohiṇī's son, Baladeva, again challenged Rukmī to roll the dice.

Text 38

ityevam āhvayāmāsa
rukmiṇaṁ rohiṇīsutaḥ
anuktvā vacanaṁ kicid
vāḍhamitya bravīta punaḥ

In reply, Rukmī did not waste any words but simply nodded in assent. Thereafter, he rolled the dice once again.

Text 39

akṣān rukmī tato dṛṣṭaḥ
pātayāmāsa pārthivaḥ
cāturakṣe tu nirvṛtte
nirjitasya narādhipaḥ

This time, Rukmī rolled a four. According to the rules of the game, he lost. Still, the cunning king of Vidarbha proudly announced: Again You have lost!

Text 40

baladevena dharmeṇa
netyuvāca tato balam
dhairyān manaḥ samādhāya
sa na kiṁciduvāca ha

Balarāma again carefully controlled His anger and didn't object, so that the game could continue. After the next deceitful roll of the dice, Rukmī smiled and sarcastically announced: I have won this time as well!

Text 41

baladevaṁ tato rukmī
mayā jitamiti smayan
baladevastu tacchrutvā
jinham vākyaṁ narādhipa

Upon hearing these deceitful words spoken by Rukmī, Baladeva became extremely angry, but did nothing to express His rage.

Text 42

bhūyaḥ krodha samāviṣṭo
nottaraṁ vyājahāra ha
tato gambhīra nirghoṣā
vāgu vācā śarīrinī

At that moment, an announcement was heard from the sky that simply fueled Balarāma's anger.

Texts 43-44

baladevasya taṁ krodhaṁ
vardhayantī mahātmanaḥ
satyamāha balaḥ śrīmān
dharmeṇaiṣa parājitaḥ

anuktvā vacanaṁ kiṁcit
prāpto bhavati karmaṇā
manasā samanujñātaṁ
tat syāditya vagamyatām

(The unembodied voice said:) Lord Balarāma is the actual winner and His words are always truthful. The truth is that Rukmī has lost this game of dice. Although at the commencement of this match, no rules were laid down, it can easily be understood by the way he threw the dice that the king of Vidarbha has cheated. Although he lost, he is claiming to be the victor.

Texts 45-46

iti śrutvā vacastathyam
antarīkṣāt subhāṣitam
saṁkarṣaṇas tathotthāya
sauvarṇeno ruṇā balī

rukmiṇyā bhrātaraṁ jyeṣṭhaṁ
nijadhāna mahītale
vivāde kupito rāmaḥ
kṣeptāraṁ kila rukmiṇam
jaghānāṣṭā padenaiva
pramathya yadunandanaḥ

After hearing this celestial announcement, Lord Balarāma picked up the golden dice board and after standing up, struck Rukmiṇī's elder brother, Rukmī, on the head with it. In this way, after becoming enraged by Rukmī's cheating and insulting words, Balarāma killed Rukmī.

Text 47

tato'pasṛtya saṁkruddhaḥ
kaliṅgādhi paterapi
dantān babhañja saṁrambhād
unnanāda ca siṁhavat

After striking Rukmī, the enraged Lord Saṅkarṣaṇa knocked out the teeth of Jayatsena, the king of Kaliṅga. Being not yet pacified, He continued roaring like an enraged lion.

Text 48

khaḍgam udyamya tān sarvāṁs
trāsayāmāsa pārthivān

stambhaṁ sabhāyāḥ sauvarṇam
utpāṭya balināṁ varaḥ

Lord Baladeva then unsheathed His sword, greatly frightening all the assembled kings. He then uprooted one of the golden pillars from the gaming hall.

Text 49

gajendra iva taṁ stambhaṁ
karṣan saṅkarṣaṇas tataḥ
nirjagāma sabhādvārāt
trāsayāmāsa kauśikān

When Lord Saṅkarṣaṇa came out of the gaming room pulling that golden pillar like a king of elephants, all the members of the Kauśika dynasty became filled with fear.

Text 50

rukmiṇaṁ nikṛti prajñaṁ
sa hatvā yādavarṣabhaḥ
vitrāsya vidviṣaḥ sarvān
siṁhaḥ kṣudra mṛgāniva

Thus, after killing Rukmī, whose nature was exceedingly duplicitous, Balarāma, the foremost of the Yādavas, instilled fear into the hearts of all His enemies just as a lion frightens all the other animals in the forest.

Text 51

jagāma śiviraṁ rāmaḥ
svayameva janāvṛtaḥ

nyavedayat sa kṛṣṇāya
tatra sarvaṁ yathābhavat

Thereafter, Balarāma returned to His camp, surrounded by His relatives. In the camp He narrated everything that had taken place in the gaming hall to His younger brother, Kṛṣṇa.

Text 52

novāca sa tadā kṛṣṇaḥ
kiṁcid rāmaṁ mahādyutiḥ
nigṛhya ca tadā'tmānaṁ
kṛcchrād aśrūṇya vartayat

Supremely powerful Lord Kṛṣṇa did not say anything about this incident to Balarāma. He controlled Himself very carefully but could not check the tears that rolled from His eyes.

Texts 53-54

na hato vāsudevena
yaḥ pūrvaṁ paravīrahā
jyeṣṭho bhrātātha rukmīnyā
rukmiṇī snehakāraṇāt

sa rāma karamuktena
nihato dyūtamaṇḍale
aṣṭāpadena balavān
rājā vajra dharopamaḥ

Rukmī, who was as powerful as Indra, the wielder of the thunderbolt, and the destroyer of his enemies, whose life had been spared by the Supreme Lord, Vāsudeva, because of His affection for Rukmiṇī, was now killed by Lord Balarāma with a golden dice board.

Texts 55-56

tasmin hate mahāvīrye
nṛpatau bhīṣmakātmaje
druma bhārgavatulye vai
druma bhārgava śikṣite

kṛtau ca yuddhakuśale
nityayājini pātite
vṛṣṇayaścāndha kāścaiva
sarve vimanaso'bhavan

King Bhiṣmaka's son, Rukmī, was a greatly powerful king. He received instruction on the use of weapons from Druma and Paraśurāma, so that he became equal to them in prowess. He was learned, very expert in the art of fighting, and a regular performer of sacrifices. After his death, all the heroes of the Vṛṣṇi and Aṇdaka dynasties became morose.

Text 57

vaiśampāyana uvāca
rukmiṇī ca mahābhāgā
vilapantyārtayā girā
vilapantīṁ tathā dṛṣṭvā
sāntvayāmāsa keśavaḥ

Vaiśampāyana said: When the greatly fortunate Rukmiṇī heard the news of her brother's death, she began to lament pathetically. Seeing Her crying and lamenting profusely, Lord Kṛṣṇa began to pacify Her.

Text 58

etat te sarvamākhyātaṁ
rukmiṇo nidhanaṁ yathā
vairasya ca samutthānaṁ
vṛṣṇibhir bharatarṣabha

O foremost descendent of Bharata, I have thus narrated to you the killing of Rukmī, which was the ultimate result of his having created enmity with the members of the Vṛṣṇi dynasty.

Text 59

vṛṣṇayo'pi mahārāja
dhanānyādāya sarvaśaḥ
rāmakṛṣṇau samāśritya
yayurdvāravatīṁ prati

O King, the members of the Vṛṣṇi dynasty collected all the wealth from Rukmī's palace and then returned to Dvārakā under the protection of Lord Kṛṣṇa and Lord Balarāma.

Thus ends the translation of the sixty-first chapter of the Viṣṇu Parva of Śri Harivaṁsa.